GOD'S
REJECTED KING
A Story of Saul

Ron Baesler

ISBN-13: 978-1541159112
ISBN-10: 154115911X

ACKNOWLEDGEMENTS

The funeral song in Chapter Twenty-six is based on Psalm 91. David's wedding song in Chapter Twenty-six uses verses from Song of Songs, Chapters 2 and 8. David's lament in the Epilogue is from II Samuel, Chapter 1. All quotations are from the New Revised Standard Version Bible, copyright ©1989 the Division of Christian Education of the National Council of Churches of Christ in the United States of America. Used by permission. All rights reserved.

Cover art: **David and Saul**, an 1878 oil painting by Ernst Josephson, located at the National Museum in Stockholm Sweden. The image is in public domain.

AUTHOR'S NOTE:

The stories in **God's Rejected King** are drawn from the Hebrew Bible's books of Judges and Samuel (Judges and I Samuel in the Christian Old Testament.) I follow the order of events as found in those books. However, I add characters and scenes not found in these texts and omit some that are recorded there. Unlike the Scriptures, I try to imagine the thoughts and emotions of the characters, especially those of Saul, son of Kish. This book is not a work of biblical scholarship. It is an exploration of the conundrums of life, calling, failure, faith and God through the experience of one of Scripture's often maligned characters.

PREFACE

Josephus in *Antiquities of the Jews*: He [Saul] therefore seems to me a uniquely just, courageous, and prudent man.

Proverbs 19.21: The human mind may devise many plans, but it is the purpose of the LORD that will be established.

What portion of life is by God defined? What portion is the product of the human mind?

Two travelers reach a fork in the trail and they must decide. The right branch curves downward and follows the valley back toward home. The left branch climbs the ridgeline forward to the next village. Which branch will they take? Has God already determined their choice or has God given these two men the power to choose? Will their choice change God's actions? If they choose the right-hand path how will God shape that history? We will never know for the men are already moving. They turn left and walk up the ridge. This is the story of that choice.

GOD'S REJECTED KING

A Story of Saul

Chapter One

"I could just as well spend the night here. Maybe tomorrow the donkeys will find us." Jakeh, speaks as if to himself, but loud enough for his master to hear. The two weary Israelites plod toward the sun-steeped village alongside the trail: a dozen simple stone houses, a few groves of arthritic olive trees, a hard-baked little plaza with a covered well in the center.

Saul flashes his white teeth in a broad grin at the old manservant. "I'm sure everyone in this great city will take one look at us and see that we are clearly royalty and give us nothing but the best." His eyes dance at his own joke. The tiny settlement is clearly no city and this land of Israel has never had royalty. Nonetheless, attention is guaranteed. Saul is already shaking the dust from his blue robe and running his fingers through his thick black beard. He unwinds his turban and shakes out his long dark hair. His mane ripples with a coppery sheen in the sunlight. He throws out his chest and adds a swagger to his lengthy strides.

The children playing in the plaza and the scrawny village dogs are the first to notice the two strangers on the trail. The children's shouts quickly fade into awestruck murmurs.

"Ohh, look, it's a giant." "He's as tall as two men!"

It's a childish exaggeration, but Saul does tower head and shoulders above every other man in the region. Women's faces appear in the windows and eye the tall, powerful stranger. A few men emerge from their homes and stand in the doorways. A stocky elder, gray bearded but still erect and imposing, strides across the plaza toward them. Saul tries to read the approaching elder's face.

Saul's impressive appearance usually provokes one of two immediate responses from men. Some grant him quick deference, assuming he's an important clan leader. Others note his thrown out chest and swagger, assume he is a bully, and immediately decide to confront him. Saul discerns this elder belongs to the latter group. He stops in his tracks and bows deeply as the elder approaches.

"Shalom to you and your village." With practiced ease, he slips into the self-effacing tone he uses in encounters with anyone in authority. "I am Saul, son of Kish, from the tribe of Benjamin. This is my servant Jakeh. We apologize for entering your village looking so bedraggled and dusty, but we've been days on the trail, hunting for three stray donkeys." He rolls his eyes in mock exasperation, "they're lousy donkeys, but the best of our vast herd of six!"

The elder's tight jaw relaxes as Saul grins down at him. He bows stiffly. "Shalom to you both. Welcome to our humble village. We can offer you food and drink, but we've no news of runaway donkeys. Come!" He leads them toward a bench set against one of the stone houses. He shouts and a young girl in a dark robe shyly emerges with a jug of cool water and two bowls. The thirsty men draw long draughts and sigh as the chill water sluices through their bodies.

A gray cloaked figure crouching with a basket near the well slowly stands and hobbles toward them. The aged crone, as wrinkled as the dates in her basket, stops a few yards from their bench and bows. Her voice is as cracked and dry as ancient leather.

"Shalom, my lords. Forgive me for intruding but I heard you speak of donkeys. This morning as I was filling my basket with dates, I thought I saw some donkeys on the hillside moving that way." She points a gnarled finger to the south. "I saw only two but my eyes are often cloudy in the morning. Maybe there was another."

Saul looks over at his manservant with a wry grin. Jakeh shrugs his shoulders in resignation and slowly levers his body up off the bench. Saul takes another long gulp of water, thanks the elder, and the two men hurry southward along the dusty trail.

Chapter Two

By the time the sun slides down behind the distant mountains, both men are exhausted with still no donkeys in sight. They make a simple camp a few yards up from the trail. They lie next to a huge granite boulder hoping that some of the day's heat in the rock's stony heart will seep out and warm them in the chill desert night.

Melancholy ghosts stranded from long ago battles whisper in the darkness. Two-hundred-year-old wraiths sigh in the night breeze, ghosts of Canaanite men, women and children wiped out by the bedraggled tribes of Israel under the banner of their god, The Lord. Decades old spirits of surly Philistines, Israel's perpetual enemies, invaders intent upon conquest, hover in the chill velvet air. The Philistine survivors were driven back to the shores of the Great Sea, and though traveling merchants bring occasional rumors of renewed army activity, the region is still calm. None of these apparitions disturb the sleep of the two exhausted men. They would still be sleeping if not for the tinkling bells on the goats being led out to graze by a young shepherd boy.

The golden stallion sun charges into the crystalline sky. It splashes amber onto the distant hills and pours honey into the valley beneath the little campsite beside the trail. Jakeh sits huddled in his gray robe, still in the dark shadow of the ridge, slowly wiping the dream webs from his mind. Saul stands on the trail and stares out over the rough folds of scrub land stretching below out to the west. In the early light and from this height the land is a rolling ocean of brown and tan waves.

Saul throws his long arms up and roars in frustration. "Three days! Three days we've been scouring the land and we've not seen one hair of these damned beasts. By the Holy Ark of God, I swear those stupid she-asses have sprouted wings and flown to Joppa."

Saul stands in his dark blue robe, silhouetted against the brightening pale sky. He is far from home and family, far from responsibility and the authority of his father. The air has a crisp edge redolent with the fresh scent of cedar. He slept deeply and now stretches and roars like a lion. He turns to Jakeh, a sly smile gleaming in his dark beard. "What do you say? Is it the curse of the Benjaminites, to always be chasing after fleeing females?" He chuckles at his own wit. The old servant shakes his head in quiet disgust.

Saul breaks the God-blessed morning silence by swearing on the Ark, the most holy object of our people, the Ark that languishes in the hands of the Philistines—ai! That is offense enough. But now he dares to make a jest of the nightmare that forever stains the entire tribe? Why is this towering man's humility so stunted? Has he no respect for the God of our people?

Jakeh still remembers his own grandfather Eliab, a hardened stump of a man, telling him the story with tear filled eyes. More than once Eliab gathered his sons and grandsons around the fire, reciting the grim tale of how one night, over a generation ago, their own fellow clansmen, the Benjaminite men, violated the sacred duty of hospitality. Eliab always began in a raspy whisper.

"The story begins with Amran, a gaunt, somber man. He had a thin beard, watery eyes and tried to live a quiet, invisible life. He belonged to the clan of Levi and was pious. One day, Tizrah, a women in his household ran away, back to her parent's home. You can imagine how the village buzzed. Amran was deeply embarrassed. Tizrah was a young, talkative girl, with flashing dark eyes whom he'd brought into his family as a second wife. Evidently she found the household too subdued for her taste, or maybe Amram's demeanor was too grim. For whatever reason, she slipped away. More to restore his honor than to regain his property, Amran made the trek to reclaim her. Negotiations took more days than he imagined and more discussions than planned. At last he managed to satisfy both Tizrah and her family. He extricated himself from the lengthy, clinging farewell ceremonies and the two of them started their journey home."

Grandfather Eliab paused, looked out at his audience from under his bushy white eyebrows. His voice dropped lower. "That's when the trouble began. Amrah and Tizrah walked through the gauzy orange air as the sun settled over the hills. They'd gotten a late start on their homeward journey. It was nearly dark when they arrived in the mountain town of Gibeah in Benjaminite territory. The Levite hoped that someone in the village would offer them lodging for the night. Welcoming the stranger is our law is it not?"

Once again, his eyes swept around the circle of men and boys gathered around him. They all nodded and grunted assent. Eliab shook his head. "But not one Benjaminite offered lodging. The sky faded from silvery gray to mauve and the night chill crept upon them. The two travelers began preparing themselves for a night in the plaza. Then, just as the first stars gleamed in the sky, an old Ephraimite who lived in the town, hobbled in from the fields. He was appalled to see strangers standing alone and unwelcomed in the square. He insisted that they spend the night with him. Soon Amran the Levite and Tizrah sat on mats in the old man's house, eating bread, sharing wine, laughter and stories with him and his family."

Eliab paused again and raised his thin arms. "If the night had passed quietly then our tribe would have had to bear the humiliation of poor hospitality. Serious enough, but this is not the end of the story. Somewhere in that town a dark spirit stirred. Was it spawned by a feud between two hot headed men? Or a dare gone berserk under the power of wine? No one will ever know. But without warning shouting filled the dark village. A brawling, rowdy clot of men surrounded the Ephraimite's house. They began to shout, 'Hey, old man, send out the traveler. We want to show him what studs we Gibeanite men are! He's in for a real ride!' The mob's shouts and animal growls filled the house. Amran wrapped his arms around Tirzah, and the man's daughters whimpered."

"'I'm going out to them.' The Ephraimite pulled away from his family's embrace and slipped outside. He stood with his back to his door. His sudden appearance silenced the horde. He could hear them panting, see the lust burning in their eyes. He did his best to sound courageous. 'Brothers, I've given this man shelter in my house. It's my duty before God to protect him. You know this, you know this in your hearts. I cannot give him to you. Take my daughter, take his concubine, but leave the man alone.'"

"The man closest to him was red-faced with drink and lasciviousness. He snorted in disdain. 'Old man, give us the traveler!' He shoved the Ephraimite and his head bounced off the door behind him. The mob roared like a wounded bear and he quickly slipped back inside. Now the villagers began pounding on the boarded-up windows and the door. Panic swept over the family and its guests. The door began to crack. With a groan, Amran leapt up, jerked hysterical Tirzah to her feet, threw open the door and shoved her out into the rabble. Her screams mixed with cheers from the pack of savage men, and with the sobs of the women inside the house."

"An endless cacophony of moans and bestial grunts ravaged the night. A travesty had been avoided, only to be replaced by a gruesome depravity. By the time the sun rose, the streets were silent. Amran opened the door. Tirzah lay raped and bloody, stretched out in the dust, her limp hand lying on the threshold...."

Eliab paused, choking on a sob as tears zigzagged down the furrows in his cheeks. Young Jakeh and the other listeners wiped tears with the backs of their hands. But then the grandfather would begin again, and tell the rest of the grisly tale.

"Amran carried home Tizrah's corpse. He cut her body into eleven pieces. Yes, he cut her body apart and sent one piece to each of the Israelite tribes. With this ghastly gesture, he summoned them to unite and punish the clan that had committed such an evil deed. By the hands of their eleven brother tribes and by the power of the Holy God, entire Benjaminite cities were leveled and their inhabitants slaughtered. The clan of Benjamin was punished to the edge of extinction. Ai! Extinction might have been a better fate than what followed."

"The eleven tribes took an oath not to allow any of their women to marry any of the pitiful men of our perverted tribe. We Benjaminites would have disappeared entirely had not the victors shown mercy. And it was mercy, though of a deeply perverse kind. The victors discovered that the city of Jabesh-Gilead had sent no soldiers to join their army. So they marched into the city and slaughtered every living person saving only four hundred virgin girls. They delivered these women to the ragged remnants of our tribe. But four hundred virgins still left too many men without women. To heap shame upon our shame, the desperate men of Benjamin were given permission to hide in the vineyards of Shiloh during the harvest festival. When the evening dances began, they were given permission to pursue and kidnap the young women and claim them for their wives. Desperate ancestors running through the darkness after frightened women solely to keep the clan alive: this is the legacy of the Benjaminites."

By the time Grandfather Eliab finished the story, his thin caved in chest always heaved with pent up sobs. Even this morning, forty years later Jakeh can hear the old man's choking voice. Jakeh sits in the gathering light and shakes his head at the memory.

This is the besmirched history that Saul so flippantly mocks. This legacy is our shame, whether he cares to acknowledge it or not. And the God of our fathers hears such idle talk, whether be believes it or not.

Jakeh sits hunched inside his robe on the blanket that was his bed through the chill desert night. Saul squats down beside him. "Do you think we should turn around? We haven't found the wretched donkeys. Still, it's been good to get out, get away for a few days from…" His voice trails off. He abruptly stands and gazes back along the way they came. He sighs, "I suppose by now Father Kish is more worried about us than the asses." The sun has topped the ridge and bathes the entire valley below with golden light. Today will be another hot day.

From his seat, Jakeh speaks in a voice as dry as the air, "The next village is Ramah. A seer lives there. Honorable man, they say. Sees things and speaks truth. Maybe we could ask him… before we give up." That tiny pause and the last phrase has its intended effect.

Saul spins and strides back toward Jakeh and growls, "I didn't say we were giving up. I was just asking—." He catches himself.

Yes, Jakeh is a servant, but he's also older. Some say he's even a distant clansman whose family was forced into slavery by poverty. Respect is due. Saul shakes his head, annoyed as always by his own quick temper.

"So, an honorable man you say. If he can see things he must be God favored…its worth a try." Then he slaps his hands on his thighs. "Ahh, but we can't just appear at his door empty handed. We need to offer him some sort of gift. And we've got nothing, not even a bit of stale bread."

Jakeh grimaces and moans as he struggles to his feet. He reaches a bony hand into his waistband, pulls out a coin and smiles crookedly up at Saul. "I've got a bit of silver here. Maybe it'll be enough to find those donkeys."

Saul roars with laughter and throws his arm over Jakeh's thin shoulders. "Lead the way, old man, lead the way."

They roll up their blankets, stuff them into their bags and return to the ragged, dusty trail. Saul's mercurial spirits rise as the sun heats up the morning. Days ago, when they began their journey, his face had been clouded and baleful. Now he steps lightly and playfully imitates the flitting sparrows that flutter in the breeze. As usual the farther he travels from his father the more frequent his smiles and the more boisterousness his enthusiasm.

Chapter Three

In the village of Ramah, Samuel the seer steps from his house and squints up at the sun. Noon has passed and yet no one has appeared. He is bald, his beard is hoarfrost white and as wispy as the high clouds in the washed-out sky. Age has stooped his back but there is still energy in his frame and his eyes are still sharp. He scans the small village and the path to the gate. No strangers in sight. He wonders if he is losing his hearing.

For most of his life he's heard the Voice. The Voice speaks slowly, never in a rush, always calmly, never fevered. It speaks confidently, without hesitation or stammer. Long ago, he was told by the priest that it was the voice of God and if you can't trust a priest who can you trust?

The first time he heard the Voice he could have sworn it came from outside of his own head. He'd been a boy then. He rolled off his mat, still half asleep. With his heart throbbing he dashed to the bedside of Eli. The decrepit priest was snoring fitfully, obviously in deep sleep. But Samuel was utterly convinced that the priest had called him. He clutched the old man's bony shoulder and shook until the holy man opened bleary, filmy eyes. Eli was not happy to be dragged out of his dreams which evidently were more appealing than his day time duties. He rebuked the boy and ordered him back to sleep. This happened more than once, until finally Eli told his overeager young assistant that if he heard a voice it must be a voice meant solely for him, in which case it must be the Lord's own voice.

From that day forward Samuel has heard the Voice. He can't describe its location. It is inside his being but not part of his being. It's a voice meant for him but it does not belong to him. The Voice doesn't always speak, it isn't constant. But when it speaks he listens. The Voice never speaks in conundrums or riddles, in abstractions or generalizations. It speaks about the events and people in Samuel's world and directs his actions and his words. Throughout his life Samuel has been convinced that the voice is the Lord's and that it speaks the truth. He has always listened and obeyed.

But today he stands in front of his house in the glaring afternoon sun and he wonders if he is losing his hearing. Has he heard the Voice correctly? Maybe his mind itself is going deaf and he's jumbled the words into some bizarre message. Or even more disconcerting: What if this is a different voice, a counterfeit voice? In all these years, he's never had any doubt about the Voice. But today he wonders. If the Lord can speak into his mind, can some other power do so too? The priests and everyone who counts tell him there is no other power in the creation. He has always believed that. But today, today his certainty wavers like the heat shimmering off the city wall.

When this particular conversation began some weeks ago, he'd recoiled. He'd been seated on the rooftop, welcoming the evening breeze's first whispers. He heard the nighthawk's whoop as it plunged out of the darkening sky to grab an insect. The Voice began as it always did—as if it had always been there, listening intently; as if Samuel's everyday life was one side of the conversation and now the Voice would take its turn.

You know you are getting old.

Samuel smiled to himself and thought, "You don't need special power to see that."

Your sons will not carry the people forward.

He stared out into the dying light looking for the first star. He took in a deep breath and slowly let it leak from pursed lips. "Ahh, everyone in the village and in the land can see that too. They are my sons, share my blood, but, they don't share my heart." He sat for long minutes. The only sounds were of the village's evening routines: a baby crying, a mother's lullaby, some men laughing. Then the Voice spoke. In the days that followed, as he painfully and repeatedly returned to that speech, Samuel convinced himself that the Voice had spoken with a deeper intensity.

Samuel your days are ending, your sons will not follow you. The people want a king so I have decided to give them a king.

His mind flinched as though lashed by a whip. His gut clenched as if punched. Never in all his decades had he protested the Voice but this, this…. He groaned, pinched his eyes shut until his temples ached.

"How can you give the people what they want? Their faith is feeble, their hearts fearful. They covet the kings of the pagan nations around us. They close their ears when the prophets speak. Don't give in to their whining!"

He hunched lower into his robe. The evening breeze chilled his neck as his thoughts swirled. Minutes past. At last the Voice answered, measured and calm as always.

Why are you so dismayed? Have they battered your pride? Do you think they're rejecting you? I should be the one distressed. Once my kingship was enough for them. But now… Now, for good and for ill, they shall have a king.

An entire night of rooftop wrestling began. The hours passed, the stars spun in the heavens and Samuel grew more and more desperate, confused and angry. That night he'd not questioned the legitimacy of the Voice. But he had challenged the decision. The seer had lived with the Voice for many decades, had trusted, obeyed and reverenced it as God's own truth. After such a long history of faithfulness he felt entitled to express his disapproval. But the Voice never wavered, never cajoled. And when the eastern sky began to grow pale, Samuel wrenched his aching bones up from where he'd sat wrestling, slowly shuffled down the stairs and threw himself on his mat. He felt twenty years older than the night before.

In the weeks since that night, the Voice had been silent, not absent, he was sure of that, but silent. Last night, as he sighed and stretched out on his sleeping mat, a few simple words slipped into the silence like a boat on a glassy lake and rippled across Samuel's thoughts.

He will come tomorrow. He will be exceedingly tall. Tell him his donkeys have been found. Invite him to stay the night. The next day you will anoint him.

He waited for more, but the glassy silence was broken only by the crickets gossiping in the sand outside. He lay on his back, staring into the darkness. He imagined himself feigning ignorance and asking who 'he' was. He smiled ruefully at his own ridiculous notion. That would be as laughable as Adam and Eve trying to hide from God behind the bushes.

His dreams that night teemed with hands groping endlessly in clouds and fog. He awoke early with an ache in his head. The morning passed and now noon too was gone. Still no tall man looking for donkeys. Once more the blasphemous thought ripples across his mind.

What if that voice was not the true voice, what if it was the voice of a pretender? How would I know?

He shakes his head at the futility of his own questions. He grabs his staff and begins marching to the house of worship.

I still have work to do and can't spend all day waiting for some wandering stranger.

Chapter Four

Saul and Jakeh move southward along the trail to Ramah. The midmorning sun heats the grassy fields and locusts whir across their path. They pass sun bleached olive trees laden with fruits only weeks away from picking. Saul continues his whistling and striding. Jakeh does his best to keep up.

Jakeh was twelve years old when he came to serve the family of Kish. Saul had just been born. For the last thirty-eight years Jakeh has been a faithful and wise servant. He's taken advantage of a servant's invisibility and after decades of observation fathoms the heartbeat of this clan better than anyone else. The seeds of Saul's confused feelings for his father were sown early and often. Jakeh remembers one day….

From the door to their courtyard, Kish called out, "Saul, come! You need to work today." Ten-year-old Saul was supposed to be studying his Hebrew letters. The village priest, a nervous young man who reminded Saul and his classmates of a skinny raven, had used a piece of charcoal to write out the alphabet on a piece of a clay from a broken pot. Saul had dismissively tossed the piece of clay against the side of the house and was playing a target game with his little brother. But when Kish called, the boy did not hesitate. He spun away from the games and jumped to his feet. No time for childish games when his father needed him. He dashed out into the pale sunlight toward his father.

Saul ached to be a man like Kish, and to be a man was to work. They neared the city gate and he was so full of tingling delight that for an instant he was tempted to grab hold of his father's hand. He quickly quenched that thought. Such things were for little boys, but he, he was almost a man. Kish walked as he always walked, as though he were late for an urgent gathering. Saul tried to match his strides but had to run every few steps to keep pace.

They emerged from the gate just as his mother and the other village women were returning from the well, carrying their jugs on their heads. Young Saul put what he imagined was a serious adult look on his face, hoping his mother and the others would notice that he was going out to work. Outside the gate, he and his father turned left and neared the sheepfold. The back side of the sheepfold was formed by the stone wall around the village. A five-foot-high semicircular barrier made of branches and brush stood with its ends against the wall. A rough gate made of the same branches stood open and the fold was now empty.

Kish stopped beside the barrier. "See how the fence is low and thin along here? If the sheep crowd against it, a gap could open and the sheep might escape and the wolves would have a feast. Or worse yet, one of those devilish bastards could enter the fold and kill half the flock just for pleasure."

Saul nodded and frowned in concentration. Kish pointed behind Saul. "We need to add branches from that pile there, weave them in to make the wall stronger and higher. Like this." Kish grabbed a branch and deftly wove it into the mesh of interlaced boughs.

"Did you see how that was done?" He did not wait for an answer but began walking and spoke over his shoulder, "You work here and I'll do the other side."

Little Saul watched his father stride away. He wished he could have seen Kish add one more branch. Or better, had his dad help him put in a branch. But it was too late. He grabbed a branch from the pile and tried to weave it in as his father had done. Kish had made it seem so easy. Saul desperately tried to do the job correctly. He studied how the branch had been placed and woven, he measured the height that his father had indicated. He interlaced a branch into the mesh. He twisted and pushed. He stepped back to examine the result, then removed the branch and tried again. Yes! Perfect. He went along cautiously and conscientiously, doing his best to emulate his father's work. The hours passed and he'd only advanced a few yards when Kish came hurrying around the enclosure. Saul stood silent and proud. He longed to say "Dad, look at how carefully I wove the branches. Tell me I did a good job."

But Kish took no notice of his son's painstaking efforts. He scarcely looked at his son. Instead he brusquely said, "Here, let me finish, we don't have all day." Saul stepped back and watched his father do the work he'd been assigned to do.

Jakeh's role as family servant gave him an insight into both father and son. Father Kish began each day with a morning prayer as had been commanded by the patriarch Abraham. With his mouth, he gave thanks for the day but even as he spoke his heart was girding itself for the day's battle. Sparse grass, predators stalking the herds, unreliable workers—Kish always awoke feeling like a general about to engage the enemy. He was driven by the conviction, unarticulated even to himself, that were he to relax, ease up or slacken off for a day, the dreaded vulture of disaster would swoop from on high and destroy everything—family, herds and his own life.

Kish's hard work earned him the respect of his clan. He was a good provider for his family. But he could not mentor his children. He could not stand alongside them, watch them struggle and learn. His belief that chaos was kept away only by the force of his will and his constant exertion prevented him from taking time to be a teacher. He knew what sheep needed to grow and thrive. But he had no sense of what a growing, desperately eager to please boy like Saul might need. He had no inkling of how his own actions affected his oldest son. He never intended to wound his children in any way, either physically or emotionally. He was not without emotions but they were obscured from his own consciousness. Thus, he barely registered the emotions of others. In this and many other ways, young Saul was his father's son. Like his father Saul could not name, must less express his tumultuous feelings.

Now as young Saul stood back from the sheepfold watching his father complete the job he'd been given, he only knew that he'd disappointed Kish and he castigated himself for his slowness. The muted sunlight set his head to throbbing. He kept his eyes on his feet and plodded toward home, left behind by a father hastening on toward the next battle engagement.

Jakeh remembers drying the boy's tears on that day and on many other such days. Saul's youth and adult life was a series of variations on that scene. The latest argument, the one they'd left behind three days ago was simply the adult version of Saul's desire for his father's approval mingled with the sense that he would never measure up. The argument's path was as predictable as the well-worn trail they were now treading.

Kish emerged from his house into the crisp morning. He was thinner now, a bit stoop shouldered but still taller than most men. Though he was approaching his sixtieth year his gaze was that of a man accustomed to commanding. The tilt of his head and the firmness of his jaw gave no doubt that he expected those commands to be obeyed. He held a steaming cup of tea and lowered himself on the bench beside his front door. The finches were holding a riotous conference in the oak tree in the plaza and the young boys were leading the flocks out to pasture.

Saul came striding across the plaza. He'd been out early, walking in the fields and sat down on the bench beside his father. He leaned back against the stone wall and spoke as though he were announcing to the neighbors, "I've determined that we should take the goats to the high pastures to the west. Three of the men can handle them. The sheep will go to the grasslands along the southern valley. I'll send Manoah and he can pick a couple of men to go with him."

Kish held his bowl of tea in both hands, sipped, and then slowly nodded. "So, you think this is the best choice?"

Saul continued to stare straight ahead and said, "Yes, father, I do."

Kish turned and tilted his head to look up at his son. "And what has led you to this decision?"

Saul raised his eyes to the pale morning sky and lowered his voice. "Don't you trust me? I'm thirty-eight. Aren't I old enough to make such decisions?"

Kish put out his hands, palms out, "I didn't say that. I simply wanted to know the reasons for your choices. I assume you have thought this through."

Saul gritted his teeth. "Well, yes. I suppose…I…" He sat in painful silence for a moment then abruptly stood. "I don't know why you always try to come at me like this, why you always attack me."

Kish set his tea down on the bench and with a sigh stood up and turned to face his son. He growled, "And I don't know why whenever I ask for the reasoning behind your decisions, you charge me with attacking you."

Now Saul growled, "If you'd treat me like an adult you wouldn't keep questioning me."

Kish's face reddened. "If you were an adult you'd be able to give clear reasons for your decisions. Could it be that you never give me any reasons because you have none? You think standing tall and speaking loudly justifies your position."

Saul snarled, "I didn't ask to be tall. And as for raising my voice, well, old ears sometimes have trouble hearing."

Kish coughed and spit into the dust at Saul's feet. "Oh, so now you dare to call me old. I imagine you pray for me to go quickly so you can rule the tribe."

Saul answered through clenched teeth, "Now you put words into my mouth and your own fears into my prayers."

Kish raised his ragged sandal and stomped into the dust. "Fears? I fear only the Almighty. I'm a just man and I stand before you and anyone unafraid. Have you forgotten that I am head of this tribe and head of my household?"

Saul grunted, "How can I ever forget. Do what you will with the flocks." He spun on his heel and stomped toward the pastures.

That had been four days ago. Jakeh had seen this drama played out often enough to know how to proceed with this latest blow-up: steer clear and keep mute. Then came an unexpected blessing: the donkeys escaped and the still fuming Saul was sent to find them. The trip began in ominous silence. But as the trail opened before them, so did Saul's spirit. Now after three days on the road, as they near the town of Ramah, the tall and handsome son of Kish is singing bawdy songs into the summer sky.

It is midafternoon when Saul and Jakeh reach Ramah. They begin ascending the hill toward the single gate piercing the nine feet high rough stone wall surrounding the town. A band of young women heading down to the well meet them as they climb. The women quickly pull their colorful veils over their faces and drop their eyes but not before hastily scanning this handsome tall man who approaches.

Saul stops and with exaggerated formality, says, "Good afternoon, daughters of Ramah. Might you be able to tell us if the seer is present today?"

After some shy giggling, one young woman replies from behind her veil, "Yes he is here, in fact he's just going up to the shrine to carry out the sacrifice so the banquet can begin. If you hurry you can catch him before he gets there."

Saul replies with a deep bow and a chuckle, "We thank you most deeply, o beautiful daughters of Ramah." Saul marches up the hill followed by Jakeh who shakes his head at the way this husband and father who should conduct himself with dignity, often acts like a callow youth.

They pass through the gate and see ahead of them an old man stepping out of his house. He grabs his staff and begins walking up the hill toward the center of the village. Saul hurries toward him, reluctant to disrespectfully shout. But when he is still a distance away, the old man stops and pivots toward him. Even at this distance Saul feels the elder's gaze. It exerts a squeezing pressure that slows Saul's hurried trot. He approaches in what he hopes is a deferential manner.

"Good afternoon, O lord, if you are the seer, then we, my servant and I have come to seek your services. We have some silver…"

The man raises both his hands, one to shield his eyes from the sun, the other, the one with the staff, to halt Saul's speech. He stares for some moments at Saul, sweeping his eyes up and down Saul's length several times. When he speaks, the words seem to be dragged from his throat.

"I am Samuel, seer of Ramah. I need no silver. I can tell you all that is on your mind."

Samuel's slow and solemn words tickle Saul and he can't help smiling. "Honestly, O lord Samuel, I have little on my mind but my three rascally--."

Again, the old man raises his staff and cuts off Saul's speech. "As for your donkeys, you may rest easy, they've been found."

Saul's grin lights up his dark face. "Great news! At least we don't need to return with bad tidings! Thank you and excuse us for interrupting your duties. We heard as we entered that you were going to…"

Once again Samuel raises his staff and now speaks ceremoniously, as if he's memorized the words. "On you and your ancestral house, all of Israel's desire has been fixed."

The character of Samuel's latest words is so different that Saul doesn't immediately register their content. But when he discerns that the words are in fact directed to him personally, he grins again and shakes his head.

"Lord Samuel, you may know about the donkeys, but I think you may be mistaking me for someone else. I'm of the tribe of Benjamin, our history is besmirched, in fact we are the lowest of all the tribes and, our family… well we're among the humblest. Why would you even say something like this?"

The seer intently peers up into Saul's face and opens his mouth as if to speak. Instead he steps forward, grabs Saul's elbow and begins walking up the hill. "Come, both of you. We go to the shrine. You will be honored guests at tonight's banquet." Saul shoots a puzzled glance back at Jakeh. The servant shrugs his shoulders and follows the two men up the hill.

Chapter Five

Dawn is a mere hint of grayness in the east. Saul pulls his long legs up against his chest. His rooftop bed, a straw mat laid on the mud dried roof, was refreshingly cool last night when he stretched out with a groan of pleasure. Belly full of rich food, good wine, and a clean bed after three nights in the sand. This was luxury. Now the desert dawn chills him beneath his robe and he wistfully thinks of that olive-skinned beauty who served the food at last night's banquet and how warm her body would be next to his.

The doves begin to murmur in the dim light. The goats are clearing their throats in the fold outside the wall. He begins to drift back down into sleep. Then, like a rusty sword a voice from below slices into the quiet morning,

"Saul, son of Kish! Saul, son of Kish, wake up and come down." Saul rubs his bleary eyes and groans.

"Saul, son of Kish, come down so I can bless you and send you on your way."

Saul rolls over and mutters, "Yesterday, feted and treated like a favored guest, this morning rousted out like a slave before dawn. Is this old man crazy?" Saul is a man accustomed to do what needs doing. If there is an animal that needs killing or a wall that needs mending he will be on his feet, robe belted, and ready for the job. But he is no reader of situations, not one to spend time ruminating upon the motives of others. And yet… several times yesterday Saul caught the seer squinting at him with narrowed eyes, as though trying to bring some blurry vision into focus. Then there was the embarrassing, extravagant treatment Saul received at the party—the choicest meat, the sweetest wine. And now this—an early morning wakeup call in total violation of village hospitality. All of this is as baffling as the man's absurd pronouncement yesterday that he was Israel's desire.

Saul rises and rolls up the mat. He shakes out his heavy hair, yawns loudly and stretches his long arms into the pale sky.

No sense fretting about it. Either it all means something or it doesn't. I'll find out soon enough.

He skirts the mat full of grain drying on the rooftop and walks down the steps that hug the wall. He delights in the simple beauty of the little houses whose stone walls look rosy in the dawning light.

"Hey Jakeh, how was your rest?" The servant has just emerged from the seer's house where he'd slept on a mat in the front room.

"Fine, but short," he grumbles, "And you, my lord, how did you sleep in your place of honor?" His words hold just a whisper of sarcasm but he is certainly correct in calling Saul's rooftop bedroom the place of honor. Last night, after they'd returned from the banquet, Samuel had been adamant that Saul take the choice spot.

"Well, I slept well, no dreams of lost donkeys, at least." Saul grins boyishly and can't resist irking his servant, "Other than I had to sleep alone, my night was fine!"

It is too early for fresh baked bread so Saul and Jakeh chew yesterday's flat bread and sip the hot tea served by a silent withered woman. They sit cross-legged on mats laid on the hard packed and swept dirt floor. Samuel sits quietly across from them. Before they began their meal, he recited one of the ancient familiar prayers, but now he does not eat. A few scant rays of the morning light filter into the room, but even in the dimness, as Saul works his jaws on the bread, and bends to his cup, he again senses the pressure of the Samuel's squinting eyes as they scan his face. They eat in silence and scarcely have swallowed the last swallow of tea when the seer scrambles up, staff in hand. Saul always defers to his elders but this man's impatience borders on rudeness. For whatever reason, Samuel is overly impatient to escort them out of the village.

Saul stands and stops mulling over the seer's motivations. As the three men walk toward the city gate, he sheds the puzzling hours he's spent in Ramah and is already planning the party he will have for his friends when they reach home. He grins as he imagines the wineskins being passed and the embellished stories he will tell. Just as they reach the gate, the seer grabs Saul's robe and jerks him to a stop. In a hoarse whisper, he says, "Send your servant on ahead, I have something for your ears only."

Saul is irked at this interruption but also curious. He expected the customary blessing for the two of them so they could be on their way. What could this aged seer have to say of importance to a wandering donkey herder? He shrugs and waves Jakeh on through the gate. He stands in the shadow of the wall, turns and looks down at the Samuel. He towers more than a foot above the elder planted before him.

Samuel squints up at him. "Yes, it is true, it must be true." He is murmuring to himself and nodding his head. Then he straightens his slumping back, takes a new grip on his weathered staff. His dark eyes flame like an ember in a breeze and his nostrils flare. The quiet murmur disappears and is replaced by a sonorous, stern command. "Saul, son of Kish, kneel down!"

Saul is tempted to roll his eyes and smile. But when he stares into Samuel's blazing eyes he feels a clutching inside his broad chest. The soft morning sounds of a village coming to life suddenly cease, as though everyone and everything is holding its breath. Time pauses at a crossroads and for an instant the two men are locked in the power of each other's gaze. Saul and old Samuel--young giant and old prophet.

A choice has already been made, and neither the young, restless giant, nor the weary grizzled seer has made it. Both will have enough years to rue that choice, and suffer because of it. That choice was not theirs to make, but it encloses them and clutches them in its grip. Now it is they who must choose. The next fearful choices will be theirs, and many of them will be dark, and bloody.

Still holding his riveting stare, Samuel tilts his head, points to the ground with his wispy beard. Time hangs like a raindrop on the tip of a leaf. Finally, slowly, Saul bends his knees and lowers his lanky body onto the gravelly soil. He fixes his eyes on the prophet as he kneels, hoping to discern what will happen next. He is bound to fail, because what comes next is beyond all discerning.

The seer's eyes pierce Saul's soul. His gaze grips Saul's dark staring eyes as he fumbles at the cloth tied around his waist. "Bow your head." A trickle of sweat slides down the Benjaminite's broad brow and a shiver slithers down his spine. This is no mundane traveler's blessing. Some spirit is spinning; some unseen wheel is turning. He bows his head and waits.

Samuel holds the small jar of oil and looks upon the bowed head before him. Even kneeling Saul's head reaches the seer's chest. Samuel knows his assignment, but he cannot help himself. After a lifetime of listening and serving doesn't he have the right? He murmurs, "O Lord, again let me ask: Who is being rejected here? Who is being received? Are you sure? Is this truly what I must do?" But the answer to this prayer, one he's prayed hundreds of times these last few days, is always the same: a distant thunderous silence in his own ears.

At last, he surrenders. His hand, as tough and thin as the foot of a chicken, trembles as he slowly tips the jar. The oil pours out silky smooth onto the crown of Saul's head, then trickles down his cheeks and drips off the end of his beard. Old Samuel speaks again but now the vitality in his earlier command has disappeared. Now there is weariness, and the craggy edge of bitterness riding on his words. "Saul, son of Kish, you are anointed by God to be king over his people. Rise now as King of Israel."

Saul sits back on his heels and tips up his head. Drops of oil fall off his beard and darken his robe. He stares up into the figure silhouetted against the silvery blue sky. Confusion, anguish and anger sweep across his face. His voice is flinty, "Prophet, what have you done to me?" Like every Israelite, Saul knows that a word once spoken, goes out into the world and does its work. Words are so much more than sounds that strike the ear. Words, especially words spoken by people like this seer, have the power to create what they announce.

Did the prophet actually say, "Rise up as King of Israel"? Sitting on his haunches, in the shadow of the village wall, with olive oil darkening the front of his dirty robe, Saul wonders if he should laugh, cry or curse. He can't decide, so he repeats the question, "Prophet what have you done to me?"

Samuel is stuffing the vial back into his belt. Like an old man who's been wakened from a deep sleep he growls, "I said, 'stand up.' And I have done nothing but what the Lord has commanded. If you have doubts or questions take them up with the Lord Almighty."

Saul swipes at his beard as he scrambles to his feet. "How can I be king? I'm no one. I came looking for donkeys and you anoint me king? I can't believe…"

"Believe or don't believe, it's all the same to me." Samuel snarls. "I didn't choose you, I didn't ask for a king. Blame your countrymen. The foolish, smug people of this land decide to conform to their neighbors. They clamor for a king." He spits disgustedly into the dust. "I'd have sent a plague of scorpions to sting their asses. But the Lord gave in to their desire. And the Lord chose you. He warned me…. told me, days ago that you were coming. This is His doing, not mine." The prophet turns toward his home. He suddenly stops, wheels around and pounds his staff into the dust, "I have done as the Lord God commanded. Now go on your way." He spins around and hobbles up the path.

For a moment, Saul's bewilderment paralyzes him. Then fear shatters his trance and he sprints after the retreating figure. "Wait, prophet, wait." He catches up to Samuel in a few strides but the seer keeps trudging up the path. Exasperated, Saul steps in front of Samuel, and dares to grab his shoulders. The elder scowls up at him and Saul drops his arms but continues to block the path.

"Please, prophet, stop. This is insane. How can any of this make any sense at all? Like lightning falling from the sky I am suddenly made king." He gasps for a breath and tries to speak in a quieter, lower tone, "or I should say, an old man in a shabby village pours oil, says words, and claims that I am king."

Samuel shakes his head and moves to step around Saul, but Saul quickly steps in front of him and implores, "Please, I mean no disrespect, but how can any of this be true? How can you call me king and then, with not a backward glance tell me to go on my way? If I am king as you claim I am, where am I supposed to go? What am I supposed to do?"

Samuel takes a step back and his eyes narrow. His scraggly beard trembles and his craggy voice bites. "O great King Saul, you'll have to ask those questions of someone else. I told you this wasn't my doing, not my idea. Talk to the Lord. Maybe you'll get more answers than I've gotten lately." The obvious pain in those last words softens Saul's response.

"Yes, I know, you told me to talk to the Lord. But I …well, I've prayed but I've never actually heard Him speak. Does He speak to you, I mean so that you hear? Are you sure you heard the Lord? Maybe it was a dream, a bad dream as far as I can see."

Samuel sighs with the longsuffering patience of a parent. "The Lord can speak and does speak, when and where He chooses. And no, it was not a dream, even though I can see why you'd wish it to be. No, my son, it was no dream just as this moment here and now is no dream. This is real, as real as the sun pounding on our heads, as real as this hard-baked earth beneath our sandals." He pauses, gazes up at Saul, then takes a step around Saul. He stops mid-step and turns back to the bewildered new king.

"If you think this is all some old man's demented ravings let me tell you what's going to happen as you head home." He raises his staff and points to the north. "When you leave here and head toward home, you're going to pass by Rachel's tomb in Benjamin territory, at Zelzah. Some people there will tell you that your donkeys are found and now your dad is worried about you. You'll keep going and when you get to the oaks of Tabor you're going to meet three men, not two, not four, but three. They'll be on their way to worship at Bethel. One man will be carrying three kids, another three loaves, the third a skin of wine. They'll greet you and give you two loaves of bread which you will accept…

Saul throws his hands into the air. "Wait! Stop!" His eyes flutter in confusion. "What if I don't accept the bread? What if I take a different road home? Will this cancel this…. this curse, this anointing? Is there any escape?"

Samuel tips his head into heaven, then scowls into Saul's face and continues as if he has not heard. "You'll keep going until you get to Gibeath-elohim, you know the place, where the Philistine soldiers are garrisoned? As you approach the town, a band of prophets will be coming down from the shrine. They'll be playing harps, banging tambourines, piping on flutes. As they come down the hill toward you, a mighty spirit will fall upon you and you too will become a prophet. You, Saul son of Kish, will become a prophet."

He stops and takes a breath so deep his body trembles as he releases it. "There. Are these enough signs for you? Will they convince you? Now please, let me go, I must rest."

Saul steps aside to let Samuel pass, but before he moves on, the prophet quietly murmurs, "Saul, when you see these signs, do what you think is right, for God is with you." Then his shoulders slump and he plods home. His battered sandals barely lift out of the dust. Saul watches him go and then turns and stumbles toward the city gate.

Chapter Six

Saul reaches the gate and a wave of nausea engulfs him. His stomach and head ache as though he's awakened from a night spent drinking too may skins full of bad wine. *The last words the prophet said to me were, 'Saul, when you see these signs, do what you think is right, for God is with you.' Did Samuel mean them as an encouragement or maybe even as a blessing? To me they're a vicious curse. 'Do what you think is right.' How am I ever to decide what is right? I'm always bedeviled by that dilemma. I'm never even sure of exactly what I'm thinking. How can I think my way to what is right?*

And then there was the seer's last utterance: 'God is with you.' His temples pound and he squeezes his eyes shut until his head shivers. *I've always done my religious duties, made the appropriate sacrifices at the birth of my children, kept the Sabbath. God and I... we've always had a safely distant relationship. But now, now Samuel announces that God is attached to me, always looking over my shoulder. No escape, no more carefree hikes into the wilderness*

Unnerved and terrified, Saul staggers out through the city gate toward Jakeh. The manservant gapes at a man transformed. A few minutes ago, Saul was striding with a boyish spring in his step and a heading-home grin on his face. Now, he walks like a man desperately trying to move a body wracked with a new pain in his gut. A frightening grimace has displaced the broad grin.

"Lord Saul, are you sick? You look like you've been struck by a fever, or maybe... seen a ghost." The leathery servant adds that last in a harsh whisper. For a generation, the Lord's priests had been telling the people that all such talk of ghosts and mediums is forbidden. Orthodoxy is an implicit duty. But this, this goes beyond pious priestly dictums. Only a few minutes earlier this young giant was swaggering down the path, a brawny brash lion. Now he comes reeling out through the gate, pallid and grim. If he hasn't met a ghost he must have encountered something even more horrifying.

Saul approaches and Jakeh hears him drawing deep breaths, as though he's trying to keep from vomiting. Jakeh smells Saul's sweat, the sweat of days of travel, but now also the sharp, bitter tang of fear. Before he can ask another question, Saul lurches past him and grunts, "we're leaving this place, we're going home." He straightens up, thumps the sides of his head with his fists, then stalks down the hill, past the well and back onto the worn track homeward.

Jakeh does his aged best to keep up. He is baffled. How can this rugged man whom he has known all his life suddenly mutate into a weakened stranger?

The sun melts the few early clouds and leaves an empty sky, so unlike Saul's mind full of billowing, roiling thoughts. He desperately tries to bring order to his thoughts. Yet the mere idea that all the while he is thinking, the Lord, the great God of the people, is evaluating his feeble mental efforts---this sends his reflections skittering in a thousand directions, like a terrified rabbit dashing from one stunted shrub to another. He shakes his head and his long hair snaps like a whip across his shoulders. A few hours ago, he welcomed the morning sun with delight but now it batters his head like a smith's hammer. He trudges homeward with bowed head.

Near midday they crest the ridge and see the small shrine of Rachel's tomb alongside the road. Rachel, patriarch Jacob's favorite wife is buried here, and not in some hallowed place. Some storytellers say this was because she died suddenly and unexpectedly and so was hastily buried where Jacob and the herds happened to be camped. Others tell a more religious tale: Jacob did not want to draw attention to the fact that he'd married sisters. Burying his Rachel alongside the forefathers at the cave of Machpelah would certainly have done that. No one knows which tale is true, or if either of them is correct. But everyone accepts her as the matriarch of the chosen people, and cherishes her as the consoler of the lost and desperate. Saul always imagined Rachel as a kind mother who would have understood his heart and would have comforted him. But today as they near the simple stone structure, his legs and heart petrify.

Jakeh notes Saul's slowing steps and calls hopefully ahead, "Shall we rest here awhile?"

Saul only grunts, "No, we keep moving" and quickens his pace.

They draw even with the ten feet high limestone enclosure. It's face glows white in the noonday sun. But Saul does not glance at it. He averts his eyes and surges ahead. As they pass the tomb a voice sounds behind them.

"Saul, son of Kish, is that you?" Saul ignores the shout and keeps charging forward but Jakeh hurries up to him and clutches his robe. "Master Saul, someone calls for you." Saul turns and winces. His eyes adjust and he spies the man standing in the shadow of the tomb.

"Are you Saul, son of Kish?" Saul nods and stands tensed as though preparing for an enemy attack. "I've been sent to tell you that the donkeys have been found and now your father worries about you. You're supposed to hurry home."

Saul not only refuses to acknowledge the message; he spins as though slapped in the face and stalks down the path. Jakeh scurries to keep up, perplexed by what has just happened. *Wasn't the stranger simply echoing what we heard from Samuel? What has happened to Saul? What power strangles him and sends him scurrying like a hunted deer?* Jakeh is curious enough and old enough to transgress the boundary between servant and master. He would grill Saul on the spot if only he could catch up to him.

Saul's chest is tight and his heart pummels his ribs. This morning when he left Samuel, he'd grudgingly accepted the prophet's incredible assertion. But once they marched out into the open country, once the horizon stretched out so generously before him, once his tense muscles loosened and sweat soaked his robe, he began to question the entire surreal scene. As he replayed the episode out here in the clear light of day he could almost convince himself that it had all been a dreadful dream. He began to hope that maybe this was all a massive mistake, a misbegotten farce. But now as he flees from the fulfillment of Samuel's first sign he begins to lose his fingertip grip on that desperate hope. *No, this morning's drama was more than a senile man's ravings. What will become of me? Am I marching to my doom?*

The next hour they walk in silence. Saul slows his pace and Jakeh walks alongside him. The questions he was determined to ask stick in his throat as soon as he looks up at Saul. His master's eyes are fixed on some empty space in the distant future. His jaw works as if he is chewing on an old piece of leather and he breathes as though working a Philistine iron maker's bellows.

By midafternoon they reach the fork in the path marked by the ancient oak of Tabor. This morning Saul raced past Rachel's tomb but now he slows down. They step under the shadow of the sprawling branches of the great oak and Saul gazes first at one, then the other path. They stand only a minute when they see three men descending the path from the east. Saul draws in his breath, then releases it in a long hiss. The youngest of the men is a slim youth with the beginnings of a man's beard. He carries in his arms, wrapped in a bundle, three very young goat kids, white and gray with sharp black eyes. The oldest man is a short, gray bearded elder with a wide smile and a skin full of wine slung over his shoulder. The third man appears to be about Saul's age. He is well built and tall though still nearly a foot shorter than Saul. He carries loaves of bread in a bag on his shoulder.

Saul speaks first, "Greetings, pilgrims, the Lord's blessing to you." He bows his head stiffly and keeps it bowed.

The old man speaks, "And greetings to you, travelers. You look as though your journey has been long." Saul looks up and silently nods. He holds his breath, fascinated and yet dreading what may come next. He does not need to wait long.

The tall pilgrim looks at the gaunt old servant and the haggard giant. "Would you accept some bread? We've eaten and have some to spare. Will you take these two loaves?" He pulls two browned and hard crusted round loaves from his bag and holds them out to Saul. Saul tips back his head, peers up into the thin blue sky. Every sinew and muscle in his body screams to him: Run! Scream and run down, down into the valley, over the hill, and lose yourself in the wilderness. But now he's convinced. *It will not be that simple, not now, not ever. I've been chosen, branded, marked. For some unknown reason, I've been grabbed by the Lord. I'm not my own man anymore.*

He does not run. He lowers his head and his eyes well with tears. He extends his powerful hands, gently takes the loaves and murmurs, "Thank you and the Lord bless you." The men smile and reply, "And the Lord bless you," then hurry away on their pilgrimage. Saul and Jakeh watch the three until they are mere dots on the hillside. Without a word, Saul gestures to Jakeh and they continue their journey home.

Chapter Seven

They make their evening camp in the shade of a clump of tenacious plane trees that tap into deeply hidden moisture next to a canyon wall. The light dwindles and the cloudless sky's blue is swallowed up by purple. The airy heavens transmute into an ebony bowl studded with stars. Each man eats from a loaf of the bread given to them by the pilgrims. Jakeh silently chews on the tough crust and on the puzzling change that had fallen like a shroud upon Saul. He is bursting with questions but one glance at Saul's masticating jaw and his glassy, distant eyes warns him off. His has been a life of patient waiting and that is what he does.

"Jakeh, have you ever talked to God?"

The question astonishes the servant more than if a star were to detach from the firmament above and plummet to the earth at his feet. Naturally all of Israel's children acknowledge the God of their fathers: Abraham, Isaac and Jacob. They all worship this God who led them out of slavery. God is as real as the firmament above and the earth below. God simply is. But this is different. Jakeh stares slack-jawed at Saul. During the nearly four decades he has lived with the family of Kish, never has Jakeh heard any member of the clan raise a religious question.

He clears his throat and searches for words. "Well, on the Sabbath, when we pray, aren't we talking to God?"

"I don't know. Are we? I suppose. That's what the priests tell us to believe." Saul takes a swallow from the nearly empty water skin, then wraps his long arms around his knees. He stares out into the dark night. He is wandering in unexplored territory. Foggy tendrils of disquiet invade his voice.

"But Jakeh, isn't there's supposed to be something more than just a roomful of men mumbling prayers together. Some people say they truly talk to God. Like I'm talking to you. Even if I don't look at you, I know you are here and I can talk to you and I know you can hear me. You've heard the stories... father Abraham--God talked to him and he talked back, even bargained with God. Moses, they say, even argued and disagreed with God."

Now Saul's words are more combative than plaintive. "Come on Jakeh, tell me, have you ever had a **conversation** with God?"

"Well.... I... not really." The servant's head drops and his thoughts step gingerly into healed, but still tender territory. He lifts eyes brimming with tears. "Three years ago, a fiery fever swooped down upon Aliu, my youngest son. Struck him with a flaming sword. He lay in our tent too weak even to groan. He teetered on the knife edge of death. I was distraught, frantic. I dropped to my knees and threw my face into the dust. I entreated God to spare his life. I begged, groveled, made promises… I suppose that was the closest I ever came to a real conversation."

"And did God answer?"

Jakeh smiles into the darkness. "My son is alive."

Saul plunges ahead with impatient intensity. "Yes, yes, I know Aliu's alive. I've seen him, that much I know. But Jakeh, did God speak to you? Did you hear words, a voice, a whisper, a sound in your head, a feeling in your heart, in your gut? Did God tell you what He was going to do? Did He tell *you* what you should do?"

A sad blanket of silence settles over them both. Saul releases his knees and claps his hands over his ears. "Not a word, not a murmur, not a buzzing in your ears or a rustle in the trees. Why doesn't God speak up? If God wants us to do something, or be something, why this damned silence?"

Saul stands and gazes up at the faint river of light arcing across the firmament. The malevolent spirits lurking in the darkness already are casting doubt on the words he heard from Samuel in the morning light. Already he's tempted to consider the encounters at the tomb and under the oaks as mere coincidences. "Is God dumb or are we deaf? Or maybe we're deceiving ourselves. Maybe God isn't speaking at all. Maybe God is watching, simply watching. Maybe God is sitting on his throne up there above the firmament, waiting to see what we'll do. Watching us parade around and make a shamble of our lives."

Jakeh wants to object, to warn Saul against such blasphemous words. But Saul wanders out into the darkness muttering to himself. As Jakeh watches him leave he is reminded of termite mounds he's seen in the south. Reddish towers, taller than a man, seemingly sterile clumps of soil. But when the tower's hard outer crust is shattered, the surface teems with frantic termites. A shell inside of Saul has cracked and his mind is flooded with questions and swamped by feelings he did not even know he possessed. Jakeh lies down, wraps himself in his cloak and drifts into sleep wondering, *what or who has broken into Saul's soul?*

Saul stands in the cooling night air. The silence is broken only by the chirps of lonesome crickets exchanging messages. Was it only last night that they'd had the wonderful feast hosted by Samuel? He remembers as if it were a dream, a picture viewed through a watery screen, a fragment clipped from his previous life. But this morning's scene…. Ai! That is chiseled into his memory. That surreal moment at Ramah's city gate---was it the entrance into a new life or was it an unhinged man's illusion? *How can I be a king? Impossible. And yet. The signs…*

He sits down on a rocky shelf still warm from the day's sun. He rolls his neck, reaches up and tries to knead his coiled shoulder muscles. He has borne this new burden only for one day and already he is exhausted. He's trod the clearly demarcated life trajectory of his culture for thirty-eight years. No forks in that road, no optional routes, no real decisions required. He followed his father's profession, as custom demanded, married the bride chosen by his parents, and sired children. Who needed introspection? But as he sits in the cooling silence of the night with the events of the day churning in his soul, he steps back and looks at himself. A distant memory flits across his mind, like heat lightning dancing across the sky.

He was eight or nine years old. It was the first time he'd been allowed to join his father and other men on a journey. They were traveling south to trade for salt. He shivered like a new born lamb, trembled with excitement and gulped down every new smell, sound, and sight. Three decades later he still remembers the unbridled, rolling laughter of the men out on an adventure. He still smells the pungent sweat of the mules as they scaled the hills and descended into the verdant valleys. He can still see the glorious soaring of the majestic eagles in the cerulean sky.

On the third morning of their journey, as they broke camp, his father said, "This afternoon we come to the great Salt Sea and you will see another wonder. But first we must pass through that…and it is never easy." He pointed from their point on the hilltop down to what seemed to the boy an undulating plain. To young Saul's eyes it appeared much like the terrain they'd already traversed.

At home he seldom questioned his father, but journeying together, traveling with the other men emboldened him, "Father, why won't it be easy, it looks just like all the other land?"

Kish smiled and then grunted as he loaded the donkey, "Not all things are what they appear to be. You'll see soon enough."

Their small caravan followed the switchback trail downward, toward the plain. From the back of his donkey, the boy's eyes widened in wonder. What from above had seemed like an unbroken tan blanket slowly revealed itself to be a maze of canyons, wadis, and ravines. The trail soon disappeared in the sandy soil at the base of the cliffs. Random tracks splayed up each gulch. The temperature rose as the high walled chasms stifled the breeze. The men's voices echoed eerily all around them. Some of the canyon floors were littered with stones. The hooves of the donkeys clattered across them and the air reverberated like the clacking of dried bones. A few valleys hid trickles of water. Saul could hear the secret streams murmuring beneath the stony floor. He marveled at how quickly and completely the terrain had changed, how what had appeared familiar and simple was in fact strange, complex, and mysterious.

Saul sits on the stone shelf staring into the night. In the last twelve hours, he's been carried into bewildering terrain. His mind seethes with unanswerable questions. *This morning I knew myself, but now, who am I? Does my life truly have a trajectory that I do not see? Is God truly at the heart of all of this? Can I run away, avoid what Samuel insists is my destiny? Can I thwart what is supposed to be God's will? Am I truly a king? Will I become a prophet like Samuel? Will tomorrow bring clarity or more confusion?*

If at this moment Saul could see what his tomorrows will bring, he might scream and run headlong down the slope into the purple darkness. But like most humankind, he is not blessed, or cursed, with such vision. He sees only the flicker of the stars and the ghostly rising of the moon. Its pearly luminescence gives depth and contour to the dark countryside. Bushes and boulders materialize faintly in the night. But Saul's tomorrows are shrouded in blackness. Gradually the weariness in his body trumps the maelstrom of his emotions. He sighs, wanders back to camp, lies down on his sleeping mat, wraps up in his cloak and sleeps.

Chapter Eight

The trail toward home winds across the lower hillsides, just above the valleys. Alongside the shallow stream that meanders through the tall grass on the valley floor yellow melons wink amidst the dark green leaves and vines. The two men awoke early and have walked for hours in near silence.

Finally, when the afternoon sun is the hottest and the traveler's legs are the weariest, the town of Gibeath-Elohim, the Hill of God, comes into view. It perches on a ridge high above the trail and is surrounded by a rough stone wall. Saul peers up at the town and hears the echo of Samuel's predictions. Yesterday he swung between stubborn denial and humble acceptance. Yes, the first two signs foretold by Samuel occurred. But the roads are always full of travelers and pilgrims. Saul is not completely resigned to accept the inevitable. And yet. What if Samuel's final prediction is fulfilled? "You, Saul, son of Kish, will become a prophet."

Saul pictures Samuel the prophet and then conjures up an image of himself as a fierce, sharp tongued speaker of the truth. *Would I have a clear vision of the future? Would I know the Lord's will with unshakeable certainty? Would the Lord literally speak to me as Samuel claims He speaks to him? If I became a prophet could I be bold and decisive?*

He chews on the notion as if it were a ripe fig and it grows ever sweeter. He sees himself standing fiery and stalwart in front of his clan, in front of his father, uncles and cousins. He imagines himself speaking a word from God. *Conceivable? Possible, yes!*

They begin the trek up the ridge. Sandals on tired feet slap in the dust. Then the chittering sound of tambourines comes drifting down the hill, rising and falling like the murmuration of a flock of starlings. They soon hear the shrill trilling of flutes and the dulcet tones of harps. Down the hillside trail swarms a band of men. They are enveloped in swirling clouds of dust and they surge down toward the travelers. Saul scowls. If these are prophets, they most certainly do not look or act like Samuel. They are dressed in brazen yellow and glowing white robes. They are barefoot and their hair is tousled and wild. They leap, twirl and shout out unintelligible words.

Saul cringes and steps back. This anarchic spirit terrifies him. He wants no part of this chaotic display. He frantically tries to encase his heart, raises up an internal shield so he can deflect whatever spirit they might fling out at him. The band of men gyrates down the pathway toward them. Saul lowers his shoulder, widens his stance as though preparing for an enemy assault. He clamps his jaw, contorts his face into a warlike scowl. He will defy these men with body, mind and spirit. He will not yield.

But his shield proves irrelevant. The spirit he fears doesn't radiate from these strange ecstatic prophets. They aren't burning bushes threatening to sear him with God's flaming spirit. To Saul's horror, the spirit's attack comes from within. He senses a movement within his chest, a stirring inside, as though something, or someone is alive at the center of his very being—a fluttering of wings, a stretching of limbs. His legs and arms begin to tremble. The fire he feared would attack him from without ignites within his own bloodstream. Abruptly his soul resonates with the exotic music, his feet move to the riotous rhythm. The pulsing melody and spinning movements send his mind's conflicting thoughts skittering into the dusty air. An ecstasy of wind and fire explodes in their place. The unwieldy, leaden chain he's staggered under since leaving Ramah drops into the dust. Saul is as exuberant and light as a fork tailed swallow. He twirls and shouts like a young man filled with strong drink.

Jakeh backs off the trail, sits on a boulder, thoroughly dumbfounded. Never could he have imagined this man, this Saul overcome by the turbulent spirit of the *nabi*, the ecstatic prophets.

The swirling, cacophonous band of fifteen men now surrounds the gyrating Saul. He leaps head and shoulders above them all, his thick mane swirling and bouncing about his shoulders. Abruptly the harp and flute stop. The tambourines begin pounding a steady beat that grows in speed and intensity. Everyone begins to spin in place. Tambourines pound, men shout and twirl, dust swirls. One of the dancers opens his mouth and a shriek born in the deepest corner of his soul explodes into the dusky sky and he collapses in a heap in the dust. The pounding of the tambourines and the shouting reaches an even higher pitch. Another dancer falls. For Saul, there is no thinking or pondering, no confusing examination of self. Now there are only feet dancing, arms flying, and body pulsing. Ecstasy has granted him the freedom of forgetfulness. The beat pounds and the shouting throbs until finally, with eyes white and wild, and saliva strings flying from his mouth, Saul bellows like a raging lion, leaps into the air, and spirals down onto the dust. The spirit's flaming wind blazes white before his eyes; a curtain swiftly falls and he is wrapped in blessed silent blackness.

Thirty minutes later, Saul moans and rolls onto his back. Strands of wet gritty hair lie across his face. His fingers wriggle, then his toes. He hesitantly reconnects with his body. His eyelids flutter and he opens his eyes. Jakeh's creased face hovers anxiously over him.

"Ai, Jakeh, what in the name of the Lord happened to me?"

"Here, sit up, drink some water." The old man holds out the water skin and Saul clutches it with shaking hands. He takes deep gulps and the trickles carve pathways through the coat of dust on his face.

"Jakeh, why am I…who..what…" The relaxed, placid face that slept in the dusty trail for half an hour twists and tenses.

The servant scarcely knows where to begin. "What do you remember?"

Saul stares up and away into the afternoon sky and tries to recapture a few strands of memory. A flock of finches sweeps across the sky. He follows their joyous, effortless flight. Now he turns back to Jakeh and stammers, "The noise, I remember the noise, music and shouting. Yellow and white robes. Fire, somehow, fire inside. And then…no… nothing more."

Jakeh could fill in the details for Saul, but intuitively he realizes these are of minor importance. Instead of describing Saul's ecstatic explosion he softly asks what he's been waiting to ask for a day and a half. "What did Samuel say to you yesterday inside the gates of Ramah?"

For a few confused seconds Saul stares into Jakeh's concerned face. Then his eyes flare wide and he scrambles to his feet. He begins to pace in a ragged circle and mutters to himself. He stops, points to a rock shelf in the shade of the cypress tree alongside the path. "Come, old friend, sit. I'll tell you everything. But you must swear on your life that you will tell no one."

Chapter Nine

Ahinoam looks up from her grinding stone as her husband walks through the village gate. Twenty-three years of marriage and a lifetime of silent observation equip her to see what he may be able to hide from others. Some sort of calamity has befallen her Saul. His broad shoulders slump under a leaden weight, a burden heavier than the usual tension after a stiff argument with Kish. His head is tipped forward and his smile is wooden. Her heart tells her his distress lies in a region beyond exhaustion.

Ahinoam rises as Saul plods toward their house. She is taller than most of the village women, though she barely reaches her husband's chest. Bearing and raising six children has taken its toll on her, grayed her hair and wrinkled her skin. She is both proud and envious of her husband who usually looks so much younger and stronger than she. She smiles to herself when she sees how he still captures the glances of women and allows herself to secretly gloat. She daily thanks the Lord God and her parents for arranging this marriage. Saul is always gentle with her. His occasional dark moods never spill into abuse.

As he crosses the plaza and draws near, she can see new wrinkles on his brow. How can this short trip have aged him so? She keeps her observations and questions to herself and steps into his embrace. "So, the donkeys beat you home. Now I suppose you want to do nothing but eat and sleep for a week."

He groans and grins. "Two weeks would be better."

She feels his stiff body soften against her. They walk arm in arm to the bench beside the courtyard door. Saul slowly lowers himself down and heaves a deep sigh. Ahinoam brings out the basin as he slips off his sandals. Dark brown eddies swirl in the cool water as she scrubs the dust off his feet.

"The boys are out with the flocks today. Kish sent them out to the Kinnoah fields." She still calls her sons boys though they are grown men. Abinadab, Malchisua and Ish-boseth are already married. Only Jonathan remains unattached.

Saul growls, "Of course the old man would send them out to the farthest field, even though the grass is better closer in." She wipes his feet and holds her tongue. Any comment she makes will only fuel Saul's frustration. She deftly changes topics.

"The girls are weaving with Abner's women. They should be home soon." After bearing four sons, she was blessed to have two daughters. Merab and Michal are lithesome teenagers. They chatter like excited sparrows and their laughter sparkles like a sunlit brook. The very thought of them invariably brings a smile to Saul's broad face. But not this afternoon. Saul's only reaction to his wife's comment is a worn-out grunt. Ahinoam picks up the basin and pours the water at the base of the fig tree that stands just outside their courtyard. Saul slumps forward with his elbows on his knees and stares at the ground. She has seen his dark moods before. But this heaviness is new. She returns and stands beside him, hand laid gently on his shoulder. At last she leaves and goes inside to prepare the evening meal.

The girls return as Ahinoam sets the food out on the mats. "Welcome home, father." They kneel in front of Saul and kiss him on the cheek. He smiles but says nothing. The girls chatter, sharing the latest gossip of the village. Their laughter fills the mellow evening air but Saul seems oblivious. He methodically chews a handful of dates, tears off a piece of bread and eats not out of hunger but of habit. His gaze loses itself in the fluttering flame of the oil lamp. Repeatedly he sighs as though his lungs are too big for his chest.

At last the girls are asleep and the couple lies on the sleeping mats. Ahinoam turns on her side, lays her hand on his great chest, and softly asks, "Husband, what's troubling you?" The omnivorous darkness swallows her words and leaves a long and painful silence. She begins to wonder if he even heard her question. Finally, his chest heaves in one more of those deep, searching-for-breath sighs.

"Not what. Who. God is troubling me." Her hands stiffen on his chest. They both know how odd this sounds. Never in their decades together has the subject of God entered their conversation. He stares up into the dark night. "According to the old seer at Ramah, God has decided to give our people a king." He props himself up on an elbow and gazes into her dark eyes. "And what's more, supposedly God has already decided that I am that king."

Now she rolls onto her back, sputtering in confusion. "But that's crazy…I mean…How can you…?" She snickers in disbelief. "Hold on. Who is this seer? Who gives him this authority?"

"I told you. His name is Samuel. He's been the judge of the people for years. He claims that God speaks to him."

Ahinoam throws her hands into the heavy air. "Doesn't there have to be a ceremony or….?"

Saul snorts, "Ceremony? Oh, of course there was a ceremony. If you could call it that. Samuel poured oil on my head, it streamed down my face and dripped off the end of my beard. While he was anointing me, he announced that I was the king of Israel. Sure, there was a ceremony. But only he and I and the pigeons on the city wall witnessed it."

"So maybe the old man isn't in his right mind. Maybe he doesn't---"

"Speak for God? I challenged him on that too. But before I left he told me what would happen on the way home and every detail."

Saul sits up and for the next hour unleashes the torrent of emotions, words, and images dammed up in his soul since his encounter with Samuel. As he speaks of the whirling prophets and his own ecstatic experience, his voice rises.

"Shhh, shhh, shhh! Don't wake the girls." Ahinoam sits up beside him. All this talk of God and king baffles her. But beyond her perplexity lurks a fear that jabs chills into her heart. "What will your father say about all of this? What will our clan say?"

Saul is abrupt and blunt. "Nothing, nothing at all. They don't know. I've sworn Jakeh to secrecy and you mustn't say a word, not even to our children. Can you imagine Kish's mockery? Can't you just hear the elders' scornful braying? Besides, remember the story of our ancestor Joseph who bragged about his dream of being a king? Remember what his brothers did to him? They almost killed him, then sold him into slavery. No, I'm not telling anyone a word."

He drops back down on his mat. "Besides, I wouldn't know what to say. How would I even begin to explain? If this is the gibberish of a demented old man, then it'll come to nothing. And if it's God's doing…well, then God will have to speak up and give me instructions."

They lie in silence. The cool night air carries only the usual sounds: a dog barking at the scent of an invisible enemy, a baby crying to be fed, and palm fronds whispering secrets to each other in the breeze. The couple holds hands in the darkness, mutely posing their questions into the gloom. *What does this all mean? Is God here now? What will happen next?*

Chapter Ten

The world-weary prophet eases himself down on the rock ledge. His right knee pops and his left knee clicks. Samuel is determined to fulfill his duty to the Lord, despite his body's protest. He grins wryly to himself, "To grow old you need to be as stubborn and as stupidly courageous a rock badger!"

Samuel has been coming to Mizpah for years to hear the people's complaints and settle disputes. The mountain city is one of the stops on his annual circuit: Bethel, Gilgal, Mizpah and finally home to Ramah. He's been gone now for weeks. Today will be his last day in Mizpah. Tomorrow night he can sleep on his own mat in his own house. At every stop on this entire journey, he ordered the leading men in each village to gather in Mizpah on this day. He promised them a special word from the Lord.

He sits on the limestone ledge on the crest of the hill. The slope below is dotted with clumps of men. The air is full of buzzing conversations and laughter. Yesterday sheets of rain swept across the hills, today the sky is clear blue crystal. The farmers all agree, "now the storms have the smell of summer." Throughout the land it is the season of change.

Today's sun warms the prophet's back, but it is no match for the fire that has been smoldering in his gut for the past weeks. Before he began his latest journey the Voice had come to him. Its usual measured and calm tone ordered him to announce to the entire nation what he had done to Saul last summer.

He raises his arms for silence. He looks out over the hundreds of men silently looking up at him. He speculates on how much longer he will have enough power and respect to hush crowds with a simple gesture. Flaming words pour from his mouth, bearing the sharp acid of his own rancor.

"Sons of Israel, here is God's word to you: 'I, your God, carried you out of slavery in Egypt. With the back of my hand I swept away other nations who tried to stop your march to freedom. I drove back the Philistines from your land. Over and over again you've gotten yourself into all sorts of messes and every time I've lifted you up and saved you.'"

The crowd nods and murmurs assent. Fire flickers in Samuel's eyes as he raises his staff and spits out the next words: "Today God says to you: 'All this I have done, but now you people, you sons of Israel, now you want a king.'" The fire in Samuel's belly spills out and he nearly shouts, "Obviously having a God like ours is not enough for you. You don't want to be unique among all nations. You don't want to be chosen and set apart. No, you want to fit in, you want be like everyone else. You want to be like all the pathetic pagan nations around you. You want a human king.'"

Eyes once fixed on Samuel now drop, and sandaled feet shuffle in the dirt. No one dares deny the words, for they are true. No one dares mount an argument against the blazing words of the prophet. An apprehensive silence carpets the hillside. Obviously, he is not finished. What will come next?

Far down the hill, near the back of the crowd, out of range of Samuel's fading eyesight but still close enough to feel the heat from his words, stands Saul. He tried every argument to convince his father that he should stay home. 'Someone needs to manage the boys who tend the flocks, someone needs to supervise the servants.' But the result of all his justifications was predictable. He silently and sullenly submitted to his father. He stands behind Kish, surrounded by the rest of the Benjaminite clan. The crowd does not know the prophet's next move, but Saul has his suspicions. Since the day he heard of Samuel's summons, he's lived in dread of the "special word" of the Lord the old man promised to deliver on this day. Samuel's words crackle over the crowd and Saul is certain he knows what will come next. Nervous sweat trickles down his cheeks, his robe sticks to his back, and a fist of panic clenches in his chest. He furtively works his way backward beyond the edges of the crowd.

On the hilltop, Samuel's fire now appears to be doused. He lowers his staff, and clings to it simply to keep from toppling forward and tumbling down the slope. The throng holds its breath. "You want a king. So be it. Gather up by tribes and clans and stand before me where I can see you." Hundreds of pent up breaths whoosh out at once. The bluster and buzz of men organizing themselves into groups reaches Saul who has arrived back at their campsite in a shallow valley. He pulls some of the packs and bedrolls around himself and lies down on a sleeping mat. His panic has subsided and been replaced by a dull throbbing in his head.

Lying on his back, he begins a harangue or a prayer. "How crazy, utterly absurd is all this? Here I lie, paralyzed by fear. God, are you senile or simply insane? Why not pick an old, wise elder? Why not choose someone accustomed to giving orders? Why pick a man like me? I've only taken orders and can hardly make any decisions at all?"

He hears Samuel calling out names, "the tribe of Benjamin." Even from his baggage hiding place, Saul can hear men's voices and he's convinced he can hear shock and disbelief in their tone. He imagines more than one elder muttering, "Benjamin? That pitiful tribe of losers?" After a few minutes, the seer's raspy voice sounds out again, "out of the tribe of Benjamin the clan of Matri".

Saul shakes his head in bemusement. *Why is the old man playing this pathetic game? Is he so unwilling to give up the center of attention that he's dragging this out as much as possible? Is he delighting in playing god? Is he determined to make a fool out of me? I should run, I should get up and run and never look back.*

On the hillside Samuel shouts, "Saul, son of the family of Kish." Saul yearns to flee, to run like the wild donkeys into the wilderness, to take flight like the falcons and soar above this confusing maelstrom. But he only groans and lies on his mat, his powerful legs paralyzed by his own indecision and fear. He remains frozen as he hears the men muttering as they trot down the valley to fetch him. "Saul from the tribe of Benjamin…the seer is a cynical bastard, or God has done this to punish us." Transfixed on his mat, Saul can't help but agree with them. The men excitedly shout, "he's here, we've found him."

They drag him to his feet and Saul is mute. He climbs the hillside in a trance with the men surrounding him so he doesn't flee. He is petrified with terror. His mind is lost in a dense cloud. The shouts of the men scarcely penetrate his fog, "Long live the king!" His own mind whimpers, "May I die quickly and without pain." Today there is no repeat of the fire and ecstatic freedom he experienced in Gibeath-Elohim. Instead of fire and freedom his heart is chilled and burdened with something new: the heavy stone of responsibility. He stands on the hilltop, towering over the prophet at his side. He sways and struggles to breath under the pressure of a thousand eyes. He doesn't know where or how to look. He doesn't even know where to put his own hands. He stands immobile as a statue, while Samuel prattles on about kingship regulations and documents.

Saul stands tall and imposing upon the hilltop. But his thoughts are as desperate and frantic as a bee trapped inside a jar. *What will come next? Will I have to say something to this crowd? Am I supposed to do something? If this is truly God's doing, shouldn't God give me a word to speak? I hear nothing, feel nothing. Absence. God's absence is all there is.*

His buzzing thoughts are interrupted by silence. Samuel has stopped speaking and Saul holds his breath. What next? He doesn't dare turn and look at Samuel. He doesn't even have the temerity to look down on the faces gazing up at him. His tongue is leaden; his mouth is as parched as the Negev. But then Samuel heaves a deep sigh, "Now men of Israel, go home. Go home to your families and flocks."

Saul stands shocked and momentarily relieved. It's over. Samuel is already descending the hill and heading home. Most of the men simply turn around without a second glance. The spectacle has ended, time to get back to fields that need planting, flocks and families that need tending. The air throbs with conversation as most of the men gather their baggage and start their homeward journey. Most of the men, but not all. A dozen strapping men, some of them about Saul's age but most younger, gather their things and climb back to the hilltop. They stand beside the stunned giant, waiting to follow him.

If he had the temerity to interrogate these men, Saul would ask "What has convinced you that I am your king? Were you moved by the prophet's words or by God himself or do you simply think I'm

56

tall enough?" Another group of men cluster lower on the hillside, spit into the dust, glare at Saul, and mutter, "How can this guy save us?" Saul yearns to say to both groups, "Just go home and forget about me." But confusion and trepidation imprison his tongue. He mutely gathers his baggage and follows his family home, trailed by those few men who are already convinced he is their leader.

Shouts, laughter, and boisterous conversations tumble through the air as the clans of Israel scatter to their homes. But the Benjaminite clan plods home quietly. They are trying to cope with a new and unfamiliar sense of notoriety. In decades past they carried the onus of their ancestors' abomination. Lately they have simply been regarded as insignificant minor partners in the loose brotherhood of tribes. When Saul was dragged to the hilltop they all stood with mouths agape. That they were now to have a king was a thunderbolt. But that this king would be one of their own? This news is as unsettling as the earth tremors that plague their land. And what about this cluster of men from different tribes that trail after their caravan? The clansmen mumble to each other under their breaths and sneak sidelong glances at Saul who marches stiffly in their midst. His glazed eyes and locked jaw ward off any attempts at conversation. Before long Saul stretches out his lengthy stride and walks alone, a dozen yards ahead of his clan.

Kish gazes at the broad back of his eldest son. He is both apprehensive and proud. The patriarch's beard is long and gray, and his knees ache every morning. But his back is still straight and he still holds pride of place in his family. For Kish, and for any elder head of the family, stability and control are what make life possible. Count the herd meticulously and often, plow the furrows straight and sure, set clear boundaries for children and wives. How else can anyone fight off the chaos that always swirls beyond the horizon? But today's events…The bizarre scene he's just witnessed…. Where does it fit into his world? What does it mean? His gut cramps with anxiety. And yet, and yet…this is Saul, this is *his* son…summoned, summoned out by the prophet surely, and …by God, possibly.

Finally, about an hour into their journey, Kish defies all propriety, hikes up his robes, breaks into a shuffling trot and runs up alongside his towering son. Saul shortens his pace to accommodate his father's stride but he does not unclench his jaw. They walk in silence accompanied by the sound of gravel crunching beneath their sandals and the occasional cry of a hunting hawk. Father and son have entered an unfamiliar landscape. The familiar territory of their relationship had plenty of well-worn conversational trails and recognizable landmarks. But they now face unexplored terrain. Finally, the clan leader, so inured to speaking with authority, dares to voice his confusion.

"Son, what does this mean? A King? How…who… I don't understand."

The bewilderment in his father's voice is so real and so new that it shocks Saul out of his mute marching. His voice is rough with emotion.

"*You* don't understand? You think I do? This angry prophet claims to speak for God. Who can prove it? Or disprove it? Why would God even look in my direction? Who are we? Who am I? Now you see why I wanted to stay home!"

Kish hears, for the first time, the deep pain and bitterness in his son's voice. "So you knew? You knew this would happen? You've met Samuel before?"

Saul shrugs. "Seven months ago, on the last day of our hunt for the donkeys. Yes, I met him. He declared this same absurdity." He hesitates. He yearns to tell it all but is embarrassed. The power and the intimacy of that event defy words. At last he murmurs, almost under his breath, "Then he made me kneel and he…he anointed me."

Kish gasps. Anointing is a sacred act, a God infused ceremony. Only a raving maniac would dare to perform an anointing without some sign from God. And Samuel, from what Kish has seen, is no maniac.

"Anointed…and now proclaimed…. Then it's true, it must be true. So now…?" The question hangs in the dusty air and Saul snorts.

"So now…So now what? … Samuel never answers that question and the God who supposedly speaks to him hasn't yet chosen to speak to me. So now, now I go back to the fields and the flocks and I do my job. What else can I do?"

Kish has never seen his son vulnerable, or perhaps he's never looked. In the house of Kish, vulnerability has always been equated with weakness. But now the father looks unwaveringly into the confusion assailing this giant, this king, this son of his. Instead of turning away or attacking, he ponders how he might help. On impulse, or incited by some spirit beyond his reckoning, he draws his sword from his scabbard. This weapon is a rare thing in Israel. It is solid steel, forged by the Philistines who've mastered this art and whose armies now grow more dangerous. Kish paid dearly for it and proudly displayed it to his clan and to the other clans gathered at Mizpah.

He grabs Saul's arm and tugs him to a stop in the middle of the trail. In front of the approaching clan he holds out the smooth sword. It gleams with menace. He presents it to his son. "A king must have a kingly sword." Saul's unbelieving eyes travel from the sword to his father's eyes. Saul takes the blade and hefts it, while Kish unbuckles his scabbard, steps close to his son, reaches around him, and silently buckles the belt. Kish stands inches from his son's broad chest and softly murmurs, "Take the sword. You will need it."

Chapter Eleven

Saul is plowing in the shallow valley north of Gibeah. The single plow point easily turns the gray brown soil. Most of the rocks have been taken out years ago and deposited on the edges of the field. His stolid, steady oxen have pulled the plow through this field for many seasons. The routine is printed on their sturdy oxen hearts. Saul keeps the plow upright and plods along behind them.

The rains have stopped and the days have grown hot. Months have passed since the gathering at Mizpah. Neither Kish nor his clan have been able to digest what happened there. They were perplexed on that day and nothing since has helped explain its meaning. When they question Saul he simply shakes his head and refuses to speak of that strange spectacle. The men who followed him to Gibeah have found work in the surrounding villages. The flocks need tending and the fields need tilling. The daily demands force them all to return to their normal routines. So today Saul plows.

In his mind the anointing at Ramah and the proclamation at Mizpah stand like isolated stelae, those slabs of stone poking up from the earth to mark a grave, or a great victory. The surface of his life is still filled with contours worn smooth by decades old routines and relationships. But now, thrusting up from this familiar landscape are these two pillars. Though he refuses to talk about them, (what could he say, anyway?) his thoughts keep returning to them like a tongue finds an aching tooth.

King of Israel? Preposterous. What would a king of Israel act like, what would he do? How would I even begin? He tries to strangle these troublesome questions and focus instead on his work and his family. He has fields and flocks to tend. He tries to be a helpful father to his youngest son. Jonathan is already a grown man, not as tall as his dad but more aggressive and less concerned about Saul's opinions than Saul is of Kish's. There is no lack of daily matters to attend to.

But his mind is magnetically drawn to those peculiar pillars. And when, like today, he is engaged in some activity that requires no mental concentration, he puzzles and wonders. Some days he even allows himself to imagine what being a king might feel like. He has never seen a king, nor even known anyone who has seen a king but traveling storytellers, passing caravans have told tales. And when the elders of the clan gather, someone always tells the story of the king of Egypt who enslaved the sons of Israel centuries ago. As he plows his thoughts drift through images of finery and thrones, attendants and servants.

No matter where his musings wander, they always return to the kernel of this mystery. *If I've been chosen by God to be king, then where is this God? If I've been selected to rule over God's people, then why doesn't God speak to me? Lord God, are you hearing me?* Hour after hour Saul follows his patient plodding beasts around the field. He scans the silver blue sky, probes his roiling mind and troubled heart. Not a word, not a whisper. The silence is empty.

Saul finishes the field, unhooks the plow from the yoke and walks the two oxen along the path back to the village. In between the steady plodding of the beasts and the chuffing of their great lungs, he hears a new sound, a clamoring disturbance. He halts the oxen, turns his head and strains his ears. A subtle shift in the breeze and…? Yes, now he can clearly hear shouts and wails coming from the houses up ahead. He urges the oxen to a trot. He and the two beasts come thundering into the village square. Men and children, even women carrying their babies are gathered around a messenger who stands under the great oak in the center of the plaza. The women are weeping, their babies whimpering in sympathy, some of the older men have ripped their robes in grief.

The crowd parts as Saul and his gasping beasts skid to a halt in their midst. They all begin to chatter at once, competing to tell Saul the tragic tale. Saul throws out his arms, tips back his head and bellows, "Silence." They are shocked by his uncharacteristic outburst and the cacophony abruptly dies. Only the babies continue to whimper. Saul marches up to the travel weary young man beneath the tree. The fellow's eyes are red with weariness, his robe is dusty and sweat stained, and his sandals are mere scraps of leather.

"Who has sent you and what is your news? I want to hear it from your own mouth." The youth straightens up, sweeps the hair from his face and recites the message he's repeated in every village in the region. He speaks directly to Saul, not shouting as he did when he first entered the plaza.

"The elders of Jabesh-Gilead in the east have sent me. They beg for help. Nahash, king of the Ammonites came up against your brothers of the tribes of Gad and Reuben. He not only conquered them but viciously ordered that every man's right eye be gouged out. The land weeps in pain and anger, but everyone fears to protest, lest they be totally blinded. Now this vile snake Nahash has laid siege to Jabesh-Gilead. The elders have tried to negotiate with him. They plead for their lives and have offered to serve him. But Nahash will not agree to their terms unless they surrender their right eyes. The elders have asked for seven days to consider his demand. They sent me and others to ask every tribe for help." He stopped his recitation and shouted now for all to hear, "In the name of the elders of Jabesh Gilead I ask, does the tribe of Benjamin have a deliverer?"

"Deliverer", "Meshach", "Messiah." As the syllables strike Saul's ears, a vibration begins deep in his bones. Like flint striking steel, the words strike his heart and sparks fall into the tinder of his soul. His lungs begin to work like a smith's bellows and the fiery spirit of the Lord surges through his veins. His eyes smolder with passion. The crowd hushes and edges back sensing the heat of a blazing power. In one swift blur Saul draws his sword, raises it high over his head and points it heavenward. The summer sun transforms it to silver fire. Saul's head tips back and he gazes into the pale blue. His eyes roll in a frenzied ecstasy. Then his head drops and soundlessly he abruptly steps between the two oxen. He grabs the horns of the ox on his right, tips back its head and with an upward slash, slices open its neck. The beast makes no sound as its blood begins to spurt in great bursts onto the dust. Before its buckling knees even hit the ground, Saul turns, grabs the horns of the other ox and slashes its neck.

The two huge beasts slump grotesquely in the dirt and blood gurgles and pools blackly around them. The village dogs begin sniffing at the scent of hot blood and flesh and edge closer, but the crowd, as one body, gasps and retreats further, terrified by Saul's frenzy.

Now completely possessed, Saul bellows out orders. "Ropes! Bring ropes!" His command unfetters the paralyzed crowd and the village men break for their homes and return with cords, some of leather, some of woven fibers.

Saul stands between the two bloody beasts as the men return. Their tall clansman has become a giant. His eyes are dark flames. He tosses his thick dark mane and flings sweat into the air.

"Drag the beasts to the oak tree and lift them by their back legs." A dozen men surround each beast and with grunts and shouts tug the slaughtered oxen beneath the limbs. Two men clamber up into the branches, catch the ropes as they are tossed up. With ropes attached to their hind legs the beasts are hoisted up by men caked in blood, dust and sweat. The ropes are fixed and within minutes the oxen are hanging, nearly severed heads grazing the dust, and hind legs touching the lowest branches.

The men gaze at the carcasses. They pant with exertion and adrenaline. They have been infected by Saul's passion though they do not yet understand what it means. They quickly discover his plan.

Moving with the authority of a priest and the precision of a butcher, Saul takes the tip of his razor-sharp sword, inserts it an inch into the underbelly of the first beast, beneath its hind legs and slices downward. With a great sucking, sloshing sound the entrails flop onto the ground. Saul cuts the viscera free and the entire mess now lies in the dust beneath the carcass. He waves his sword and nods to the men. Without a word, several come forward and drag the guts to the edge of the plaza where the dogs already drool and growl. He repeats the process on the second carcass.

He stops now and his chest heaves with exertion and fury. He turns toward the crowd and stands between the freshly butchered animals. He speaks in a voice as razor-sharp as his sword. "I am Saul, son of Kish, of the tribe of Benjamin. I will go and free my brothers in Jabesh Gilead. Now, I want eleven men to step forward."

Some of the men who followed Saul from Mizpah immediately separate themselves from the crowd and stand before him. More slowly, a few of the village men join them until eleven men stand facing Saul and the two bloody slabs. Empowered by the Spirit and instinctively guided by ancient memory he announces to the men and to the crowd. "I send this message to every tribe of the family of Israel. Whoever does not join me as we march against Nahash, let him be as these oxen." He turns and begins hacking at the carcasses. First, he hacks off the heads and casts them aside. Then he makes several deep slashes and severs one front shank and hands it to one of the men. "Take this to the tribe of Zebulon and give them my message." He severs the other shanks, the ribs, the loins. As each piece is severed, a man steps forward, receives his commission and his burden. Eleven bloody chunks of meat, eleven messages sent to the eleven tribes of Israel.

It is late-afternoon when the last messenger leaves. The villagers stand aghast and mute. They have seen God's power at work, God's lightning strike one of their own, one who is not a holy man or an elder. As they gaze at Saul, their sweat soaked, blood drenched clansman, the fire in his eyes flickers and dims. His head droops and his shoulders slump in exhaustion. He moves toward home and throws one arm over his son Jonathan's shoulder and then, to the bewilderment of the villagers who know of the friction in that family, Saul drapes his other arm over Kish's shoulder. They watch Saul shuffle across the plaza. Everyone in the village has heard the stories of the Samuel's announcement made months ago in Mizpah. Now they themselves have witnessed an astonishing event. The prophet's declaration must be true.

Saul leans against the stone wall of his house, in the shadows and out of view. He is drained. His soul has been singed. He peels off his gore soaked robe, crouches beside the clay water pot and begins scrubbing blood from his face and arms. His earlier musings of what kingship might mean are washed away by the wine-red water that sluices off his arms and disappears into the sand. *Does God peer into my heart and mind? I don't know. But this much I believe. I will be king. And there will be blood.*

The next morning Saul quietly rolls off his mat, silently unbars the courtyard door and steps out into the gray morning. Ahinoam and his daughters still sleep within. Jonathan sleeps on the flat roof. Murky clouds blanket the sky and only a faint blur marks the hidden sun. Scenes from yesterday's bloody rite scudded across Saul's dreams throughout the night and now his head is wooden. Jonathan descends the staircase and joins his father. He is nearly twenty. His beard is still short but already it glimmers with a reddish sheen like that of his father. He has the smooth, supple movements of his mother, and though his shoulders and chest will never match those of Saul, he is clearly strong and quick.

"Shalom, father. Did you sleep well?" Saul smiles ruefully and slowly shakes his head. They stand in silence as the village stretches and awakes. Women fetch water, dogs arch their backs and yawn, chickens scratch in the dust. Jonathan raises his arm and lays a hand on his father's shoulder. "What will we do next?"

Saul turns and looks down at the smooth, eager face of his youngest son. "We? What will WE do?" He tips his head back and stares into the blank gray sky. "Don't think that you have to be part of this……"

Jonathan pulls back his arm and lays it across his own chest. "I'm your youngest son, but I'm also a Benjaminite man. Last night you called this tribe to arms and I will come with you. I'll follow you because you are my father, and….my king." Those two words hover and buzz in the air before Saul like a hummingbird. His thoughts spin. *"'My king,' how strange to hear these words. How strange to hear them from my own son. The words are more natural in Jonathan's mouth than they are in my heart."*

"Jonathan, I'm still trying to understand what it might mean to be a king, but I've no doubt that you are a man." He puts his long arm over his son's shoulder determined to give him something he himself has never received. "You don't need my permission to be a man…or to be a soldier."

Chapter Twelve

"Shalom, Saul, son of Kish."

Even before he turns, Saul recognizes the scratchy, dusty voice of the seer.

"Shalom, Lord Samuel. Why am I not surprised to see you?" The elder merely grunts, draws up alongside Saul and they continue hiking up the hill. This is not a morning for small talk. The day will be scorching. Locust whizz out of the grasses as they make their way to the summit. Will the enemy be so quick to flee?

They reach the summit and Saul stands with legs apart, fists planted on his hips, head swiveling back and forth as he gazes down at the seething plain below. The prophet Samuel, wiry and weary, leans on his staff beside him.

Three days ago, Saul sent out his bloody declaration of war. Each gory slab carried a foreboding weight. It recalled to the collective memory of Israel the story of the Levite and his concubine. Then a hacked off body part had summoned the land to rise up against the Benjaminites. Now a Benjaminite was doing the summoning. In every town and village men felt the crushing burden of the call.

Samuel smiles sourly at the crowd below. "You see how the people rally to you? Surely God has lifted you up as their leader."

Saul shakes his head. "They don't come out of allegiance to me. I'd wager that for most of them the fear of saying no was greater than the joy of saying yes." He imagines the men hugging their wives and concubines and receiving from them the hard loaves of bread baked for the journey. He envisions the men gathering their children and making them promise good behavior and obedience. He visualizes those men who have swords sheathing them and tying on their scabbards, then reluctantly marching out to Bekah, the appointed gathering site.

Saul glances over at the hawk-nosed, aged prophet and for a moment turns his thoughts away from the looming conflict. *What makes a man a king? What transformation elevates any man from simply being an exceptional human specimen to a king? This old man, God's holy prophet… must I accept him as that? He anointed me. Just the two of us, simple oil, simple words. But still, it was a sacred ceremony. Must I admit that? Samuel claimed it was a divine act announcing God's decision.*

But that earthquake moment in the shadow of Ramah's walls didn't make me a king, at least not in my own heart. Then came Mizpah. Once again, this same holy prophet drags me before the tribes and proclaims, "Here is your king." Unnerving public proclamation. But it didn't convince all those who heard it. It certainly didn't persuade me. I neither saw myself, nor felt myself to be a king.

But now as I stand on the crest of this hill, something has shifted. Look at the thousands of men who've gathered in the cramped valley below, thousands who've responded to my summons. I'm forced to accept it and admit it. I will be their leader in battle, and maybe their king.

Saul shifts his thoughts back to the present and his eyes back to the troops below.

"Samuel, I've no illusions—I doubt that many of those gathered below recognize me as king. But they've responded to my call, whether out of fear or duty or devotion, I don't know. But they've come and now I feel responsible for them."

The prophet speaks quietly, and Saul hears sadness seasoned with sarcasm in his voice. "Responsibility. Yes, this is the gift God has now given to you. You'll do what a prophet can't do. You are a king and a king leads his people into battle."

Saul slowly nods. "So it seems. I've committed myself to do this, so I suppose, yes, I've accepted that I'm now the king. But you should know I'm not embracing this responsibility as if it were some alluring woman. I take no pleasure in this. Back home, when I look out over my flocks in my heart I feel joy and pride bubbling up like a spring of clear water. But I don't feel any of that here. And you should know this too. Even though you keep insisting that this is all the plan of God, I haven't found any sensation of relief since I said yes to being king. I thought that once I gave up resisting, once I stopped fighting against what you declared as God's will, I thought my anxiety would disappear, I thought I might even feel some relief, some comfort. But I haven't had any of that.

Samuel's neck is clearly stiff. He turns his head slightly and tips it back with a grimace.

"Relief? Comfort?" He looks down to the valley below and snorts out a contemptuous laugh. "Whoever promised you that? Did anyone ever suggest that doing the Lord God's will would give YOU anything at all? Don't say that you got that idea from me, Saul, son of Kish. This isn't about what you will get. It's about what you will give, what you will do. When I was a boy I was taught that simply knowing you were doing the Lord God's will was reward enough. I was captured by God's will a long time ago and all I can say is this: Don't expect anything for yourself. That way you won't be disappointed."

Saul throws up his arms in exasperation. "But am I doing God's will? How do I know? *You* have said so. *You* claim God has chosen me. But God hasn't said a word to me, not a whisper in my ear, not a thought in my mind!"

Samuel is not dissuaded. "What about the prophets of Gibeath-Elohim? And these bloody tokens that you sent out into the land?"

Saul shakes his head. "How can you call these words? I swirl and dance and fall drooling in the dust. I explode with blazing rage and slaughter my own oxen. Fury and fire invade my bones, lift me out of myself. But is this the Lord God's doing? Who's to say? Is this the Lord God's word? Is this all I get? I can't accept that."

Now it is Samuel's turn to shake his head. His words slash the morning air. "And who are you, Saul son of Kish? You may be a king but who are you to say how God's word will come to you?"

Saul opens his mouth to respond then slowly chews on the bitter naked truth of the old man's question. *Who am I after all? A Benjaminite, the least of the tribes, a plower of fields, a tender of flocks, a tiny ant ordered to do an oxen's job. This may be unjust, unfair, and ridiculous. But what right does that give me to question God? All I can do is act and hope that God will be satisfied.*

Saul's ruminations are interrupted by a young man running up the hill. He skids to a stop in front of the two men.

"Sir, you asked for a messenger. Here I am." He stands at attention, puffing from his exertion. Eagerness gleams in his dark eyes. The whisper of a beard darkens his jaw.

Saul stares at the fervent lad for a moment. Then he swivels his eyes to the mass of men below. It strikes him that this is his first command, his first order. He is dispatching a fellow son of Israel into mortal danger. He squares his broad shoulders and turns toward the youth.

"Yes, my messenger, good. Jabesh lies ten miles to the east. The Ammonites have camped before the city gates. I want you to find your way into the city and give this message to the city elders: 'Tomorrow morning you will have deliverance.' Then tell the elders to go out and promise the Ammonites that tomorrow at noon the city will surrender."

Saul smiles grimly and turns to Samuel. "Maybe tonight Nahash and his cursed troops will celebrate their imminent victory and tomorrow morning they'll still be sodden headed." He turns back to the young man. "Do you understand the message?"

"Yes, my king."

Saul growls, "Then go!" The messenger begins trotting down the slope, then Saul shouts, "Wait." The eager warrior turns and looks up at this giant of a man silhouetted against the bright sky. "What is your name?"

"My name is Medad, O king."

Saul softly repeats, "Medad, Medad. Godspeed Medad."

They watch the lad trot down the hill and head off toward the Jordan valley. Saul turns toward the valley full of soldiers and slowly begins descending the hill. He mutters more to himself than to the prophet, "Now we'll see if the rest of these men are as eager to obey as young Medad."

I don't know if I'm kingly but at least I'm tall enough to be seen by the troops. Saul surveys the crowd before him. He strides through the mass of men, and is met with a few shouts of acclaim, a handful of quiet greetings, and a great blanket of disquieting silence. He fights the temptation to banter and joke and finally stops trying to read the message of this muteness. He throws back his shoulders and stalks among the soldiers with what he hopes is an air of authority. By late afternoon he gets the thousands of soldiers divided into three companies and has given each company its orders. Saul names his oldest son Malchisua to lead one company, his cousin Abner to lead another and he himself will lead the third.

As the sun slides behind the undulating horizon of the Judean hills Saul leads the troops out of the Bekah valley eastward toward Jabesh. Only the occasional whickering of the horses breaks his strict order for silence. By midnight the three companies are in place in the hills around Jabesh. Malchisua's company lies hidden to the north above the city, Abner's company to the south. Saul's company is sequestered in the hills to the west of Jabesh. Straight ahead across the plain the moonlight shines on the walls and city gate. Below their company, between them and the city, lies the enemy camp. Just as Saul hoped, the guttering dance of a few fading fires and the occasional burst of raucous laughter suggest that at least some of the soldiers are indulging in a pre-victory celebration.

Saul's troops stretch out on the grass, recuperating from their march and regaining energy for the conflict ahead. For Saul rest is futile. A torrent of anxious adrenaline surges through him. If he hadn't ordered his men to minimize movement, he himself would be frantically pacing up and down the hills. He sits with his back against the trunk of a cedar. His knees are pulled up, and his heels relentlessly jitter up and down. He broods on what he's set in motion.

As a boy, Saul often joined his friends in pushing small boulders down the steep slopes of scree. The rocks would roll and leap in unpredictable fashion. Sometimes a surprising landslide would set the boys shouting with glee. He stares at the dark slope full of sleeping men. When he ritually slaughtered his oxen, he pushed a boulder down the mountainside. He made plans and communicated a strategy, but now the execution and the outcome are no longer in his hands. He can't control tomorrow's events. As a shepherd of flocks and planter of crops, he could rely on his own resources to accomplish his goals. But now he is a king. His world has expanded. Now, despite the risks and the anxiety, he must rely on others. This new burden is a millstone around his neck. He mutters a prayer.

"Oh God, I don't know…… Is it by your power that these men have come? Is it by your power that they've responded to me? Is it under your banner that we'll charge down these hills tomorrow? If we conquer, is it you we thank? If we are defeated who bears the blame? These men will blame me, oh God. If we defeat the enemy, they may thank me but they will also thank you. But if we're crushed, there's no doubt I'll be held accountable. O God if you could only give me some assurance, some sign…."

The night breeze teases the leaves of the tree above him, the soft snoring of the men drifts up the slope. Perhaps God is speaking, but Saul hears nothing.

Waiting hours are eternal hours. The new king stares eastward until his eyes ache. Suddenly, between blinks, he perceives a subtle distinction between hills and sky. Finally, gratefully the moment for action! He quietly moves to waken his men. Their company will launch the attack at dawn, drawing Nahash and his troops toward them. Once those enemy troops are in motion, the other two companies will rush down the hills to crush the infidels.

Saul's company moves down the slopes toward the enemy camp in the half light. They have only a few horses among them. Some men carry spears while others have swords and leather shields. A contingent has bows and arrows. A few of the men are carrying only scythes brought with them from their hay fields. Only half of them have any sort of helmet. Saul looks at them from the back of his stocky red stallion and wonders how many of them will survive the day. Yesterday, before leaving, he tried to organize them into groups. But as the first rays of the rising sun illuminate his troops he grimly admits the truth: *this army, my army, is a motley, ragged horde. I can only hope their prowess and courage are in better shape than their equipment.*

Just as they reach the valley floor, the panicked blast of an Ammonite watchman's trumpet rips open the morning calm. Saul stands up in his stirrups and shouts "Shields up!" The soldiers in the front line lift their oblong shields and the troops began trotting toward the camp. The morning air now teems with avid, adrenaline loaded shouts, the sounds of clanking metal and pounding boots. Across the field, the first line of enemy soldiers begins forming. Saul bellows, "Archers prepare" and those with bows nock their arrows. He hopes their attack will be enough of a surprise to allow them to strike first.

He roars, "Shields hold." The shield carriers halt and form a closed barrier. The archers plant their feet, angle their bows upward and wait. Battle blood throbs in Saul's temples. He tracks the approaching chaotic clot of enemy soldiers and finally roars "death to the enemies of God." Like angry wasps a swarm of arrows buzz into the sky followed by shouts of anger and screams of pain from the enemy horde.

This is the signal anticipated by the other two companies. They charge down out of the hills from the right and the left, roaring with blood lust. They hurl spears and wave swords. The Ammonite soldiers swirl in confusion, sheep surrounded by wolves. Their eyes roll white with panic. Saul spurs his horse into the maelstrom, slashing with the only steel sword in the entire army. Blood spurts from slashed and severed limbs, men roll in the dirt stabbing at each other. A grotesque chorus of agonizing animal screams and guttural roars of savagery rise into the dust above the plain.

Within an hour, the slaughter is complete. A handful of Ammonite soldiers manage to escape across the plain and hide in the hills. But most of them lie here in the dirt, twisted and blood soaked. Already their corpses attract flies and eager vultures circle overhead.

Saul sits on his horse in the middle of the carnage watching his kinsmen root amongst the bodies. If they find one of their own still alive, they quickly stoop and tend his wounds as best they can. If they happen upon an enemy who still breathes, they stretch him out spread eagle in the viscous bloody soil and deliver a quick stab through his heart. He squirms and jerks like a worm on a hook for only a few seconds, then joins his comrades in death.

Saul walks his horse carefully across the gruesome plain. He is not surprised by this scene, nor is he appalled. Blood, stench, and grim horror are unavoidable. After all, this conflict is between God's chosen people and the infidels. The slaughter was necessary. What does surprise him are his own feelings. He feels a great relief. He expected that. But beyond that, he feels exhilaration. The realization that he is still alive sharpens all his senses. The sky is magnificently blue; the hills shimmer in the glassy sun. To him even the dusty, bloody air smells sweet. Most of the men around him are surely feeling the same way. He sees his sons, Malchisua and Jonathan, embracing their comrades and roaring with joy.

But Saul's exhilaration surpasses theirs. He rolls his neck and his aching shoulders, then pulls off his helmet, shakes his sweaty black hair and roars like a lion who has just brought down its prey. He has done it. He has proved to himself, to Kish, to Samuel and to God that he is a man who could be, no, *should* be Israel's king.

Like sheep released from the fold, the citizens of Jabesh-Gilead pour out of the city gates and greet their deliverers, their redeemers with cheers and embraces. Saul sits proudly grinning on his horse. A young man pushes through the crowd shouting, 'hail, King Saul'. It is the messenger Medad. He reaches Saul and looks boldly up at him and then drops to his knees and touches his head onto the ravaged dirt. Saul sweeps his long leg over the saddle, lifts the boy up and swallows him up in an embrace. "Well done, well done." Still holding the lad, Saul shouts to the crowd, "Israel needs brave men like this young man to fight against her enemies."

From the back of the pack, comes a familiar voice, "Yes, and the enemies are many." The men part as Samuel approaches Saul on his leathery mule. Saul's exuberant spirit is dampened by a blanket of irritation. The old man must have left at midnight to get here. *Why must he trail me like some suspicious parent who's not sure he can rely on his son? Or is he jealous because I'm the center of attention?* He swallows these bitter thoughts and steps forward to receive the prophet.

But before Samuel reaches the king, some of those who've followed Saul since Mizpah surround the prophet. A young, barrel chested man, whose shield bears the scars of many strikes, speaks for the group, "Lord Samuel, since the day you declared Saul to be our king, we've followed him, waiting for this day. But we've also held in our hearts the names of those who turned their backs on him. We want your blessing now so that we can hunt down and execute these traitors."

The citizens and soldiers hush, crane their necks to see the old man and hear his decision. But this is Saul's day and he will not let Samuel steal it from him. Before the weathered seer can even open his mouth, Saul holds up both arms and announces, "No! No vendettas, no killing of brothers. Today the Lord has brought deliverance to Israel. Let gratitude, not vengeance fill us all." Samuel nods in silent approval and the crowd roars at Saul's magnanimous decree. But the wily prophet is quick to refocus the attention to himself.

He holds high his staff and shouts, "Once already I've declared to you that this brave Benjaminite is your king. Who will come with me now to Gilgal to renew that declaration?" Men raise their swords and spears, their scythes and shields and shout their assent. Samuel swings his donkey around and the troops slowly follow. They step over and around the corpses of slaughtered Ammonites, leave the battlefield and march to the hallowed ground of Gilgal.

Chapter Thirteen

The caravan of men and animals moves west back toward the Jordan River. Saul rides in the middle of the crowd. His face shimmers with delight. Status and power taste honey sweet. The air is full of raucous laughter and rollicking shouts and it surrounds Saul like a warm bath. It softens and sloughs away the crust of anxiety that has surrounded his heart for the past year. For the first time in his life he dares to see himself as he believes others now see him: broad, tall, and formidable, a true man of stature amongst his people.

They are marching toward Gilgal, the circle of twelve stones, a holy place for the tribes. Saul grins at the memory of himself as a boy, sitting cross legged and wide eyed with the other boys as the young nervous village priest regales them with the story of Joshua, successor to the great Moses, leading the chosen people into the promised land. He can still hear the young priest's piercing, pinched voice.

"So, the great Lord, The Lord stops the flow of the Jordan. The water stands there like a wall. All the boys and girls and men and women and herds and flocks march across into this land where the milk flows like a river and the honey drips like dew drops in the morning. So, boys, what do you think Joshua does once everyone crossed over? Does he continue the march, order everyone back into motion?"

The teacher does not expect, nor does he wait for the spellbound boys to answer. "No, he doesn't. Here's his first official command in the new land. Joshua looks out over this mass of people and he shouts, 'Let one man from each tribe come forward.' Every tribe chooses a big, strong man to put at Joshua's disposal."

As he rides along with his troops Saul chuckles at the memory. He was only ten years old but already big for his age and still innocent enough to believe he could lead his clan one day. Like all the other boys he imagined himself standing shoulder to shoulder with the other clan leaders waiting for Joshua's orders.

The young priest's voice climbed higher as he grew more animated. "Joshua looks at these twelve men, representing all of the chosen people. And he says, 'Go back into the river bed that we just crossed. Each of you dig out a stone, a big stone and bring it here before me.' A strange command, eh?"

The teacher peered at them over his thin, sharp nose. "But they obey, oh yes, they obey. Boys, can you imagine those sweaty, muddy men, parting the crowd like God had parted the Jordan minutes earlier? Can you see them flinging down their stones on the grass? Thunk---'remember the powerful God who brought us to this land!' Thunk---'remember the faithful God who never forgets a promise!' Thunk---'remember our God who is generous beyond all imagining!' Thunk---'remember why this God brought us here!' 12 tribes, 12 stones of remembering. Never forget, boys, never forget. It is God who has given us this land. If we forget we will lose it."

Saul and his boyhood friends imitated the priest's shrill voice and retold the story, but that final injunction hadn't made much of an impression on any of them. Today as his victorious army marches westward, Saul wonders what is at stake for him and for the people these many centuries later. *Gilgal was the site of the first monument in Israel to the fulfillment of God's promise. Will it soon witness another fulfillment? This still seems murky to me. Whose will is being satisfied by this coronation? The Lord God who is seeing his divine plan moving forward? The disgruntled crowd that clamors for a king so Israel can be like the other nations? Or maybe it's an impatient Samuel, who has twice already tried twice to install me as king? Could it be all three?*

Five days ago, Saul would not have imagined that he would be comfortable with, much less looking forward to, another public ceremony. But this afternoon, as they near the holy site, he thirsts for the shouts and acclamations. God may have anointed him king, Samuel may have declared him king, but to have the people, God's people, his people, acclaim him king, that will be a true coronation.

They descend the slopes, covered with grasses and shrubs brittle now in the summer heat. Here the Jordan is shallow, but it still provides a cool refreshment as they ford across. They approach

Gilgal at dusk. The singing and shouting of the boisterous horde fades quickly. All are awed by the sacred circle of stones.

Instinctively, Saul moves to the head of the caravan. He dismounts, hands the reins to a soldier and solemnly strides to the center of the circle. The soldiers gather around the outside. The boulders are dark shadows now, the last rays of the sun skim Saul's head and shoulders. A hush, a golden silence holds for a moment. Then the emotions of the last twenty-four hours--the nighttime march, the dawn attack, the bloody victory and the triumphant journey to this holy place—all the army's pent up emotion is unleashed when one voice shouts, "Hail, King Saul, the power of God be with you!" The soldiers burst into cheers and raucous shouts. Saul glows and the towering man grows taller in their eyes.

Saul looks for Samuel in the crowd. The seer stares silently at the ground. Sensing Saul's eyes he glances up and reluctantly steps into the stone ring and walks out to Saul. He stands alongside the man he anointed and gazes out over the crowd. He sighs, then begins to speak softly, barely above a whisper, "Let us now make offerings to God, thanksgiving for the victory."

The rousing fiery prophet is unusually subdued as he leads the troops in sacrifices. He intones prayers as a slaughtered goat burns on a makeshift stone altar. The rising smoke carries up thanks to God for victory over the infidels and for raising up a leader. By the time he finishes the rituals, the stars are glimmering.

The men now gather around bonfires to share stories and wineskins. Saul wanders through the camp and is received with cheers and embraces. His bellowing laughter fuels the celebration far into the night. He falls asleep with his head spinning from the wine and his heart overflowing with satisfaction.

Chapter Fourteen

Saul's tent is already warming in the sunlight when the rusty-sword voice of Samuel rips through the camp. "Arise, men of Israel. Gather at the circle and hear the word of the Lord."

Saul splashes water on his face, combs his beard and hair and joins the yawning crowd as it makes its way to the stone circle. He steps over the outer rocks and stands beside Samuel who waits in the center. He expects that Samuel will repeat the declaration he made months ago at Mizpah. But then, does Samuel ever do the expected?

The summer sky is crystalline clear. The snorts of horses, buzzing of flies, and a few scattered yawns are the only sounds as the king stands alongside Samuel. The disparity between the two men strikes every man in the crowd.

The seer astutely homes in on that fact. "Men of Israel look at this man, what do you see?" They all see a towering Saul with shoulders as broad as the yoke for a team of oxen, dark beard and hair gleaming in the sun, cloak stained with the blood of the enemy, a man in the prime of his life.

"This man is the king that you have asked for. Remember, he is *your* idea. Now, look at me. What do you see?" They all gaze at a scraggy Samuel, shoulders rounded, wispy beard fluttering in the breeze, a worn but clean robe, an elder wearily facing his waning days.

Samuel's voice turns brittle. "When you look at me, do you see a thief? Have I ever taken advantage of my position at your expense? This is your chance. Speak up now."

The crowd had anticipated a grand coronation speech. They are taken aback by Samuel's surly challenge. A murmur ripples through the ranks and finally some men begin to shout, "No, never. You've never stolen from us."

Samuel holds up his staff and stills them. "Fine. Remember that. This king of yours, and God himself have witnessed your answer. Now, remember this."

He replaces last night's subdued mumbling with a piercing harangue that reaches the farthest ranks. "Remember when our forefather Jacob and his family went to Egypt and the Egyptians made them slaves? What happened when our ancestors cried out to God? God sent Moses and Aaron to lead them out and bring them to this land. Do you remember?"

The crowd rumbles its assent. Samuel's words reverberate over the soldiers and as he speaks, clouds arise in the west and begin to stretch across the sky.

"But then our ancestors forgot the Lord their God and bowed down to the Baals and Astartes. To punish them God sold them into the hands of the Hazorites and the Moabites and the Philistines. Then our people cried, oh they cried. And they begged God to forgive them and to rescue them. Do you remember what God did? Do you?"

Samuel is shrieking now. "Our Lord sent Jerubbaal and Barak and Jephthah and Samson and the Lord God rescued you and you lived in safety."

The clouds scud closer and a chill wind slaps the faces of the watching crowd. Cold wind and clouds in the dry season? An undercurrent of anxiety ripples through the crowd. Samuel finishes his recital of the past.

"Every time the people sinned and got into trouble, they cried out for rescue and God rescued them. But when Nahash the Ammonite king threatened you, you decided that you needed a king to defend you. A king, not God, but a king. Well, here he is, here's the one you've asked for." He taps Saul's shoulder with his staff. Saul glares down at the seething seer. He grinds his teeth and desperately longs for this harangue to end. But Samuel hasn't finished.

"Your God has relented and given you what you wanted. This king will order you around, and you'll have to submit to him. If both you and this king obey God, you'll be fine. But if either of you goes your own way…" His voice drops and he slowly growls, "there will be tragedy for all of you."

The seer glowers at the troops standing in petrified silence. Then he thrusts his staff toward the clouds and bellows, "God, send a sign. Show these people that they have embarked on a dangerous path."

A bitter wind swoops upon them with a banshee howl, clouds mass and boil, jagged lightning stitches pierce the sky, bellows of thunder roll across the plain, and icy rain pelts them all. The bewildered, soldiers crouch down, turn their backs to the wind and the stinging drops.

Saul glares at the satisfied smirk in Samuel's eyes. In disgust, he turns full face into the wind and rain. He trembles, not from the chill but in frustration and anger. The drops burn his face and torment his soul. *This dried-up seer prays to God and God sends rain in the dry season. I pray to God and get nothing but desolate drought, a parched and empty silence. I am king of Israel but I am graced only by God's muteness.*

Within minutes, as quickly as it materialized, the clouds evaporate into wisps, the wind dies, and the sun reappears. The stunned soldiers slowly rise and shake the water off their robes. They gaze apprehensively at Samuel. Saul scowls down at this man who now appears to be his adversary. His long arms tremble and he fights the impulse to pick up the seer, fling him out of the circle and claim his kingship cleanly and completely.

Some of the men begin to wail, "Samuel, Samuel, pray for us so we won't be destroyed. On top of all our sins, we've added asking for a king."

Samuel holds up both arms to quiet the shouting. "Don't be afraid. Of course, I'll keep praying for you, just as I've always done. I'll keep teaching, just as I've always done. Just be sure you stay faithful to God, both you and your king." Then he swishes his staff over the troops, "If not, you'll all be swept away." That grim warning settles over them like a funeral pall.

Samuel begins walking out of the stone circle. He stops and turns to Saul who remains rooted at the center. "Seven days after the seventh full moon, after the barley seeding, I will come here for ceremonies. You will wait for me here."

Saul watches him march away. He thought yesterday's victory and last night's heady celebration had buried his doubts. Clearly that grave was shallow. He feels the uncertainties grimly creeping up out of their crypt accompanied by a new cynicism. He might now be the king, but Samuel the prophet isn't going to sit passively on the old men's bench under the palm trees. For Saul, most devastating is the stunning evidence that while Samuel still had God's ear, he, the king, has only God's silence.

Samuel's stark figure disappears over the crest of the hill and all eyes now turn to their new king. Saul has no choice but to act. He must do something, anything to demonstrate that he has embraced his role as king. Bands of panic constrict his chest. He needs time to think. From the center of the stone circle he speaks in his deepest voice.

"Men of Israel, after the noonday rest, gather here for your orders." He nods a dismissal and without speaking passes silently through the stunned crowd and crawls into the loneliness of his tent. He sits unmoving on his mat and chews upon Samuel's words. The prophet's latest words still burn. But the words that trouble him now are not the ones spoken moments ago, but the words spoken to him by the prophet at his anointing at Ramah: 'Do what you think is right, for God is with you.'

Lord God if you are with me, then help me think. What is the right that I should do? Are you guiding my thinking? Will you bless my doing?

His fevered questions go unanswered. At last he forces himself to consider the choices before him. Many of his men, including his older sons, need to return to their land and homes. The wheat harvest is beginning and if the families are to eat through the winter, the ripening grain must be cut, gathered and threshed. But he must also keep some soldiers with him. After all, he was made king to help protect the people from their enemies.

He spends the next hour passing between the tents, speaking to a few chosen leaders. When the troop gathers around the circle he is ready.

"Brave men of every tribe in Israel. The Lord God has blessed us with a great victory over the Ammonites. You have brought honor to your tribes and clans. Now God has made me king and called me to protect our land against the enemies who still prowl our borders. I cannot do this alone. Some of you have already been appointed by your elders to stay here in Gilgal. You will receive your orders soon. As for the rest of you, I send you home to your flocks, to the harvest and to your families. Go now with God's protection."

Without cheers or fanfare, the subdued troops begin their march homeward. Saul leads Jonathan, Abner and elder soldiers from the other tribes into his tent. The sides of the tent are raised and a lazy afternoon breeze drifts through. The men sit in a circle on the woven mats. Bodies are stiff, voices restrained; the prophet's warning still reverberates in their ears. All of them, except Jonathan, have dark beards, and weathered skin.

A flash of frustration nearly overwhelms Saul. He sits down, then lowers his head so the others can't see him grinding his teeth. Samuel keeps giving with one hand and yanking away with the other. Saul is near exploding in a blaze of curses but the hooded gazes of the men restrain him. Their dark stares press against him like ill-fitting armor. Gradually he raises his eyes and sweeps slowly around the circle.

"So, brothers, most of the men have gone home. What about the thousands we have kept here with us? What shall we do? Tell me what is in your hearts?" Nervous glances flit around the circle but the men remain mute.

Finally, Eliad from the tribe of Zebulon blurts out, "Saul, you're the king. Tell us what's in your heart." Saul is encouraged by the grizzled man's words. Despite Samuel's cautions, these men hunger for a leader. He remembers the surge of savage joy he felt after the battle. He decides to test the men's will for war.

"Brothers, it grieves my heart that the pagan Philistines continue to swallow up our land. In Geba, once one of our cities, the ruler is now a Philistine. His decrees are backed by a garrison of Philistine soldiers." All around the circle beards bob in agreement and the men begin to clamor.

"These infidels are nibbling away at our territory too."

"We need to stand up."

"We need to reclaim it."

"This land is ours by The Lord's promise. If we do not defend it…."

Amid the din, Saul notices that Abner alone looks down into his lap. Saul holds up a hand and hushes the men.

"And you cousin, what do you say?"

Abner is not only solid as a brick, but shaped like one as well. His head sits directly on square shoulders; his legs are as thick as tree trunks. Of all the men in the circle, he's had the most battle experience. He raises his deep-set eyes and methodically looks at each man in the circle, stopping with his gaze locked onto Saul.

"The Philistines have caused me and my family great pain. No one in this tent hates them more than I do. But war is huge risk. You, O King, you alone have a sword of steel. But the Philistines all have armor of steel, and every soldier has a sword of steel. They can hack our weapons to pieces. I'll take the lead in any battle, but I tell you, there'll be blood and not all of it will be from the Philistines."

The group falls silent. Abner's bleak reminder slices deep into their bravado. Then Jonathan clears his throat. He dramatically raises his arms.

"Isn't the threat of the Lord's displeasure at our cowardice greater than the threat of the Philistines?" Saul smiles secretly at Jonathan's zealous and pious idealism. He himself doubts that argument, but it appears to sway the men around the circle. At least their heads nod in silent agreement. Saul embraces Jonathan's challenge and speaks in what he hopes is a decisive tone.

"We stand then as one people, twelve tribes but one people. God's chosen people against the heathens." Faces lighten and robust voices of approval fill the tent. For centuries, the tribes have shared a common history and a common God. Now resistance to a common enemy is forcing them to raise up a new nation. The men now turn to strategies. Abner's wary words dissuade them from declaring war outright. But Jonathan's challenge persuades them to take a definite stand against their common enemy. They decide that Jonathan will take a thousand soldiers and hold a position over against the Philistine garrison in Geba. Saul will take two thousand soldiers to Michmash to prevent the Philistines from further incursions. They rise from their mats and as they prepare to leave, Jonathan ventures to voice the question the other leaders are silently asking.

"King, how long will we occupy these positions?"

Saul rolls his eyes and slowly shakes his head. "Jonathan, this only God knows." He dismisses the men and watches them walk out of his tent into the afterglow of dusk. He wonders. *Does God truly know and if so, will He ever tell me?*

Chapter Fifteen

Jonathan stares up into heaven's dark bowl and traces the star outlines of the Bear and the Hunter. A few men quietly talk but most of the troops are sleeping. Off in the distance, in the hills that roll behind them, he hears the eerie, crying howl of jackals on the hunt. Their cries only add to his restlessness. For month after month he and his men have encamped on this hilltop across from Geba. They've done nothing to hide their presence. Jonathan is sure the Philistine troops knew they're stationed out here. But the pagans have shown no indication they are in any way vexed by the Israelites' presence. His orders were to stand guard on this border. He'd agreed to that without question. But then he'd been surrounded by all the elders. If he'd been alone with his father he might have spoken the thoughts that now tumble through his mind. *Why should we defend this border? This border was determined by the Philistines, not by the Lord. Why should we respect it? Wasn't all this land promised to us? And if the Lord entrusted it to us, won't He supply the power we need to reclaim it?*

Jonathan's restive blood itches in his veins. He fidgets until almost midnight when gradually the seed of a plan sprouts in his mind. He grins in the dark at the adventure ahead, then falls into a fitful sleep. In the gray dawn light, he rises and awakens Ben Amad, his second in command.

"Have the men on alert overlooking the road by mid-morning." When the groggy soldier begins to speak, Jonathan interrupts, "No questions. Just do it."

He slips out of the camp and winds his way through the dew laden grass down to the road leading up to Geba. He doesn't need to wait long before he sees what he needs. An old farmer plods up the road carrying a net bag full of melons.

"Shalom, grandfather. Your melon fields have been blessed!"

The man had been scuffling along lost in foggy thoughts. He jerks to a stop and looks up with rheumy eyes. He slowly examines the handsome young man before him.

"Shalom, son. Yes, the Lord has been kind this season."

Jonathan bathes the elder in his broadest smile, "I'd like to buy your melons."

The farmer swings the bag off his neck and sets his load on the ground with a grunt. He squints with one eye at the young man. "I'm going to the market in Geba to sell 'em. I suppose I could sell you some here. Less for me to carry up the hill."

Jonathan grins, "What if I would buy them all? How much would you want?"

The farmer straightens up. "All? But how could you carry that many?"

"Ah, of course. I'll want to buy your bag as well." Jonathan is tickled to see the amazement on the elder's face. "How much for all of the melons plus the bag?"

The aged farmer shakes his head in disbelief. But when Jonathan repeats the question he creakily stoops to the bag and at least twice slowly counts the melons. He finally names an amount that Jonathan knows is nearly double what the fruit and bag are worth. He pretends to consider it. He knows he should haggle as custom demands but this morning is no time for clinging to old traditions. He nods and counts out the coins as the elder stands dumbstruck in the middle of the road. Jonathan bows to the farmer, twines his fingers in the net bag, shoulders the load and marches up the road to Geba.

As he walks he quietly thanks God for the beauty of the day, for the energy pulsing through his muscles, and for the delicious savory mix of adventure and danger that floods his body. After an hour of steady hiking he reaches Geba's city gate. It is not a pretentious entrance: a ten-foot wide gap in the fifteen-foot-high wall, a cedar beam stretching across the top of the gap, the wooden gates lying flat against the outer walls, flanking the opening.

Jonathan takes a new grip on the net bag slung over his shoulder and joins other men and women carrying fruits, vegetables and squawking geese through the gate and toward the market square. The musky scent of the melons mixes with his own nervous sweat as walks into the city. Two bored Philistine soldiers at the gate do not bother to scrutinize the stream of peddlers and Jonathan slips in unnoticed.

His only clear goal is to venture into the city and investigate the strength of the Philistine garrison stationed there. He wonders what it would take to lure the soldiers out of the city but has no inkling of any possibilities. Whatever might happen in the next few hours will depend on doors that the Lord might open.

Jonathan carries his burden through the winding, narrow walk ways between the stone houses and shops. He is struck by how few Philistine troops are about. The streets teem with the usual mix of women on the way to market, surging flocks of giggling children and peddlers carrying their wares. Then he sees three soldiers strutting toward him. Each one has a metal breastplate glinting in the morning sun and the red crested helmet of the Philistine army. Jonathan tries not to stare at their menacing steel swords. As they drew near to him he can hear them laughing boisterously among themselves. They pay scant attention to the crowds. As far as Jonathan can see the merchants and the customers generally ignore them and go about their business unperturbed. The residents and the soldiers seem to have arrived at a truce, at least on the surface. He wonders how the citizens would react if the garrison soldiers were attacked?

He shifts the melon bag to his other shoulder as he emerged from the narrow street to the central plaza. Some of the fruit sellers have set up simple shelters against the walls and laid out their wares on swatches of cloth. Others simply arrange their produce on the hard-packed earth and squat behind it.

Now what? If I carry this bundle away from the market, I might attract the soldiers' attention. If I just leave the melons and walk away, people will notice that too. Guess I'll be a fruit merchant for a while and see what happens.

He swings the bag off his back and claims a spot beside the wall of a tannery shop with leather bridles, reins, belts and harnesses on display. He lays out his melons and squats back on his heels and wonders what to do next.

"First time seller?" The squat, swarthy man beside him is leaning against the wall with two baskets full of dates in front of him.

"Ah, yeah, is it so obvious?" Jonathan had hoped he'd go unnoticed.

"Well, the melon sellers usually all set up on the opposite side of the square." Jonathan reached for his bag. "Oh, sorry, I--"

The date seller interrupts, "No problem, you can stay here if you want. Not the best spot though. The soldiers often come to the tanner's shop to outfit their horses, so some shoppers stay away."

Jonathan settled back on his heels and struggled to sound casual. "Oh, sure, thanks. So….Lotta soldiers in town?"

"S'pose that depends on how you look at it. Far as I'm concerned one is too many, but we got at least a hundred of the pagans here."

The man spits into the dust. The peddler's vehemence and fearlessness startle Jonathan. Clearly the Philistines haven't cowed all Geba's citizens, at least not their spirits!

"If you ask me, the worst one is their commander. Why he--." He glances past Jonathan, snaps his jaw shut, and slides down the wall until he is sitting in its shadow. Two armored soldiers come toward them leading a white horse. Riding the horse is a thin man with a sharp nose. His neck is long and his head is nearly bald. His lips are thin and pressed together in a perpetual pout. As the horse slowly approaches, the man holds his chin high, only occasionally lowering his eyes to the peasants below.

"Speakin' of the snake..." The date seller mutters and pulls his robe tight around himself. Jonathan's heart pounds and his head throbs with adrenaline. He tenses his legs, ready to blast toward the gate. But the soldiers veer off and stop in front of the tannery shop. One of the soldiers holds the reins while the other helps their commander dismount.

The commander walks into the shop and without even turning his head snaps, "I'll be a few minutes. Stay alert."

Jonathan gasps for air. The Lord has not only heard his prayer, He has brought the enemy right to him. How can he not act? He steadies his ragged breathing, checks his galloping mind and considers his next move. The two soldiers stand with their backs to him, off to his right. One of them holds the horse's reins loosely in his hand. Jonathan turns to the merchant beside him. He draws in a sharp breath and the peddle looks up. Jonathan's eyes flame with intensity and the man's body stiffens. Jonathan cautiously reaches under his robe, pulls out his knife and shows it to him. Then he tilts his head to the tannery shop. The man's jaw drops open but he does not move. A mix of fear and delight gleams in his eyes.

Jonathan stands quickly and backs against the side wall of the shop. Then he points to the fig baskets and mimes pushing them over. Puzzlement gives way to understanding. The merchant nods once, then stands and shoves over the basket. He begins shouting curses as the figs roll out into the dirt. As the soldiers turn to the noise, Jonathan glides around behind them to the front wall and slips into the shop. His entrance is silent but the Philistine commander, alerted by the noise outside is already moving toward the door. Jonathan holds back the roar lodged in his throat, takes two steps and plunges his knife inward and upward into the man's chest. He grabs the man before he can fall. As he holds him, he looks over the dying man's shoulders and sees the shopkeeper backing away in horror. Jonathan hisses and with his eyes pleads for silence. He yanks out his knife and lowers the body to the shop floor. His own robe is smeared and spotted with the pagan's blood.

Through the doorway, he can see the tail of the white horse. He takes a deep breath, sprints out of the shop, leapfrogs over the horse's rump onto its back, and roars with the fervor of a lion over its kill, "The Lord alone is our God." The horse shoots forward in terror, tearing the reins from the soldier's hands. Jonathan grasps desperately for the reins as the stallion streaks across the plaza. He finally manages to grab the lines and charges through the crooked streets, scattering dogs, children and screaming women.

90

If he is to escape he must outrace the ruckus. He and his mount zig-zag around corners in the race to the gate. The horse slides on its haunches coming around the last corner. The soldiers see the commander's horse charging toward them and instinctively snap to attention. Too late they realize that a stranger is in the saddle. Jonathan dashes through the gate with the shouts of the frantic Philistines behind him.

His robes snap in the wind as he gallops down the road. He pumps his fist and yells into the heavens, "Aii, praise be to The Lord! Aii, death to the pagans!" The Philistine garrison will soon be charging after him. He slows his horse down to a lope. He needs to give the enemy time to spot him on the road. Ben Amad and his men will be ready to pounce. The war against the Philistines has begun.

Chapter Sixteen

The sides of the tents pitched above the pass at Michmash snap and boom in the icy wind. The chill wintery blast sweeps across the encampment and the soldiers shiver. But inside the black goat skin tent of the king, a fiery volcano threatens to erupt. Saul has just dismissed the messenger and now sits alone. His fists clench and unclench in frustration. His eyes flicker with the desperate rage of a cornered wolf.

Jonathan, Jonathan. Not only do you violate direct orders, you throw a flaming torch into the volatile warmongering heart of the Philistine military. If you and your men had been crushed in the skirmish at Geba, many families would've grieved, I would've grieved. Yet at least Israel might have avoided further conflict. But now...Now not only do you defeat the garrison soldiers but murder the Philistine commander...

Saul gnashes his teeth. Jonathan's ardor and daring has forced them all into full scale war. He growls to himself over the howling wind, "If I can't command obedience from my own son, how can I expect these troops to obey me?" He grimaces at the vagaries of leadership. He's the king, but circumstances outside his control continue to batter him. He'll have to react, like it or not.

He slowly uncoils his taut muscles, and steps out of his tent into the raw humid air. Gray clots of cloud whip across a filmy brown sky. Rain is near.

"Medad, grab the shofar and summon the commanders."

The young aide runs to his tent and emerges with the ram's horn. He raises the long, curved horn to his lips, fills his lungs, puffs out his cheeks and blasts twice. The piercing cry echoes across the pass, catches the wind and soars like an eagle across the hills. Within minutes the eleven commanders trot eagerly up to Saul's tent. To a man they are weary of this tedious months long border posting. They hunger for a mission, a challenge to heat up their chilled bones.

Saul sweeps his gaze across the eager faces. The wind whistles and swirls as he hunts for words that might carry a semblance of truth.

"Brothers, the battle has begun." An immediate buzz fills the air. Saul raises his arms to quiet his commanders. "Yesterday, under my secret orders, Jonathan led his troops in an attack upon the garrison at Geba. The garrison was destroyed and the pagan commander of the city executed."

The men cheer and exultantly shake raised fists. Saul interrupts their celebration. "Of course, now the Philistines are mustering a counterattack. We will need to summon all the men of Israel."

Saul's pronouncement is solemn but again the men respond with enthusiastic shouts. All except for Abner. The somber soldier doesn't join in the cheering. His face is impassive, though his dark eyes are intensely alive. Saul feels them drilling into his mind. *Has this cousin of mine already seen through my lie? Is he preparing to challenge me?"* He holds his breath as Abner raises his arms to silence his fellows. But when Abner speaks, it is as a soldier already plotting the next move.

"King Saul, where do you think it best for our troops to gather?" Saul stares at him. He suspects that Abner has seen through the deception. He will probably use it against him someday. Saul also guesses that Abner already has his opinion and is waiting to see how battle wise his new king is.

Saul sidesteps Abner's gambit. "I summoned you all here, so that we can decide on that and the other preparations. Abner, what is your suggestion for a battlefield?"

Saul detects the icy glint of cynicism in Abner's tight grin. But the veteran soldier dispassionately growls out his opinion.

"I'd say let's go back to Gilgal. That would be our best staging area. We'd have enough room to gather and hopefully organize our men before the Philistines show up."

Saul enters his tent followed by his commanders. Outside, the gray clots of cloud have merged into mountainous rainclouds and the afternoon sky grows dark. Inside the tent walls puff like bellows in the wind and the leaders of God's chosen people ponder how to confront the most powerful army in their world.

***

The plain surrounding the stone circle of Gilgal swarms like an agitated ant hill. The enthusiasm of the twelve commanders has awakened Israel. Thousands of men--fuzzy chinned youths, gray bearded elders with creaky joints, sun bronzed shepherds and farmers, even some merchants and peddlers--pour across the landscape. The twelve tribes pulse with righteous rage against the fearsome pagan Philistines.

Jonathan came into camp with his men shortly after noon. Tales of his escapade in Geba had already swept through the troops and he was welcomed with boisterous shouts and a clattering of swords. Not until evening does Saul find the opportunity to speak with him in private.

Now they sit together in Saul's tent. A guttering oil lamp casts fitful dancing shadows on the walls. Saul speaks and hears in his own words an eerie echo of father Kish's bedeviling question.

"Son, why did you choose to do this?"

In place of the defensive and often vague answer that Saul used to give Kish, Jonathan simply smiles.

"I felt the Lord was leading me."

The diatribe Saul prepared sticks like a fishbone in his throat. The Lord, Samuel's God, the people's God, and by heritage, his own God. What argument can he muster against Him? He looks across the flickering light at his handsome son's calm face. Anguish and anger sweep across the father's face.

"And when I commanded, when all of us--the commanders, and you and I, --decided that we would not attack but only stand firm at the borders, where was the Lord then? Wasn't the Lord leading us then? And didn't you agree, along with all the others?"

Jonathan's grin fades but the light doesn't leave his face. He leans forward his words brim with passion. "Yes, but out there, on the border, on that border forced upon us by the pagans, I felt the Lord was giving me a new order."

Saul's restraint bursts and he bellows like a wounded beast. He hurriedly chokes off his roar, acutely conscious of the hundreds of ears within listening distance. His whisper is husky and harsh. "Then tell me son, what is the point of a king giving orders, if each soldier is free to follow every whim and whisper in his heart?"

Now Jonathan's face darkens; his voice grows stony.

"It was no whim, no fleeting whisper. Look at the result. We won back Geba. We reclaimed one of our cities. The Lord blessed our courage."

Saul drops his head and glares at his son from beneath scowling brows.

"You call it courage. I could call it disobedience, or recklessness. You want to talk about results? Look farther than Geba. Your little adventure poked a stick into the face of a ferocious bear. You've roused the Philistines and now we'll all have to deal with the results, and they might not be so gratifying."

Jonathan opens his mouth but Saul cut him off.

"Enough of this. Tomorrow before the sun comes up, I want you to take two of your men and scout out the Michmash region. I'm sure that's where the Philistines will be gathering their troops. We'll need to know what we're facing."

Jonathan slowly uncrosses his legs and stands, nods and murmurs, "Good night father," then steps out into the night. Saul stares into the light of the lamp until it burns itself out and the acrid smell of smoke fills the tent. The image of his passionate son claiming to have been led by God swirls into the memory of Samuel standing over him, vial in hand, announcing that God had chosen him to be king.

Evidently God is everywhere except where I happen to be. What have I done, or not done, to cut myself off from this Lord whom others claim to hear and follow? Have I been too proud or disobedient? Maybe I have some deformity in my soul? Some children are born with twisted limbs or feeble minds. Maybe I was born with some spiritual distortion, a deafness of the soul. Maybe that's why I can't hear God.

Saul throws himself on his mat, first lamenting then cursing his fate. Sometime past midnight, despite his swirling agitation, he remembers what Samuel told him the last time they'd been in Gilgal. 'Seven days after the seventh full moon, after the barley seeding, I will come here for ceremonies. You will wait for me here.'

How did the prophet even know we'd be here in Gilgal? And ceremonies? I didn't pay much attention to his talk of ceremonies. Did Samuel foresee all of this? Does he intend to bless the armies before the battle? Last night was the seventh full moon since out last meeting. Will he be here in one week? If God reveals all of this to his prophet, why does he keep his king in the dark?

The nighttime chill does cool his fevered thoughts and he is up and dressed before daybreak. He leaves his tent, mumbles a greeting to the guards at the edge of the camp and climbs a small bluff. He fixes his gaze on the eastern horizon's gauzy pink blush. He recites the Shema into the chill clean air.

"Hear, Israel, the Lord is our God, the Lord is One." He stops and groans. As a young boy and man, he never considered the presence nor the absence of God. God simply was. Since Samuel had anointed him, Saul believes that God had besieged him, hemmed him in, assaulted from every side and yet, and yet… He cannot feel, sense, or hear this invisible One whom he, along with all the tribes, calls 'Lord'. How often in these past months has he shouted his thoughts and prayers into the night and heard only hollow echoes of his own anguished voice?

This morning as the first streaks of light shoot above the horizon, Saul bows his head. Is his own pride sealing his ears? He ruefully admits to himself that he chafed when Samuel pronounced his 'thus says the Lord'. *Maybe the Lord is waiting for me to be patient. Maybe the Lord will speak to me only after I humbly accept Samuel's word.* Saul lets the rising sun burn into his eyes, then strides back to the wakening camp with a new resolve.

"The troops will be ready and organized by tomorrow." Abner announces as he and the rest of the commanders sit cross legged in a semicircle in front of the king's tent. Saul nods.

"Good work. Jonathan left this morning to determine the Philistine troop strength. When he returns we'll discuss how do deploy our men. Then on the seventh we will attack these enemies of God."

The commanders lean back and shoot questioning arrows at each other with their eyes. Abner blurts out, "The seventh? That's six days away. Why wait that long? If we are to attack why not go tomorrow?"

Abner's protest opens the mouths of the rest of the commanders. "Feeding this horde is no small thing. The sooner we can move the better."

"The morale of the men is high now. But in six days?"

Saul sits silently as the flurry of objections pummel his early morning commitment to patience. It is no surprise that one sunrise resolution cannot undo a lifelong disposition. He growls in his throat and springs to his feet. The commanders struggle to stand. He glowers at them and his words are as ominous as distant thunder.

"You wanted me to be king, to lead you into battle. You declared it. I didn't seek it. Samuel the prophet told me that on the seventh day he will come to bless us. We will wait here for his blessing. I've decided. Go. Deal with your men."

Chapter Seventeen

Ahinoam hears voices in the square, puts down her loom and goes to the door. Kohath, her neighbor's husband stands beneath the oak tree in the plaza. He flaps his arms as he speaks to the crowd clustering around him.

Why is he here? He left along with my sons for Gilgal to battle the Philistines. Is the battle already over? Where are my men? Fear and excitement hasten her steps. From the edge of the crowd she can hear Kohath's shrill voice.

"Then Jonathan returned to camp with the news that the Philistines had chariots--thirty thousand chariots, and six thousand mounted soldiers and foot soldiers..." His high voice cracks, "so many foot soldiers he couldn't count 'em."

The crowd moans as one agonized body. Even from the gathering's edge Ahinoam is tall enough to see the scrawny and trembling Kohath. Like everyone else her concerns and thoughts are personal. *What about my husband, my sons?* But she speaks as the wife of the king. "Neighbor, what about the battle? How did it go?"

Kohath looks out at her. His words drip with disdain. "What battle? There has been no battle. King Saul keeps waiting and waiting."

Ahinoam responds to his venom with a shot of her own. "If the battle hasn't yet begun, what are you doing here? Our sons and husbands haven't run like rabbits."

Kohath drops his head for a moment as though humbled by Ahinoam's reproach. But after taking a deep breath he looks up and shakes his head.

"No, I didn't run to save my life, I ran to save yours. I came to tell you that when the Philistine army begins to move it'll overrun Gilgal and sweep across this land like a cloud of locusts. Every village will be razed, every woman raped, every child slaughtered. I came to tell you to gather what is valuable to you and hide in the hills. Find a cave and pray that this plague will not find you."

Woman wail, children whimper and cling to their mother's robes. Ahinoam lifts her shoulders, steels herself against this mass grief, and shouts above the sobbing.

"No! I will not run like a bitch with her tail between her legs. I am a daughter of Israel, the chosen people. Didn't God destroy Jericho and give us this land? Didn't God send Gideon and Samson and all the rest when we were threatened? How can you doubt that our God will help us defeat these pagan Philistines? I am staying right here. I will prepare my home to receive my husband and sons after the battle."

She spins on her heel and walks home with what she hopes is a regal air, all the while muttering to herself, "Why does Saul wait to strike?"

Twenty miles to the northeast, on the plains of Gilgal, Saul asks himself that same question, as he has asked for the past six days. Every agonizing minute of every day erodes another chunk of his early morning vow of humble obedience to Samuel's word. He hardly dares walk through the gathered troops. He doesn't know, and is afraid to ask, how many soldiers disappear each night into the darkness. Once Jonathan's report on the Philistine army filtered through the camp, a tense silence settled in.

But, today is the day, the day Samuel said he'd come to bring a blessing. Today is the day that Saul can demonstrate to Samuel and to God that he is humble and obedient. As he's done for the last five days, he arises before dawn and hikes up the bluff overlooking the plain. He raises both arms, gazes up into the faintly glowing sky and in a low rumbling voice recites the Shema and one of the traditional morning prayers.

"Blessed be the name of the Lord from this time on and forevermore. From the rising of the sun to its setting the name of the Lord is to be praised."

Morning after morning he hears only echoing silence but the prayers give him a bit of comfort, a sense that he is an obedient child. He briskly marches back down to the camp as the sun rises and the dew steams off the plain. He summons commanders Abner and Eliad.

"Prepare an altar, a large one and solid. Find the sturdiest bull and secure it. Today there will be ceremony and sacrifice."

The commanders march off and now the camp is abuzz like a hive during the flowering of clover. These men came to fight. They are ready and beyond ready. Adrenaline ignites horseplay and laughter throughout the ranks.

Though it is winter, the noontime sun scorches the plain. The troop's early exuberance wilts into lassitude. Saul has not eaten, his belly grumbles, his intestines clamp. *Six hours ... in six hours this day is done. And if the old man doesn't show....?* He paces up and down before his tent. He can hear the pounding of his heart in his ears. *What will I do? How will I know?*

The sun slides inexorably toward the western horizon, dragging Saul's vow to a fiery death. The hill to the east still glows pink with the sun's dying rays but the camp sinks into glum shadow. Saul summons his commanders. They stand before him in sullen silence. His own words are terse, flat and just as sullen.

"Tomorrow, first light, we make the burnt offerings, I myself will recite the prayers and pronounce the blessing. Together we will shout 'Amen' and then together we march to Michmash."

The men nod and silently slip back into the gloaming. Saul hears them murmuring to each other as they go. He guesses their words are as thorny as the sabra cacti dotting the steep hillside that surround them.

Saul's jaw works as he watches the troops gather in the soft morning light. He has washed and combed out his hair and it glimmers in the rising sun. His oiled beard glistens against his blue robe. This morning he made no trek to the bluff to pray before dawn. Today he will pray for the entire army. Yesterday's high spirits have been doused and the soldiers move slowly and stiffly. They gather together by tribes in a semi-circle around the stone altar. They stand in uneven ranks, each man dressed in his own version of battle gear—some with shields of skins or wood, some with breastplates of leather, some with simple burlap vests, each one clutching his own preferred weapon—lances, spears, axes. Every jaw is set, every eye focused on Saul and the altar. The field birds too must sense the sacredness of the moment. They cease their wheeling and chirring. Only the warning growls of dogs gorging on the bull's entrails break the silence.

The chosen bull was slaughtered and butchered by firelight before dawn. Now two commanders carry a wide board piled high with chunks of bloody meat. Saul picks up each piece, holds it for the troops to see, then raises it into the air, turns to the altar and places it on the crackling fire. As the meat burns black, swirling smoke spirals lazily into the crystal blue sky. After all the meat is in the flames, Saul raises his long arms, tilts his head back into the cerulean air and speaks words that the smoke will carry up to God's ears.

"Now I know that the Lord will help his anointed; he will answer him from his holy heaven with mighty victories by his right hand. Some take pride in chariots, and some in horses, but our pride is in the name of the Lord our God. They will collapse and fall, but we shall rise and stand upright. Give victory to the king, O Lord; answer us when we call."

He lowers his eyes from the heavens, sweeps his gaze around the circle. With hands still raised he roars "Amen!" Thousands of echoing voices thunder across the plain. "Amen!"

At that instant as though summoned by the shout, a lone figure materializes on the bluff above them all. Saul spies him first and his arms freeze above his head. Every eye tracks Saul's stare to the bluff top. Like breeze on a pond, a murmur ripples through the crowd. The figure thuds his staff on the ground as he trudges down the slope. Samuel has arrived. Saul drops his arms, moves away from the altar and waits. His mind is a wasp's nest.

Damn, here comes the old man. Why does a fist clamp on my heart whenever he stabs his staff into the ground and strides toward me? Where was he yesterday when we all expected him, all of us sitting in the shadows with rabbit ears and hawk eyes? Now he plows toward me with flint in his eyes. By the God of our fathers, where was he an hour ago when my clenching stomach could not bear to see another one of my clansmen slink off into the shadows and scurry home like a fearful mouse? The old man said, "wait for me on the seventh day." So, I waited. He himself has called me king, appointed me king, anointed me king. But when he said, 'wait for me on the seventh day,' I waited. I vowed humble obedience. I stand naked out here-- the king and the general of an army of shepherds and farmers, men once eager for battle. But he said 'wait' and so we waited…waiting seven days with nothing to do but watch the horizon and envision the enemy gathering, nothing to do but imagine the sunlight flashing on the enemy soldiers' polished shields. This damnable waiting is like a hyena eating the guts from a wounded deer. It devours courage from the inside. But all of those waiting days passed and then he didn't come. What did he expect? What did God expect? Was I supposed to sit under the fig tree until every one of my ragged soldiers slithered on home? Oh, damn him, look at how he comes charging toward me as though I were a rebellious, impetuous boy. See the spittle flying from his lips. But I am the king. Three times they've hailed me as king. By God, I did what needed doing. I gathered my men, ordered the sacrifice, said the prayers. These aren't secret words in some strange tongue. Every soldier who's entered battle has these blessing words in his ears and on his heart. So yes, I prayed, then I blessed, then we all tightened our belts for battle. And then the old man comes striding over the hill. He stands before me. I am the king. I am the general. I lower my head. Damn him, I'm afraid.

As he scuttles down the slope, Samuel's mind too is abuzz. *God, I'm tired of this journey. No, not this one to Gilgal…well yes this one too. But God, I mean the entire journey. These years and miles and miseries—all that you've seen fit to give me—I'm weary. My bones and sinews sigh for rest. The days stretch too long, they never end. I collapse onto my mat, roll over and it is day again. And now O Holy God of the Fathers, now, now that my journey nears its end, now you give me this bitter mission: name the king, acclaim the king, anoint the king. And for what end? So that you in your justice can consume these senseless children when they forget you? Ai. If I'd been a better father to my own sons, if they'd been sons after my own heart, maybe then the people wouldn't have whined and clamored for a king. Is the failure mine? Is this my burden to bear? Is that why you have given me this bitter charge at the end of my days? Is this my punishment? Now you order me to march up to this young giant, this one whom you chose—not me, but you O God—and I must smash his hold on kingship. He's not even firmly gripped it and already I must slam your iron will upon his hand. I must grind your will, not mine upon his fingers until they bleed.*

The prophet stalks down the hill and crackling energy pulses around him. The troops back away. The two men stand facing each other in the dust pulverized by the feet of a thousand anxious soldiers. Saul bows his head and opens his mouth to greet him but before he can utter a syllable, Samuel growls, "Saul, son of Kish what have you done?"

For one half of a heartbeat, Saul is tempted to claim ignorance. After all what does the old man know anyway? But when he lifts his head and sees the flames in Samuel's eyes, his intention wilts like a plucked flower in the desert heat. Saul tries to suppress his belligerence and defensiveness.

"I did what I had to do. You told me to wait for you until the seventh day. All week my men have been slipping away into the shadows. You told me to wait but when the seventh day came and went and you did not appear, I did what I had to do, I prepared the sacrifice. I went ahead and----."

The prophet sputters, "You say, 'I told you, I told you'. Who are you listening to? Are you the king, or aren't you? In Ramah, on that very first day, when the oil was still dripping from your beard, on that day I told you, 'do whatever your hand finds to do for God is with you.' But here you sit. Then at Mizpah I stood up, yes, I stood up and all the people looked to me and I told them, I told all of them, 'look now, O Israel at this strong man. This bold Benjaminite is now your king, he will save you from the pagan Philistines." But do you leap like a lion at these filthy dogs? No, you fuss like an old crone tending her chickens."

Saul's eyes widen, he tries to swallow but his mouth is Negev dry. The seer's vehemence blasts him like the sirocco wind and he takes a step backward. "Yes, but I thought you said I was supposed to wait."

"Do I give orders to you? Who are you listening to? To me or to God? By the God of Abraham and Isaac and Jacob you were called to be the king, not me. But do you act like a king? Do you rouse these men? Do you stand tall and bold and enflame their passion to fight? No, you sit like a petulant child and fret because you think some old man has told you to wait. This is what you call being a king? Where is the fire in your belly?"

Saul stammers, "but the blessing, the, the sacrifice…"

Samuel splutters in his rage, "By God's decree, that is my job, not yours. In this you have surely sinned. But the greater sin is not leading these men into battle. You already had God's blessing. How could you be so deaf, so blind, so dull?"

Saul's eyes flutter. His head feels hollow. Samuel, the troops, and the sky waver and swirl before him. Like the pillar of salt that was once Lot's wife he stands paralyzed. His jaw works but he is mute. Samuel closes the gap between and their chests touch. Saul smells the air of the old man's dying as he hisses up into his face.

"God would've made your family the royal family. Your son Jonathan would've ruled after you and after him his son. But you…. You've not listened to the Lord's command. You've lost the right to be king. You may be a big man but your heart is the size of a shriveled grape." He drills his gaze up into the Saul's eyes, lifts his staff and slams it down on Saul's foot. Saul winces and grunts but does not groan.

Be damned if I'll give the old man that reward. Besides I don't want my men, if I can even dare to still call them mine, to know how gravely the prophet has wounded me.

Samuel's fiery energy is abruptly extinguished. His hot anger transmutes into chill sadness. He pulls back his staff and clings to it with both hands. He wearily shakes his head and sighs.

"God is going to find a new king to succeed you, a king with a heart like God's heart." And then his voice alters as if his role in this drama has ended and now he can return to himself. He drops his head and quietly murmurs. "I'm sorry, I must go. May God give the enemy into your hands."

He abruptly turns, then stiffly climbs the bluff he's just descended. He does not glance back nor hesitate. Saul silently watches his hobbling ascent. He hears a restless muttering from the troops. *Did any of them capture the gist of Samuel's rant? Most of them probably assume his anger was sparked by the sacrifice. That's what I thought. How was I to know? How am I to know? 'Do what you think is right for the Lord is with you.' Nothing but a wicked snare...that's all those words are.*

The soldiers stare uneasily at Saul who stands immobile where Samuel left him. They see a man with a stiff back and a mask for a face. They do not know that the prophet's blazing anger has set the king's mind aflame. Confusion roils the molten metal of Saul's anger.

Who is to blame for this disaster? Should I blame Samuel for giving ambiguous commands? Should I blame himself for showing too much deference to the prophet and his words? Why not blame God and his damnable divine silence?

Saul's unfocused fury congeals into a lump of poisonous lead. Its toxic venom begins to drip into his blood, drop after drop after drop until the end.

Chapter Seventeen

Saul urges his horse up the slope then slumps in the saddle. This morning he began the ride from Gilgal to Michmash with six hundred men. He does not dare turn and count how many are with him now. The late winter air carries a promise of spring warmth and the afternoon sun stings his brow. His lips are chapped and the acrid after burn of bile sears his throat. His foot throbs from Samuel's staff and his head pounds with the seer's words.

Is God with me, or has He already abandoned me? Bah, as if I would know the difference! God present and God absent feel entirely the same. But yesterday's words leave me in darkness. Am I or am I not the king?

He reaches the crest of the hill and swings his horse around. Hundreds of men pick their way up around the boulders and brambles. *These poor men still take me for king. Maybe God has abandoned me but I'll not be so fickle and abandon them. Is Samuel the only one who speaks for God? I've got to find a way around this dour prophet. Ah, yes there is another path…*

He calls out to young Medad. Since the battle of Jabesh-Gilead, the young man has been his eager aide and messenger. Saul explains his assignment, sends him off, and watches him spurring his requisitioned horse southward.

He returns his gaze to the slope before him. The sun stabs at his eyes. Every rock and plant seems edged in fire. He pinches his eyes tightly shut. A faint throbbing begins in his temples and a vise slowly tightens on the back of his neck. He plods on, impelled by duty to his men and his father's dictum drilled into him since childhood: 'Finish what you begin.' He will stubbornly end this venture, even if the only end he can imagine is the wholesale slaughter of his army.

By late afternoon they reach the crest of the plateau upon which Geba lies. In the distance to the north, across the Valley of Hyenas, on the plateau of Michmash they can see the Philistine encampment.

The soldiers' shields flash in the waning sunlight, the glinting fire dances across the entire plateau.

Saul's army stops outside Geba's stone walls. On the west side of the city lies a hard-packed square of ground. It is the city's threshing floor which also serves as the gathering place for citizen's disputes and appeals. The troops camp in the large open field surrounding the floor and Saul orders his tent pitched alongside it, under a lone pomegranate tree. He hopes the location will bring added weight to his orders. But when the commanders gather at sunset, his head is throbbing so intensely that even the slightest turning sends stabs of pain throughout his frame. He sees all things through a gauzy haze and fights off waves of nausea. His only order is to count the men and meet back at the threshing floor in the morning.

Jonathan gradually opens his eyes, slowly surveys the tent ceiling, then abruptly sits up. He peers out into the bracing predawn air. A faint brushstroke of light tinges the eastern horizon. He hears the faint snoring of his father in the next tent. He sits back on his heels and tilts his head skyward. He closes his eyes and silently moves his lips. Several minutes later he taps the shoulder of Benadad, his armor bearer who sleeps on the far side of the tent.

"Wake up, we're going to visit the pagan Philistines. No noise now. It's just the two of us." Like Jonathan himself, Benadad is young, only eighteen, but he's been Jonathan's armor bearer for three years. He grins and his dark eyes gleam. Quickly and skillfully he readies Jonathan's weapons. The two walk noiselessly past tents and men snoring on their pads under the open air. They keep their weapons wrapped in cloth, lest the clink of metal betray their passing. They reach the edge of the camp, but instead of going north down into the valley and then up to Michmash, Jonathan turns east along the plateau's rim. They walk in silence until they come to the Suwenti Wadi, a steep gorge that separates the two plateaus. Rocky crags top each cliff: Bozez crag on the Michmash side, Seneh crag on the Geba side. The sun has spilled over the horizon now, sharp shadows and sun struck rock formations stand in crisp relief.

"Benadad, God wants us to remove these uncircumcised dogs. It doesn't matter if we've only got a few soldiers. God is the true warrior here. Remember the story of Gideon? He had half as many men as we have and yet God gave him a great victory."

Benadad nods and his teeth shine in the sunlight as he grins. "My lord, I'm with you wherever you go."

"Here's my plan. We'll stand up in plain view. The infidel dogs on the other side will see us. If they say, 'Stay there, we're coming over to see you,' that's a sign that this isn't our day. But if they say, 'Come on over,' that's the sign that God is going with us and will deliver these pagans into our hands."

Jonathan and Benadad scramble to the top of the Senah pinnacle and wave their swords until they flash in the sunlight. They can see the platoon on the other side of the gap, alongside the Bozes peak. A couple of men separate themselves and scramble to the top of the peak. They shout across the wadi, and their mocking voices are sharp in the still, dry air.

"So you Hebrews are finally crawling out of your hidey holes! Why don't you come on over? We've got something to show you!" The entire platoon roars with laughter.

Jonathan and Benadad exchange excited grins and deftly pick their way down the scree and boulders. They reach the narrow slit at the bottom of the wadi and cautiously pick their way up the slope. They near the top and stop beside a boulder to catch their breath. Above their heads, they can hear the boisterous laughter and conversation of the Philistines.

Jonathan's whisper is fierce, "Now, the Lord has delivered the enemy into our power. We attack."

He scrambles up the last few feet and flies over the edge. Before he even gets to his feet, he slashes the Achilles tendons of the first two soldiers who meet him and they tumble over the precipice. He leaps to his feet swinging his razor-sharp sword. He severs wrists, cuts arteries and fends off blows. At that moment, Benadad flies up to the top of the plateau several meters to the left of the camp, unleashing one arrow after another. He manages to kill three Philistines still lounging on their sleeping mats. Benadad keeps shooting until his arrows are spent then begins stabbing with his knife. Jonathan's slashing is so frenetic that the soldiers began to back up. A couple of them throw down their weapons and run back to the main camp. In a matter of minutes twenty Philistines are dead, and between their bodies the dust has become a deep red paste.

Jonathan and Benadad sit on their haunches, gasp for breath and beam at each other. Sweat glistens on their foreheads, their eyes are glazed with blood lust, and adrenaline slowly ebbs in their veins. They hear chaotic shouting and horrifying screaming coming from the Philistine camp. Then they feel a sudden jolt and topple to all fours. The horizon dances, a sudden boom sweeps across the plain and is followed by three sharp jerks. The earth shivers and then there is a moment of stillness. Every living thing trembles in hushed fear. This sacred silence is shattered by the din of convulsive wailing from the enemy camp. Jonathan and Benadad clamber to their feet. Their limbs tremble with weariness, but they wave their weapons into the sky and shout, "The Lord is our God, the Lord alone." They have no doubt. The Lord has given them an amazing triumph.

Chapter Eighteen

The pounding drumbeat of pain tortures Saul's head and weary battles invade his dreams. Hordes of grinning, cursing foes swarm around him. He swings his sword but the helmeted fiends dissolve into hollow laughter. His limbs grow heavy with fatigue. Finally, a few hours before dawn the dreadful throbbing in his skull diminishes to a sad pulsing. The baleful dreaming dissipates into a fog. He plunges into a leaden sleep.

"Saul, Saul. It's time." Jakeh is the only one who dares waken the king these days. He kneels beside Saul's pallet, ignoring the pain in his knees and hopes his voice will not gouge too deeply into Saul's aching soul. He lays a hand gently on the king's shoulder.

"Saul, the priest is here, and the commanders. They're already waiting." Saul blinks bleary eyes and then gasps as though surfacing from deep underwater. He scrambles to his feet, growling.

"The priest, yes. You should've awakened me to greet him."
Jakeh is ready with an excuse but Saul sweeps past him and bursts out of the tent and pauses, blinded by the piercing sunlight.

His commanders stand in twos and threes, voices low, shooting curious glances at the figure sitting on a stool under the pomegranate tree. When Saul opens the tent flap, the soldiers all turn and arrange themselves in a semi-circle and face their leader. But Saul does not return their look. He is staring at the man on the stool. Emotions swirl in his sluggish mind, a stew pot full of despondency and grim, desperate hope.

Ai, this is how desperate I've become. Resorting to this...this character...all to bypass that odious prophet. Or maybe to reach this maddening, silent God.

Ahijah the priest rode into camp this morning with Medad. Now he sits astride a creaking stool. He is a corpulent Hebrew with dark, heavy-lidded eyes that blink like a cat ready to sleep. Saul shifts his eyes and swiftly glances at the commanders' faces. Some of them have dropped their gaze to the packed ground below them. Others stare with dark skepticism at the porcine priest. Despite his own desperation, Saul appreciates his commanders' doubts. What's more he suspects that Ahijah's standing in the priestly community must be quite low. Why else would he be willing to show up on such short notice on a bedraggled battle field where the enemy outnumbers Israel by hundreds to one?

If Saul would know the sullied credentials of this portly priest he would personally shove him back up on his horse and send him down the mountain. Ahijah is the great grandson of the discredited priest Eli, the man who mentored the prophet Samuel.

But on this bright morning as he tries to clear the fog from his head, Saul is not concerned with the priest's appearance or credentials. The office of high priest is regularly rotated among all the priests and today Ahijah has exactly what Saul believes he needs. Ahijah is wearing the ephod. Ah, the ephod! What Israelite child doesn't know the story of the ephod. During the long years in the wilderness, when God was making His covenant with them and creating them as a people, God designed this sacred garment especially for the priest. Today the elaborate, bejeweled vest flops heavily on Ahijah's belly. Despite the plainness of its wearer, the ephod pulses with numinous power. Its jewels seem to throb, to breath. But Saul barely notices the malachite and onyx stones nor the scarlet, golden and silver threads. His dark eyes bore into the ephod's two pockets. These contain the Urim and Thummin.

Saul, like most of his people, is convinced that these two stones are the Lord's way of answering important questions. Saul still dares to believe that even if the Lord has a grudge against him, he might wring answers out of Him by means of these sacred stones. Put the two stones in a bag, ask a yes or no question. Withdraw a stone. If it is the black rock Urim the answer is no, if it is the white rock Thummin the answer is 'yes'. Succinct, sharp answers. No more hollow, lingering silences, no more nights of strained listening, no more hearing only the pounding of blood in his own head. Urim and Thummin: Yes or no, up or down.

Saul coughs and tries to clear his sleep-encrusted throat. He gives a slight nod to the priest, then turns to his men. "Priest Ahijah has joined us here today and you see he wears the Lord's ephod. Commanders, in your presence I will seek the Lord's will regarding our fate today." Saul steps toward the bulky priest and sees the glint of malicious delight in his eyes. How this unctuous man relishes his power. Saul tries to keep the venom out of his voice. "O Holy man of God, seek now from the Lord an answer to our question: shall we enter into battle today?"

As the last word slips from his lips the threshing floor shivers. The priest still on his stool, totters, and the soldiers stagger. Then follow three jolts, as though a giant hammer is smashing against the foundations of the deep. Saul and most of the soldiers fall to their knees. The priest tips over backward, limbs flailing like an upended turtle. The sacred stones escape their pockets and lie in the dust, now ordinary desert rocks. Saul stares at these mute chunks and groans at his own naiveté. Why did he ever think God would bother breaking His silence with something as ordinary as colored stones? He wearily pulls himself upright. Ahijah manages to roll over and scrambles on all fours in the dirt to recover his sacred rocks.

The soldiers break the stunned silence with whoops of relief. Then they suddenly fall silent as a wave of roaring and clattering rolls across the plain from the Philistine camp. A sentry staggers onto the threshing floor, gasping for breath. "Chaos, chaos in the enemy camp. Across the ravine on their lookout peak I saw the flash of swords, then bodies lying and then… then when the quake came I heard shouts and screams and dust from their camp. A dervish, a frenzy has come upon them."

Saul scowls, "Swords at the peak? Some of our men? Who is missing?"

Abner throws up his hands. "Look around! Do you see your son here? Jonathan is missing. What difference does this make? The pagan dogs have gone mad; they chase their own tails. We are soldiers. You ask for a sign from God and the earth shudders. Why do we waste time standing here?"

Furious blood pounds in Saul's head and his world is tinged in red. He should kill Abner where he stands. Yet even as his hand reaches for the hilt of his sword he knows that Abner speaks the truth. A bitter thought: most likely Abner speaks God's truth. He wraps his fingers around this sword and swiftly unsheathes it. Staring at Abner, he raises it high into the sundrenched morning. He draws a deep breath, then bellows, "We linger no more. Today we fight. We fight until we taste victory. No one tastes food. Cursed is anyone who even stops to eat. I am your king and I declare, 'Let God's enemies die'."

The commanders howl their agreement. The hundreds of soldiers who valiantly or stubbornly stuck with Saul, now scream with fiery lust. No one considers a battle plan. They follow their king and charge across the plain. Their whoops and shrieks fill the air like a swarm of ravenous locusts. Saul gallops at their head and draws in deep draughts of the morning air and the pounding in his head disappears. He swings his glimmering sword, his shoulders loosen, he roars like a bull. God's will, Samuel's will, his will? Who knows?

Who will ever know? Urim, Thummin, yes, no---Enough. Enough agonized discerning. Now is attacking, king leading, soldiers following.

As Saul and his avid troops pound across the plain they are stunned to see bands of men running out of the hills to join them. They are deserters who'd slunk away during this long wait but whose consciences hadn't allowed them to go home. Peering from their hideouts they see the confusion among the Philistines and the reckless charge of their comrades. Whether out of guilt or courage reborn they pick up their weapons and run to join their comrades. The numbers swell as they reach the Philistine camp. There they meet another surprise.

When Jonathan and Benadad leapt over the lip of the cliffs at Bozes peak, they not only slaughtered twenty enemy soldiers, they also sent two bloody, panicked survivors screaming into the Philistine camp. Men rolled out of their tents to shrieks of 'attack, attack', just as the earthquake sent everyone tumbling and stumbling. Horses and donkeys bucked and brayed, cooking pots tipped, chaos boiled over throughout the camp. Men half asleep blindly grabbed their swords and began blindly slashing.

As the thunder of Saul's ever growing force approaches, the Philistine army suddenly implodes. During the long years of occupation, Hebrew men recognized the military superiority of the Philistines. Many of them had joined the troops as foot soldiers. Because the Philistine control was so complete, the loyalty of these Hebrews had never been questioned.

Now, these sons of Israel are amazed at the confused maelstrom of the Philistine camp. Out through the clouds of dust they see the fearsome figure of Saul, riding his stallion, sword glittering, hair flying, eyes flaming. They hear the roar of their brother Israelites and from one heartbeat to the next they reverse allegiances. Swords and knives find Philistine backs and bellies.

The great Philistine force scatters across the hills. The more they run the larger Saul's army grows, the hundreds become thousands. Among those who join the swelling throng are Jonathan and

Benadad, still bloody from their early morning slaughter. They run alongside their comrades and are greeted with joyful roars. The bodies of the fleeing enemy dot the plain.

The panicked Philistines scatter into the brush-filled ravines with the bloodhound Israelites relentlessly pursuing. The adrenaline that fueled the men since early morning begins to ebb. Jonathan and his men push through a stand of oaks. The afternoon sun strikes gold. A honeycomb from a hive inside a hollow trunk lies on the ground. Jonathan trumpets, "Men, look, God has provided food. Let's eat up." Before his troops can stop him, he's scooping the honey into his mouth. The men shoot worried glances at each other. Saul's early morning curse is still fresh in their minds.

Jonathan swats at the angry bees and grins as he gulps. "C'mon, here's just what we need to keep running strong." But Saul's words created a taboo and despite their growling stomachs they cannot force themselves to even sample the sweet delight. One of the men blurts out, "The King pronounced a curse on anyone who would eat before the enemy is destroyed." Jonathan shakes his head and takes one more bite of the comb before flinging it to the ground. "And this will please the Lord? How are starving soldiers supposed to conquer these Philistines?" He grabs a handful of dirt and rubs his hands. "Too many of these pagan dogs have already slipped away." He tosses back his sweat-heavy hair and leads his men up the valley.

The enemies skitter through the bushes in front of them, heard but not seen. The sun is setting by the time Jonathan and his men reach the valley's end. They slowly climb the slope and see bonfires scattered on the plains below. The bawling of oxen and the bleating of terrified sheep mingle with the shouts of soldiers. The troops, staggering with exhaustion, have fallen upon the herds that provisioned the Philistine army. Jonathan and his men trot down the slope to join the feast.

They pick their way through the bushes, reach the edge of the celebration, and pause in their tracks. Their ravenous compatriots are full of shouts and guttural grunts. They grab the animals and slash their necks. Blood gushes on hands and tunics, the ground is slippery. Before the beasts even stop twitching they are hacking out chunks of flesh and carrying the dripping pieces to the fire for roasting. All the soldiers know that eating meat with its blood in it violates the Lord's sacred command. But the smell of fat and meat fills the air and every man's mouth fills with saliva and every stomach growls.

Jonathan's troops move as one toward the fires. Only Jonathan holds back with Benadad at his side. He gazes at the scene and quietly orders his aide, "Go, tell the king that the men are eating unclean food." Benadad runs off into the evening darkness, Jonathan moves among the men. Most of them barely acknowledge his presence. He eyes the gaunt faces of men who have not only ferociously fought for twelve hours straight but have spent days and weeks on soldier's rations. He watches in silence as they tear off and chew chunks of half raw meat. He shudders at their violation of the law but secretly wonders whom the Lord will blame for their sin.

On the nearby plateau, Saul and his commanders gather in a clearing encircled by tall oaks. The oak trunks are lighted by the dancing flames of a bonfire while their upper branches disappear in the darkness.

"Great work, warriors all of you, true soldiers of the Chosen people!" Saul slaps the backs and shakes the hands of his commanders. Saul strides amongst his soldiers, savoring the exhaustion in his limbs and the lightness in his heart. Even the arrival of fat, scowling Ahijah doesn't dampen his enthusiasm. The flush of the day's battle has already scoured from his mind the morning's misery. The Philistines have been routed. The enemy soldiers fled like terrified rabbits. His army has swelled in size. How could the Lord not be pleased! Why not invite the poor priest to offer up a thanksgiving prayer? Saul marches over to Ahijah and is so filled with his own magnanimity that he walks right past Benadad who has stepped into the clearing. But before he can speak to the priest the young aide runs to his side and blurts out for everyone to hear.

"King, O King, your men, they're eating, they're eating bloody meat!"

Behind him Saul hears the shocked curses of his commanders. In front of him he sees the face of the priest twist in horror. His soaring spirit plummets like a dying pigeon and his euphoria mutates into rage. He wheels about and screams at his commanders. "Have you no control over your men? Do you want to bring the Lord's curse upon us? Go down there, bring the beasts here. We've got to do this right or we'll all be damned."

The commanders trot off into the darkness. Saul enlists Benadad and under the scowling eye of the priest, they push a boulder into the center of the clearing. During the next hour, the quiet forest clearing becomes a maelstrom of exhausted soldiers who heave bawling, screaming animals onto the rock. Blood spurts and sprays into the air and paints the boulder a sticky rusty red. After the blood drains from the animals, the carcasses are carried back to the troops.

At last the commanders return to the clearing, their earlier ardor chilled by the violation of sacred law. Jonathan joins the men who sit cross legged around the fire and chew on their own portions of meat. Jonathan's face suggests that he is chewing on more than a mouthful of meat. At last he speaks almost to himself.

"We set the Philistines running but we didn't slaughter as many as we could have. We slowed down too soon."

Abner shoots a glance at Saul, then stares into the young man's eyes. "Yes, you are right."

The other men grunt in agreement but keep their eyes lowered. A chill settles over the clearing and the sweat in Saul's tunic begins to feels like ice.

Without warning he jumps to his feet. "All right, then let's go after them. Right now, this night. They've no doubt made some sort of camp on the south end of the plain. We can sneak up on them, slaughter them all in their sleep."

Saul's vehement outburst stuns the men. They glance at one another. Is he goading us? Is he serious? Is he suggesting or ordering? Saul glares down at them waiting for their response. Jonathan, and the other men scramble to find a safe answer.

At last Abner says, "Do whatever seems good to you."

Saul stares down at this battle-hardened soldier and for a second sees not the veteran Abner but his nemesis Samuel the prophet. He hears again the words first spoken months ago, "Do whatever you think is right." The words terrified him then. The same words were thrown in his face days ago and turned his heart to lead. Now they echo out here on the battlefield and they paralyze him.

How can he know what is right? How can he know what is good? Months ago, Samuel concluded the anointing by saying, "God is with you." Then Saul had been confused. Days ago, on the plain of Gilgal Samuel repeated the words and Saul was wounded. Tonight, the words fill the night air and Saul is hemmed in and isolated.

Help apparently arrives from the least expected source. Ahijah croaks from his seat in the shadows, "Let's consult the Lord God on this matter." Saul jumps as though shot with an arrow. He spins around. "Yes, priest. Of course, the ephod". But the priest glowers and crosses his fleshy arms. "No, in this matter the king himself must seek an answer from God. Go away from this light, go into the wood. Listen for a word."

Saul throws up his hands, then puts one hand on his sword. He feels the gaze of his officers scorching his back. At last his hand drops, he shakes his head and stalks into the woods. He abandons the circle of light and the heavy blanket of darkness quickly enfolds him. The distant shouting of the troops and then the closer conversations of his commanders are devoured up by the voracious silence of the forest. Saul's ears now hear the tiny sounds: the crackling of dry leaves under his feet, the frantic rustle of a night creature, maybe a mouse, fleeing across his path.

Saul leans his aching back against a tree. His eyes flutter shut. He strains to listen. A gentle night breeze stirs in the highest branches. *Lord God, are you here?* He can hear the throb of his own blood, but no other physical sound. He turns inward, listens with his mind and sifts through his thoughts. *Lord God, are you here? Where do you hide?* Everything inside is covered with his own fingerprints: his own sad anger splashed like dried blood over his emotions; vivid images of the day's carnage; his own resentments and fears lurking in the darkest corners like shrouded wraiths who've become permanent dwellers. No sign of God.   He is not surprised. He would have been astonished had he heard or sensed anything. How many time since his first encounter with Samuel has he carried out this exercise? The result is always the same: Silence, thundering silence. But this night is different. An audience waits for an answer.

Shall I make a choice and claim it as God's word? That might increase my authority, if my choice leads to victory. But what if it fails? Will I be unveiled as the imposter I often feel I am? How will the families of all the dead soldiers react if I'm as denounced as a false king?

Saul stares into the empty darkness and strains to fend off the jabs of panic in his chest. No, pretending that a choice is God's choice is too fraught with danger. Then, like a firefly flashing in front of his face, the answer comes to him.

I'll tell the truth. At least as much truth as they all need to know. And then I'll interpret the truth. Surely that is my right as the king.

He pushes himself away from the tree trunk, throws back his shoulders and strides into the clearing. The men rise at his coming. Saul steps into the light and crosses his arms cross his chest. He slowly sweeps his eyes across all of the men, then intones, "I asked our Lord. But the Lord has not seen fit to answer me today. The Lord is silent because a sin has been committed within our ranks. We will need to find out who is guilty. And I swear by our holy Lord God the guilty one will die."

Every man in the clearing saw the troops eating like ravenous wolves, saw the blood running down their arms. Every soldier who ate bloody meat violated the sacred taboo. A shiver of apprehension knifes through the commanders. Is Saul going to kill them all?

Before they can voice an objection, Saul bellows, "Priest! Step forward."

Ahijah grunts up from his stool, lurches out of the shadows and shuffles up to Saul. He looks up and croaks, "Yes, King, what do you want of me?"

Saul's mouth goes dry. A prickle of sour sweat runs down his back. Improvisation is not his gift but the act has begun and he can only move forward. Panic momentarily clouds his eyes. Then he regains his grip. *Ah yes, the ephod. Will the Lord finally speak to me? Do I dare ask?*

He works some saliva back into his mouth and swallows. "Jonathan, come stand here beside me." Jonathan shoots a puzzled look at the others, then slowly rises and moves next to his father. The two Benjaminites now stand facing the other eleven commanders. The priest wearing his ephod stands in the middle.

"Priest, take out the two stones and put them into the bag."

Ahijah widens his stance and draws from his belt a heavy cloth bag. He holds the bag open with one fleshy hand and with his other reaches ceremoniously into the pocket on his vest and pulls out first the white Urim stone and then the black Thummin. He drops both into the bag. The only sound in the clearing is the crackling of the fire.

Saul now raises his hands into the inky sky and shouts, "O Lord of Israel, why haven't you answered us tonight? Who is the guilty one? If he is among the troops below let the Thummin stone be drawn. If the guilty one is here among us, let the Urim be drawn."

The priest lifts his stumpy arms and holds the bag high above his head. He lowers it, then with head still turned upward and eyes pinched shut, he reaches into the bag. Faces tense, breath stops. The priest dramatically draws out his hand with fist clutched tight. He gradually unfurls his fat fingers. The white Urim lies ghostly in his palm.

The men gasp as one. They gape at Saul. What insanity is this? What lunacy has infected the king? But Saul is heedless of their glares. Once more, he raises his arms into the black sky.

"O Lord God, who among us is guilty. If he be of the tribe of Benjamin let Thummin be drawn. If it be one of other tribes let it be Urim."

Ahijah is savoring his moment. He raises then lowers the bag with deliberate slowness. His entire face pinches shut as he reaches in and grabs a stone. His fingers unfold and the black Thummin lies in his palm like a baleful sinister eye. The commanders first exhale in relief then gulp in dismay at the scene before them.

Like a deluge unleashed by a mountain cloudburst Saul is being swept along by a churning stream of emotion. He is beyond stopping. His eyes gleam with dark fire. He grimly declares,

"Again, priest. Replace the stones. Now, if the guilty one is Jonathan let it be the Urim, if I am the guilty one, then let it be Thummin." Again, the priest raises up the bag, again he dramatically inserts his hand. His fingers peel back revealing the deathly pale Urim stone.

Saul howls and stumbles backward. He seems to have awakened from a nightmare. The emotional deluge of the past three years has swept up too many broken plans, too many fragments of rage and sorrow. Saul's thoughts churn and eddy but cannot penetrate the dam created by his own shattered life. His heart hammers in his chest. He wants to scream out a curse or a prayer to the silent God but his tongue lies swollen and heavy in his mouth. He seeks to grasp the priest but Ahijah turns and trundles back to the shadows as a log shifts in the fire and spews a shower of sparks into the night sky.

Jonathan stands immobile, staring calmly into his father's face. Saul shifts his feet, looks down then up.

Saul stutters out, "Jonathan, I didn't, I mean… What have you done?"

Jonathan stares up at his father, speaks calmly without emotion. "Do you mean, have I sinned? I didn't eat any meat with blood. But this afternoon, when we were tracking down the enemy dogs I saw some honey and I scooped some up with my sword and I ate it. If that's a sin, then I am guilty." Jonathan takes a step back, stretches his arms out wide. "Go ahead, kill me."

Saul sways like a cypress in a windstorm. Who is this Jonathan who speaks? The whirlpool in his mind swirls and foams. Is he a pious son ready to accept the consequences of his father's oath? Is he a viperous son goading his father so he can steal his kingship? Is he a cunning son counting on his fellow soldiers to rescue him? Is he an arrogant son who believes God speaks to his own heart while dead silence reigns in the king's life? The confrontations and disobediences of the past months--Saul's thoughts boil. He has no answers, no path ahead, only this maelstrom in his soul.

Suddenly the logjam breaks. He throws back his great head and roars, "It is upon God. An oath was made before God. The king does not break a vow made before God. Jonathan, kneel down." Saul draws his sword. The dried blood of Philistines still encrusts the steel blade.

Jonathan stands frozen, staring up at his father the king. The dying flickers of the campfire dance in his shining eyes. Unhurriedly he lowers his arms to his side. Then he gradually buckles his knees. His eyes never leave Saul's face. At last he kneels in the dirt, silent and still.

The memory of himself kneeling before Samuel at the gates of Ramah races through Saul's mind. He silently curses that day and that man. He grabs the sword with quivering hands and begins to raise it.

"Nooo!" A bellow explodes from the commanders. They all begin to shout. Abner takes three steps forward and stands beside Jonathan. He grips his sword with whitened knuckles. He snarls at Saul through clenched teeth. "Who do you think set today's battle in motion? Who was it that put the pagan dogs into a panic? If it hadn't been for Jonathan do you think we'd be sitting here congratulating ourselves? God was on his side today. Nobody is going to touch a hair on his head." He raises his sword and the rest of the commanders follow suit.

Saul's eyes blaze. His fist clenches and his sword vibrates as though struck by a stone. He hunches his shoulders, a bull preparing to charge. Neither King nor commanders breathe. Once more a decision must be made, once again the road divides.

Then Saul blinks. His eyes lose their fire as if doused by bucket of water. His arms drop as though the biceps have been severed. He bows his head, and turns away from them all. The tip of his sword drags in the dirt and he stumbles silently into his tent.

Chapter Nineteen

The morning sun labors to pierce the thin clouds. Samuel tries to lengthen his stride but his body stubbornly resists. With each passing new moon every muscle grows stiffer. Some realities cannot be altered by flinty willpower.

Aii, things never change do they Lord. The melon plants still bloom in early summer and the foxes still slip through the orchards at night. Israel's summer sun is still hot and your voice never stops sending me on these thankless journeys.

Samuel approaches the end of his two-day journey up to Saul's headquarters. He has not seen the king since their caustic encounter nearly a year and a half ago. *O Lord, why me? Why must it always be me? I'm sure by now you've found younger men who can move faster than this old body. Look at me! My joints are swollen. I can barely rise from my sleeping mat in the morning. Why don't you snatch up someone else's mind and mouth to speak for you? And why must the message I carry to this man always be so dismal? And why, if you have rejected him, do you command him to another mission?*

As usual Samuel gets no answers. Three days ago, the steady calm Voice declared, **"Give Saul this command. 'Destroy the Amalekites, utterly, totally, and unconditionally—all that they are, all that they have.' They cannot escape their history. Long ago, they harassed God's chosen people when they left Egypt. Now for the good of this land these pagans and all that is theirs must be eliminated. Go now and give him this order."**

Reluctantly Samuel trudges to another encounter with Saul carrying yet another grim message. These things have not changed. But a shocking transformation has occurred since their bitter meeting at Gilgal. Days after the battle of Michmash, Samuel heard reports that Saul's commanders had united against him over the fate of Jonathan. The prophet expected that Saul's support would drift away like sand in the desert wind. He imagined that within months Saul would surrender his kingship, be killed by the enemy or perhaps even be assaulted by his own soldiers. Not even God's seer foresaw what unfolded.

The story of what happened after that night at Michmash had now spread across the hills and valleys of the land like the red springtime *kalanit* blossoms. Samuel assumed the tale had grown with the retelling. After the confrontation with his leaders, after Saul had trudged into his tent, the commanders quietly embraced Jonathan, the hero of the day whose life they'd just spared. They all tried to sleep but their slumber was uneven, and their dreams full of apprehension. Were they still troop commanders? Was Saul still their king? How deeply had Saul been wounded?

They were stupefied when Saul emerged briskly from his tent at dawn. His eyes were hooded and glowed with black fire. His voice was firm and rang out into the clear morning.

"Find four trusted soldier and bring them here."

The commanders shook off their amazement and eagerly scrambled to show their allegiance. Minutes later they returned with four young men bearing the disheveled and bewildered look of the just awakened. Saul examined them, circled them with stiff, quick steps.

"Fine. These will do." Turning to the four young men, he spoke loud enough for his commanders to hear. "You will be my body guards. Your loyalty will be to me and me alone. You will protect me with your lives. You will keep everyone—," he paused and turned in a complete circle, staring at every commander, including Jonathan, "You will keep everyone at least ten paces from me. Is that clear?"

The storytellers claimed that in the tent that night, after the battle of Michmash and the near murder of Jonathan, the Lord God appeared to Saul and endowed him new power and granted him a new heart. Samuel was skeptical. But everyone insisted that from that day forward Saul acted like a different man. Though he distanced himself from his commanders, he did not shy away from the people's enemies. In the past year, Saul had led his troops into battle against all of Israel's enemies: Moabites, Ammonites, Edomites, the kings of Zobah and the ever-dangerous Philistines. And shockingly he'd routed them all. Apparently now he led his army with blunt, dispassionate efficiency. His countrymen no longer held him in suspicion. By the thousands, young men with hot blood, thirsting for adventure, had joined the ranks of his army.

Such were the stories carried to Samuel's ears in Ramah. Today he will make his own judgments. The clamor of many voices fills the air as he draws near to the camp. The troops have set up alongside a stream and goat hide tents line the banks and creep up the slope. Small fires crackle and the smell of smoke and roasting meat fills the air. He knows Saul is somewhere in the camp, but he is reluctant to address any of the soldiers and they scarcely give him a glance as he passes. Most of the troops are young and he is old. No one recognizes him. He is chagrined at how quickly loyalty and honor have been transferred.

Samuel moves upward, away from the water. He reminds himself that he is simply a messenger, but he can't help being curious, and anxious. *Only a year and a half ago I denounced this man as a God rejected weakling. Now he commands thousands of loyal men and has the respect of the land. What kind of reception can I expect?*

He works his way up the first gentle slope and reaches the crest. His eyes are drawn to the next crest and there it is. Saul's tent is unmistakable. It has four walls of black goat skin panels and it stands alone on top of the hill. At each corner, stands a burly guard with a sword in his belt and a spear in his hand. Beside the door flap, a blue banner atop a high pole flutters in the breeze.

The prophet takes in the scene. *No matter what the Lord has decided, Saul continues to act like a king.* He starts marching upward. Abruptly a guard from the tent trots down and stands in his path. The gruff sentry points his spear menacingly at Samuel's chest. He glares mutely at the seer and the look on his face says, 'Why not try taking another step?' Samuel is tempted to clear his throat and spit phlegm into the young man's face. Instead he tips his head back to the heavens, and sighs in disgust. "Tell your king that Samuel the prophet is here with a message for him, a message from the Lord God."

Before the young soldier can turn, the tent flap lifts and Saul sweeps out. His black hair glints in the afternoon sun. It brushes his shoulders. He stands staring down at Samuel. The prophet stares back, peering over the guard's shoulder. *Is Saul considering whether to invite me into his tent? Aii, I'm too old for this.* Samuel snorts, steps to the side, away from the guard's spear, and hoists his staff into the sky. His words clatter through the air like a handful of stones.

"Saul, son of Kish, the Lord has given me a message for you." He aims his staff at the staring king. "The Lord your God wants you to go down to the Amalekite nation and obliterate it. Every person and animal that dwells there must be destroyed."

Samuel drops his staff. Saul remains motionless. A slab of granite has more expression than this man's face. His dark blue robe flutters softly in the breeze. The only sound is distant laughter from the soldiers down in the valley. Nearly a minute passes. Saul opens his mouth as though to speak but then abruptly closes it. Samuel's patience shreds. He's delivered the message. His mission is over. He shifts his staff and turns to descend the hill.

At that moment, Saul mutters to himself. Samuel's ears catch something like, "So, the Lord still speaks to you." The prophet stops in his turning and the towering king lifts his chin and booms into the sky. "If this is what the Lord wants, then this is what we will do."

To Samuel's ears the words have a cynical ring. But he simply shrugs. He's fulfilled his duty and is free to go home. He finishes his turn and steps down the slope.

Saul calls, "Wait, Prophet. Rest awhile in my tent before you return." Samuel jerks to a stop. Saul's tone is soft. The words are more an invitation than a command. He turns and with a soldier on either side climbs up to the large tent. He follows Saul into the semi dark interior. Mats and blankets cover the floor.

"Sit, prophet. Sit."

Samuel tries but cannot suppress a groan as he lowers himself onto the sheepskin. He sees Saul's bare toes and remembers their last meeting. "I'm surprised at your hospitality."

Saul notices where the old man's eyes have landed. He chuckles. "You're the first person besides me to enter this tent in almost a year. Surprised? I suppose I am too." He tips his head forward and his long hair hides his face. Then he flips his head back and gazes out above Samuel's head.

"I've become the lone wolf. Before you... When I was still free I always surrounded myself with friends and family, good food, stories and laughter. But now... I can hear better in the quiet."

Samuel asks, "So the Lord now speaks to you?"

Saul's laugh is joyless. "Ha. That's what the people think. It's the story my troops tell. I say nothing to discourage them." Saul sits cross legged only a few yards away from his nemesis. He looks down at the ground between and speaks so softly Samuel cranes forward to hear him.

"No, the Lord hasn't spoken to me. The Lord doesn't speak to me. And, I've stopped listening for the Lord." Saul sits erect and slaps his hands on his knees. "I've weaned myself. I've surrendered that desire, hopefully forever."

He sees the bewilderment on his guest's face. He hadn't planned on telling Samuel his story but he realizes they're enmeshed together in a story not entirely of their own making.

"Your strong words that first day by the city wall--they filled me with awe. They terrified me. Every day with every step I expected to be assaulted, invaded by the Lord's voice, or thought or will. I tortured myself for a year with every decision, every move; waiting and wondering when the Lord would speak. But now I'm finished."

Again, Saul slaps his knees, and grins at the silent seer. "I swear I'm finished with that. Ever since that night in Michmash." His grin dies as he relives that night.

"I crawled into my tent like a dying dog. I heard only the chattering of my own teeth. My hands, my feet-- as cold as the Mt. Hermon snow. My middle--stomach and chest--boiled with rage and confusion. What had I become? Who had I become? How had I come to nearly slaughter my own son? And why, why had Jonathan looked so calm? My thoughts tumbled like sticks swirling in a flood."

"Then outside the tent I heard my men speaking quietly. Were they still my men? I half expected them to rush in and kill me. I half hoped they would. After many hours, the fire in my middle cooled and the ice in my limbs melted. The camp grew quiet. I gradually stretched out on my pallet. I stared up into the black roof of my tent and I gave up. Yes, prophet, that's what I did. I surrendered the hope that I would ever hear from Lord God or be led by Him."

Samuel exclaims, "but the Lord God did choose you."

"Maybe yes, maybe no. You told me so. The Lord hasn't spoken to me on the matter. You also said He's turned against me. The Lord God has said nothing to me. Either way, I've decided that as long as I'm still the king, I'll be king on my own terms. There's no other way. I can't sit around waiting for God to tell me what to do. God will have to catch up or speak up. When you doused me with oil I started living in expectation and fear. First I waited hopefully for the Lord God to break in to my life and then I began fearfully trembling that He would."

Saul pauses and soberly shakes his head. "But now I've seen this isn't going to happen. No matter what you say or think, God is far away from us, at least from me. Maybe someday, when the Lord God returns from wherever He has gone, things will be different, but for now, I am free. Free to fight and lead as I see fit."

Samuel tries to interrupt but Saul shows him his palm. "You say the Lord wants to eliminate the Amalekites. Old enemies, I know, I know, enemies since the time of Moses. I've heard the stories. I've heard of how the Lord declared the Ban upon them. But these people have done nothing to me. How can I be sure this is the Lord God's idea? Does He even care about this? Is this truly a holy war, a sacred duty? Does the great Lord God hold grudges? I can't say. But, one thing I do know. I've got soldiers eager for battle. When you have an army that's what you do. You fight. You find an enemy or, if you must, you create one and then you attack. So, yes, we'll raise our weapons against them. We'll do our sacred duty."

He sweeps to his feet in one motion and glowers down at Samuel. "Tell your God that I'll obey this command, but in my heart I'm doing what's best for me and my men." He spins, stoops under the tent flap, and leaves Samuel sitting cross legged in stunned silence.

***

The warm fingers of the rising sun massage Saul's back and he rolls his shoulders with pleasure. He stands with arms akimbo in front of his tent, flanked by two of his guards. The oop-oop-oop of hoopoe birds looking for bugs on the grassy slopes fills the morning air. Saul fills his lungs, holds his breath for a second and then releases it in a long, slow "ahhh."

His twelve commanders are climbing the slope to his tent. Yesterday, after the prophet left, he sent them a message summoning them to this early morning meeting. A year ago, he'd have sat with them in a circle inside his tent to discuss strategy. No more. Now they stop the required ten paces away and stand in a silence broken only by birdsong and the exhausted chuffing from a few of the older soldiers. Saul stares at these gray-haired men and wonders how much longer some of them should be battle leaders. Does he dare remove them from their positions or should he let the brutal nature of future battles do the removing?

Abner impatiently clears his throat. Saul gives him a sardonic grin. "Yes. Good morning cousin. Good morning to all of you. Let's begin with a question: Have you all heard of The Ban?"

Ishvi, the eldest of the group, hawk faced and knobby jointed, still puffing from the ascent, speaks in a wavering voice. "What child of Israel does not know of God's Holy Ban?"

Saul is tempted to snap at the man's arrogance but the morning sun has softened his temper. "Yes, Ishvi, the Ban comes from God.

Now the Lord has decided to put the Amalekites under The Ban. Five generations ago our people marched out of Egypt. When they were weak out there in the wilderness these sons of dogs hounded them. They tried to kill our forefathers." The commanders nod. They all heard this story growing up.

Saul's voice intensifies. "We may forget but God's memory doesn't fade. God has decided that these Amalekites must be completely destroyed. We are to be the instruments of that destruction. Men, women, children, cattle, sheep, goats—every living thing must be slaughtered." He pauses, then deliberately punches out word by word. "God has commanded it."

The commanders digest this news in impassive silence. At last, Abner speaks.

"How soon do we march?" Saul surmises his cousin's question isn't motivated by holy passion, but by a veteran soldier's pragmatism.

"How soon can you be ready?" the King shoots back.

"We can break camp and be ready to march by midday."

Saul nods. "Then we march at noon. In two days, we will destroy the city of the Amalekites. Before you go...…I have one more order." His stern face hides the snicker he holds inside. Yesterday, while watching the seer depart, a scene from his childhood surfaced.

A noisy mob of men and women swarmed around a weathered, wrinkled man. Six-year-old Saul had wormed his way toward the front of the shouting crowd. The man in the center wore robes that were mere tatters, stiff with dirt. At first, he stood erect and cursed those around him. Then as stones began to smack into his body he sheltered his hoary head with reed thin arms. The stones flew faster and harder until the man crumbled to the ground. Young Saul was horrified by the brutality and fascinated that it was coming from his neighbors and from his own family. His mother tugged him away from the crowd and knelt before him. Yesterday as Samuel limped down the hill, he saw again his mother's shining eyes and heard again her earnest words. "This man claims to know the things of

God. He casts spells and speaks to the ghosts of the dead. God says such men are an abomination in the land and deserve to die."

That memory, triggered by his latest encounter with Samuel, gave birth to an idea. He's been rehearsing the decree in his mind since yesterday. "Each one of you will send out a messenger to your people with this decree: Saul, son of Kish, King of the peoples of Israel, orders that anyone practicing sorcery or soothsaying, anyone consulting ghosts or seeking to speak to the dead and then claiming to speak a word from God, that person shall be punished by death."

The men glance nervously at each other. This order is already part of the sacred law, but every one of them knows of men and women who still practice these hidden arts. Is Saul truly intent on enforcing this ancient law or is there another darker reason behind this decree? Saul interrupts their ruminations.

"Go now. You're dismissed. Send out your messengers and muster your troops. We march at noon." *Giving orders is easy when you stop worrying about pleasing others. Then what you decide, whatever you decide, is the right thing.* He watches his commanders stride down the hill and stretches his mighty frame. The blazing sun throws his shadow large and long down the hillside. It is a good morning to be king.

Chapter Twenty

Ten thousand eager, lusty men march behind King Saul. Their roars and shouts reverberate in the fall air. This is no secret assault. The troops march south to the Amalekite city with swagger and bravado

Two days ago, when the commanders told their men they were embarking upon a holy war, the entire camp simmered with rekindled fervor. Young men whose blood already surged hot for battle trembled with the passion of the pious. This unnerving power now pulses behind Saul. He does not share it, but he senses its pressure as they advance across the arid plain toward the walled Amalekite city.

Saul strives to ward off questions that shimmer in the desert heat. For so many months he's daily steeled himself against thoughts of gods or God. He tries to focus solely on the battle ahead but queries as sharp as the desert thorns pierce his concentration. *Do these Amalekites tell stories of our people? Do they even remember that they harassed the children of Israel generations ago? If the Lord God is determined to destroy this entire people, who is safe from such wrath? If this Ban is not the Lord's desire, how will we live with ourselves?*

The questions jab him mercilessly until he and his army come in sight of the doomed city. Its dark stone walls stretch east and west across the plain before them. They are still a mile away when the gates slam open and the Amalekite troops march out. Saul's commanders set their archers and loose the first volley of arrows. Then Saul raises his glinting sword and charges into the first line of troops. He swings his sword and slices the first man's jugular. He shouts as he severs the arm of a soldier preparing to throw a spear. He soon guides his horse to the edge of the battlefield. Why not give his troops the pleasure of executing their God's sacred command?

In the next hours of carnage some of Saul's men die and all the Amalekite men die. These Amalekites fight as brave men should, with hearts and muscles driven by righteous rage. They are impelled by the instinct to preserve family and home. The air is full of hacking and slashing, grunting and shouting. All of this makes grim sense to Saul and his soldiers. Man against man, parry and thrust, feint and strike. Blood and bowels turn the ground into gory mire. These Amalekite men die as men should. They are outnumbered ten to one, yet they resist with their last throat rattling breath.

Saul observes it all from a low hill, above and to the east of the city gate. By midafternoon the battlefield is quiet. Two of Saul's commanders emerge from the dust cloud. They shove a man who walks ahead of them. Even from a distance Saul can see that this man does not shuffle like a prisoner, but strides with head erect and shoulders back. The trio climbs the hillock where Saul stands beside his horse, flanked by his four guards. The commanders stop before Saul and the prisoner stares up at him with unblinking eyes.

A sweat and blood soaked Abner announces what Saul already suspects. "This one is their king. The one called Agag. He fought to the end. I could have killed him but by right he is yours to destroy."

Saul slowly examines the scowling king. His once fine linen robe is now tattered and caked with gore and dirt. Blood seeps from a wound on his arm, his elaborately embossed breastplate is dented and smeared, his bearded jaw is clenched and he rivets Saul with bitter black eyes. Saul lifts his gaze over the man's head, and stares out into the metallic blue sky above the city.

Like bubbles escaping the mouth of a drowning man, doubts pop to the surface of Saul's thoughts. *This is a man like me. We're not very different. Did he choose to be king or was he chosen? Do his gods speak to him or are they as silent as mine is? Must I take his life because my men defeated his men? Isn't he doing his duty just as I am?*

The doubts paralyze his arm and he cannot lift his sword. He curtly commands his guards, "Bind him and tie him to the tree behind my tent. I will deal with him later."

Agag makes no sound but Saul believes he sees a flicker in his eyes. Relief? Sorrow? He cannot tell. Abner says, "The troops are waiting for you to lead them into the city." Saul nods and begins marching down the hill surrounded by his guards. He wishes he could leave his doubts bound to the tree with the defeated king.

He strides in silence for several paces before speaking. "Why do they need me to lead them? The city is already ours. Only old men, women and children are left."

Abner grunts agreement. "But for some of our troops, these are harder to destroy."

Saul tries in vain to cling to his stoic silence. "And what about for you, cousin?" Saul worries that his shell, the one he's been wearing for the past many months may be cracking. Yet he is compelled to ask, "How do you feel about what we are about to do?"

Abner growls. "Soldiers don't feel. We act. We do. God has decided that these people are under the Ban. He wants them gone from the land. So we obey."

His vow of silence already broken, Saul probes further. "So why is it harder to destroy the ones who're left?"

Abner's thoughts crunch like their boots on the gravel. After a dozen steps, he responds, "Every soldier follows the king and fights for the people and for God. But most soldiers fight first to protect themselves and their fellows. When a man runs at you with a sword, you don't need to think. You raise your sword, shout and slash. You destroy the one who wants to destroy you. But now we move to kill those who don't threaten us with swords. We wipe out those whom God wants to wipe out. God says they're enemies and so we destroy them. But our blood doesn't run hot, not for most of us. We always fight because it's our duty. But it's easier to fight when that duty includes saving your own life. This…."

The icy calm Saul has maintained for nearly two years is melting, the shell he'd imposed upon his own mind to keep questions and doubts at bay is cracking with every step. He desperately wants to continue this conversation with his usually taciturn lead commander, but now they have reached the city gate. The twelve-foot high wooden doors are guarded by his own troops. These portals once kept enemies from entering. Now they keep the people inside from escaping.

Saul stands with his back pressed to the gate and swings his eyes over the thousands fanned out across the field. In the eyes of those nearest him he sees the truth in Abner's words. A few soldiers clench their swords and dance nervously, eager to enter and begin the slaughter. But most of the troops stand in silence. Sober faces, serious eyes; willing, but Saul senses, not necessarily eager. They all wait for him to speak. He does not trust his own words. He simply repeats the message Samuel brought him four days ago.

"Your God has commanded that these Amalekites be eliminated, that this land be cleansed from their impurity. Generations ago they persecuted and threatened our people when they marched out of Egypt. God wills that all living things within these walls die. Obey your God's command."

He pauses and in that sliver of silence he hears them through the heavy wooden doors: the mothers keening, mourning for their little ones who will soon die. Beneath his breast plate he feels a fist clenching, clamping, grinding. He groans but manages to raise his sword and shout "Death to the enemies of God." The troops roar in response, the gates swing open, and Saul marches in followed eagerly by the first ranks.

A skeletal, trembling grandfather staggers toward Saul. He brings a sword he can barely lift. He curses the king a reedy voice.

"Be damned, you son of a dog." He lurches weakly forward.

Saul takes a step backward. The shrunken man keeps stumbling toward him.

"Does your god smile when you kill old men and babies?" He feebly lifts his heavy weapon. Saul shakes his head, then raises his sword and runs it through the elder's heart. The carnage begins with horrific efficiency. Screams and wails echo as his troops spread throughout the city. A river of death surges down the narrow streets.

Saul backs up and stands at the gate. He sees desperate shrieking mothers burst out of their homes and attack the soldiers with knives, sticks and bare hands. Some mothers stay in their back rooms, wait for the thin doors to be kicked open, and die in a futile effort to protect their children. He watches screaming children running in terror, pursued by fearsome men.

Saul remembers Abner's words. This morning out on the battle field, the men shouted and cursed. Now they are unusually quiet. The only sounds ripping the silence are quavering cries and anguished screams. The gorge rises in his throat, he swallows and swallows lest it escape his mouth. Saul, king of the people of Israel, turns his back on this butchery and trudges up the hill.

Halfway to his tent he hears bellows and curses. Agag writhes against his bonds. He sees Saul and shouts in a voice scraped thin from roaring, "Curse you Israelite. You are no king, no honorable soldier. I spit on you and your clan!" He feebly hawks a gob of spittle into the dust. As one in a dream Saul unsheathes his sword and advances toward Agag. He should sever this pagan's head with one stroke and silence his slander. But today's torrent of blood has drowned his desire to obliterate this or any other enemy. Instead of raising his sword, he raises his voice.

"I have the sword and you're trussed like a lamb for slaughter. How is it that you dare to judge me?"

Agag's reply is sharp and brutal. "I'm a warrior. I deserve to die with my men. If you were a king, if you were an honorable man, you'd know this. Today your gods were stronger than our gods. So be it. I'm not afraid to die." His voice drops and he pleads, "Kill me now. Let me die with my people."

The two kings stare at each other. They hear the screams arising from the city, piteous cries, like the wails of rabbits in the jaws of foxes. The late afternoon sun has transmuted the dusty air above the battlefield into a lustrous gold. Saul's shadow stretches over the bound figure of Agag. He stares deep into the Amalekite's eyes and remembers Samuel's command, 'annihilate the enemy'. He remembers his own cynical response: "We will do this for our sake, not for your God's sake."

But now—now that the screeching vultures already tear at the corpses of the Amalekite soldiers, now that the floors and streets of the city are slippery with the blood of old men, women and children, now that he is face to face with this helpless man whom he is supposed to execute—now he realizes that the cynicism he's clung too for the past years is nothing more than a flimsy shield he's been using to cover his fear. *If this savage day truly is part of God's plan, then this God is a fearsome, inscrutable deity. Who will be the next target of this God's gory wrath? No one is safe, no one. And if this carnage has nothing to do with God's plan, how will I, how can I, live with myself?*

Saul's deep desire is this: to sit down on the grass and talk to this fellow king, to this man who is just as much a prisoner as he is, to ask him if he truly believes that the Amalekite god is weaker than Israel's god, if he thinks that every battle a battle between gods? He would ask Agag how he came to be king. He would ask—.

"Request to approach!" His son stands at attention halfway up the hill. Saul beckons him to come up. Jonathan is flushed and his tunic is smeared with blood. His eyes have a weary glaze; his jaw is slack and his voice scratches with fatigue.

"The men have a request. We've slaughtered most of the livestock as you commanded. But there are many fine cattle and sheep, fatling lambs. The men ask permission to dedicate them to the Almighty, to make sacrifices to God."

Saul is tempted to scornfully reject Jonathan's appeal, and remind him that "most" is obviously not "all." But Jonathan has shifted his gaze to Agag who glares up at them. Saul reconsiders the request: *Sacrifices to cleanse the soul…After today don't we all need that? And if, after the sacrifices, some animals remain, well, don't these soldiers of the Lord God deserve to eat? Besides, this will give me more time to consider what to do with Agag.*

Saul looks down at his handsome exhausted son and yearns to break the wall between them. He wants to tell him of his own fatigue. He longs to ask for forgiveness. But his courage evaporates. He simply nods and commands.

"Order the men to spare the best animals. Tomorrow morning we'll march to Carmel and make our sacrifices."

Jonathan looks back at Agag then turns and stares with heavy eyes into his father's haggard face. He opens his mouth to speak, but then shakes his head and returns to the whimpering city.

Chapter Twenty-one

You must return and speak to him.

Samuel groans, rolls onto his side and tries to cover his ears. Futile gesture, he knows. The Voice, steady and calm, dwells within him.

You must return and speak to him.

For two days, the demand has invaded every one of his brooding dreams, badgered him with every creaky movement of his aching joints.

You must return and speak to him. I regret making Saul king. He's turned his back on me. You must return and tell him.

The prophet's hip joint throbs so he shifts onto his back and stares up into the darkness. In a low whisper wrapped in the petulance of age he asks, "*You* regret making Saul king? What of me? How many times have I been sent after him? This king of yours has worn and wearied me to death. Why must I go? Can't you speak to him? Have I simply become your messenger boy? Is this how you treat your faithful servants?" Samuel fills the long, dark hours with his complaints and queries. He expects no answers and is not disappointed.

Gray morning light seeps in through the curtain across the door. He hears his wife outside, pouring water for his tea. He rises from his mat with a moan. He prepares his bundle for travel and reviews what he's heard. Yesterday a traveler came through the village and reported that the Amalekite city had been attacked by Saul's army. At least the Lord's command had been carried out. So how has the king turned his back on the Lord? What has Saul done now that has infuriated the Lord God? From bitter experience Samuel knows that he will get answers only when and if the Voice decides to give them. He snatches his staff and begins his journey in a foul mood.

Black smoke swirls and spirals into the heavens near the desert town of Carmel, half a day's journey north of the razed Amalekite city. An hour ago the troops hastily built a crude stone altar and slaughtered some of the animals. Now the flames skip back and forth across the carcasses.

The physical and emotional distance Saul tried to keep from his commanders has disappeared. The protective wall he tried to erect around himself has crumbled. When he saw his commanders and their soldiers march blood drenched and silent out of the Amalekite city the last bricks of his defense disintegrated. All of them together were instruments of this savage butchery. All of them were accountable.

He stands now alongside his troops gazing upward, watching the gray-black smoke wraiths disappear into the blue. He hears the murmured prayers of the men and he covets their faith. They believe their words ascend to God's ears with those bits of ash. They believe God sees these valuable animals offered to him and that He is pleased by their generosity.

Saul tries to pray, but the words turn to ash in his mouth. When he watched his soldiers sweep through the defenseless city, he shuddered with the realization that they all lived under the hand of a harsh and unknowable God. The distance he tried to keep from God dissolved in the horrors of the Amalekite purge. Now he is certain: no distance, no silence can protect him. And neither can words. He stands in silence before the altar, as he stands naked before God. *If only God would speak to me. But then, if God were to speak, would I survive?*

As the last wisp of smoke disappears Saul looks around the circle at his commanders. He sees exhaustion in their slumping shoulders and fatigue in their drawn faces. He decides that as they march north, each commander will take his men back to their home territory, allow the soldiers to return to their villages and spend time with their families. The commanders receive his announcement with quiet relief. The vast army dwindles as they move northward.

Four days into the march Saul and the troops from the clan of Benjamin pause on the crest of the hill. The stone circle of Gilgal lies on the plain below them. The land folds and flows endlessly toward the horizon. A breeze ripples their tunics; the sun caresses their necks. Saul gazes down the slope and recalls the many battles and deaths, all the turmoil he's endured since that day when he stood in the center of that circle bathed in the cheers and chants of the soldiers, his soldiers. He can still see their faces, ruddy and shining with pride. So few men on that day, compared to all of those who now call him king. Still, as with lovers, they will always claim a special place in his heart because they were first. But then, like the dark cloud that appeared on that next day, his mind fills with the bleak memory of Samuel beside him in that same circle, rebuking the troops for relying on a king, chastising them for their feeble faith, warning them in a harangue aimed at Saul himself. And then, despite his resistance, the bitterest memory surfaces, the memory of Samuel smashing his toe with his staff, announcing God's displeasure. He closes his eyes, shakes his head. Gilgal, layer upon layer of memories.

He tries to conjure up the life he once led, the life he had only five years ago. Always he sees it as a dream seen through morning mist: His ordered life, wife and family; months and years when his biggest worry was what pasture to use for the grazing, when his biggest conflicts were with his stubborn father; evenings spent drinking wine with friends and telling stories; feast days when he could grin and cast flashing eyes at the women, knowing that he had a warm and willing wife to share his bed. All of this now seemed to belong to another Saul, a free Saul who lived in another world. If only. If only he hadn't wandered into Ramah, if only he'd not met Samuel….

"Look King, someone stands in the circle of stones." Medad points below. An icy chill coils around Saul's neck. Before they take another step, he knows who waits there. The horses slowly pick their way down the rock-strewn slope. The troops are silent. They can feel a dangerous crackling in the air, like the air before a summer monsoon rolls in with its lightning strikes.

Saul orders his men to stop at the base of the hill. He trots toward the figure. Samuel waits, leaning lightly on his staff. Saul notices that the seer's beard is even thinner than it was only a few weeks ago. But the fiery man's jaw is still set, his chin still juts out in judgment. Saul remembers their last meeting. Then he'd felt so much stronger, even superior to the old prophet. Then he'd convinced himself that God was distant, aloof, maybe even oblivious. But like a sand bar washed away in a flash flood his certainty disappeared in the rivers of blood pouring through the streets of the Amalekite city. Today the threatening God seems nearer, and Saul is fatigued. Still, he is the king, he's completed their mission and resolves to put his bravest face forward.

He rides to the outermost circle, dismounts and marches up to Samuel. They stand in the heavy silence for a moment, the towering war weary king, and the wizened prophet. Saul bows his head. "The Lord's blessings upon you. I've carried out the commands of the Lord."

Samuel stares up at him, his face showing little emotion. Saul raises his head and stares into Samuel's eyes. *Do I see sadness there?*

Samuel holds his gaze for a moment and then shifts his eyes toward a spot above Saul's right shoulder, as though listening for a word from somewhere. The breeze suddenly shifts and the prophet's eyes widen. He tilts his head, "Wait! I hear sheep bleating, cattle lowing. What is this?"

Saul glances over his shoulder and then back to Samuel, "Ah, these are some of the Amalekite animals left after we made a great sacrifice of thanksgiving to the Lord at Carmel. The men wanted to give honor and sacrifice to God so we spared a few but we destroyed all of the rest as the Lord commanded and so…."

"Silence!" Samuel slams his staff onto the gravel and shrieks so sharply that even across the plain the animals fall silent. "Let me tell you what the Lord told me last night."

Saul's mouth fills with bile, his heart burns with bitterness. *Whether I let him or not, surely he will tell me.* He quietly murmurs, "Speak."

The prophet takes a deep breath, "Saul, you're a giant of a man, but you must seem small in your own eyes. Didn't God anoint you to be king of Israel? God gave you a command: wipe out the sinners, annihilate the Amalekites. But did you do this? No, you--.

Saul sputters, "But I--"

Samuel flames on. "You knew the command. Why did you swoop down like a hawk and snatch up booty, that belonged to God?"

Saul holds up both hands, "Wait, stop! I did obey your Lord's command. The men and the women and the children lie in their own blood, just as I was ordered to do. I completed my mission. I've got the Amalekite king prisoner but the rest are all food for the vultures. The troops wanted to dedicate some of the spoil to your Lord, so I let them pick out the best and give it to Him." Then he improvises, "we now plan to sacrifice the rest here at Gilgal."

Samuel raises his arms both hands clutching his staff so tightly that his knuckles shine gnarly and white. He raises his scratchy voice in a chant, a strange song that floats out to the horde.

"Do you think God likes sacrifice more than obedience? Obedience is better than ram fat. Rebellion is as bad as fortune telling. Stubborn people are as bad as idol worshippers."

The prophet now points his staff at Saul and his voice drops in pitch and volume. "Saul, you've rejected the word of the Lord, so now the Lord has rejected you from being king."

The chill that curled around his shoulders earlier now stabs Saul's chest like an icy knife. *This prophet, this God…there's no escape….* His men have not heard this last announcement but surely they can sense that intensity of this clash.

If I'm no longer king, what will I be? My once quiet life… I will never find my way back to it. My hands and heart are too bloody. My men? The troops? What of them? I am stubborn? Disobedient? At his word, we slaughter by the thousands, bathe ourselves in enemy blood and yet this prophet calls me disobedient? Or claims that God denounces me. God…the silent God. If I killed this prophet would God speak then? Or maybe he'd simply open the earth to swallow me and spit me into Sheol.

Saul turns away from Samuel and looks out across to the plain to his soldiers, *his* soldiers—men who've shed blood at his command, men who've risked their lives for this land. And the thousands of men in their villages who've pledged their allegiance to him? How can he abandon all of them? His heart writhes in agony. He is cornered like a rat. He can only hope that the silent God still listens. His drops to the ground and kneels onto the rough gravel. The stones grind into his knees and the words sear his throat like gall. He confesses his sin.

"I have transgressed. I disregarded your word and broke the Lord's law. I let my soldiers persuade me. I was too lenient and I heeded their voice. O Prophet, forgive me, pardon me. Let us together worship the Lord."

Samuel looks down upon the head that he anointed years ago. He remembers chafing with frustration at the Lord, but also being engulfed in deep awe. On that day, for one tremulous moment, he saw clearly that the two of them were writing the first pages of a new story. Now he gazes down at Saul's bowed head and laments. The Lord God insists that this new story is a tragedy. Samuel growls in anger mingled with grief. "No, I can't do this. You rejected the Lord and the Lord has rejected you. You are no longer king of Israel."

He spins and walks away from Saul. But Saul still on his knees lunges after him and frantically grabs for his robe. He catches the hem and the aged fiber, scrubbed thin from a thousand washings, tears off in his hand. Samuel spins back and glares at Saul, now on all fours in the dust with a scrap of cloth on the ground before him. Before Saul can utter a word, before even the Voice can speak, the prophet declares, loud enough only for Saul to hear.

"The Lord has torn the kingdom of Israel from your hand. He's given it to someone better than you. I've already told you. The Lord has decided. Do you think He's a fickle mortal like you and changes his mind?"

Saul sits back on his haunches, gasping in desperation. His chest burns with agony and rage yet he laughs at the grim irony of Samuel's words. *God chose me to be the king, then God changed his mind and so now I am not the king. But now God will not change his mind because God never changes his mind. Am I going insane?*

But he must put irony and insanity aside. He needs to act. He has men, soldiers and their families, here and across the country who still heed his voice. How will they react? What will they do to him and his family if he loses their loyalty? If he loses face completely here and now, he might never arise from the dusty circle. What will he be if he is not the king? He begs once more.

"Samuel. I've sinned. You are right. I admit it. I beg you to come worship with me. Give me that small bit of honor before the elders and the troops I've led. Let us go and worship the Lord your God."

He sits in the dust, head bowed, heart grieving and angry, furious with Samuel, raging at God, seething at the humiliation, and knowing he has no escape. He can hear the raspy breathing of the seer. He dares not look up.

Samuel sighs, "Get up. Let us worship the Lord. "

Saul stands and waves to his clansmen and they march across the plain toward the stone circle. The troops did not hear the words spoken by the king and the prophet. But even from a distance they've seen enough to know that whatever the conflict, Samuel has prevailed. They reach the two men and follow instructions, acting like people at a ceremony for the dead. They speak in hushed voices and move solemnly. They pile up stones for an altar. They slaughter the lambs and cattle and pour their quiet prayers into the sky. During the entire ceremony, Samuel speaks only what is necessary and keeps his attention focused upon the altar. At last the embers die and the smoke disappears. Now Samuel turns his piercing eyes upon Agag, who stands with hands bound, beside one of Saul's guards. He hisses like a snake, "Bring me that man."

Agag hobbles along, pushed by the guard. Saul's eyes are hooded as he watches his captive approaching the grim seer. His own knees tremble at the fate he knows is coming for this defeated king. Agag however is more than ready. He manages to croak out as he stands before Samuel, "I have already swallowed the worst part of death. Finish this now."

Samuel, always the master of the dramatic, holds out his hand for Saul's sword. Saul hands it to him and turns his face away. Samuel grasps the gleaming steel, points to Agag's chest and cries out. "Your sword made our women childless, now let your mother be childless too."

Possessed by the power of frenzied spirit the prophet raises the sword, screams and strikes Agag on the right side of his neck, severing the jugular. A geyser of blood spurts up as the Amalekite king falls. Samuel continues screaming and hacking with blind fury. Even the hardened soldiers turn away in disgust.

Samuel's screams become gasps for air and his fierce chopping gradually stops. The frenzy passes and he slumps to one knee in bloody exhaustion. He stands with a groan and tosses the sword on top of the pieces of Agag's body. He looks at no one as he wipes his bloody hands on his robe. Wordlessly he takes up his staff and turns back toward Ramah. Every joint, every sinew and muscle aches as he trudges home.

Will I ever see Saul again? Great God I hope not. My Lord, you have used me. No, you've abused me in this sordid affair. I didn't want to end my days like this. You used me to destroy this man's life. Whatever days left to him will be bitter as wormwood.

Saul watches the prophet creeping across the plain. A poisonous stone lies in his stomach. Despair, distress, fiery rage wrap around a belligerent determination.

I won't surrender, no matter what Samuel says. I didn't grab for the reins of power. They were slapped into my hand. If I release them now, my life, my army and my land will stampede into chaos. No, I can't let go. I won't let go. I'll go home, lick my wounds and lead all of those who're still willing to follow me.

Chapter Twenty-two

The march from Gilgal toward home is filled with celebrations. None of the soldiers were sure of what had happened between Saul and Samuel at Gilgal. It is no surprise that as they marched westward every village hails the great King Saul and his troops as saviors. Every evening is filled with music and dancing, feasting and drinking.

Now the troops top the last ridge. To the south, they see the expansive land of Judah. Ahead of them toward the setting sun lies the sliver of land that God saw fit to give to the little tribe of Benjamin. These remaining soldiers are mostly Saul's fellow tribesmen, plus a few whose devotion to their king transcends their tribal connections.

Cousin Abner rides alongside Saul. His usual growl is almost mellow. "Ah, it's good to be home. Too long away from family, my bed, and my wife's embrace." Saul grins at the unusual loquaciousness of his stoic cousin and at his unexpected tenderness.

Saul looks down on the hills and fields of Benjamin territory and smiles. "I see even you old soldiers grow weary of endless campaigns. Imagine those who've seldom done this before." Abner reverts to his usual form of communication and grunts in agreement.

Saul urges his horse forward and wistfully adds, "If only the Philistines would give us some time to rest and enjoy our homes."

Tonight, throughout the territory of Benjamin, laughter will bubble over as young men embrace their parents, fathers hug children and wives. But some homes will be drenched in tears as news finally arrives that this son, this husband and father will never return.

Ahinoam stands with the women and elders of Gibeah watching the troops wind their way up the slope. She can already see her Saul sitting tall on his horse leading the band. A few of her neighbors squeal with delight as they identify their husbands amidst the troops. When they come around the last turn toward the city gate the women wave their scarves and begin their joyful quavering ululation. Some women run down the slope into the arms of their husbands. Ahinoam stands tall and regal beside the gate waiting for her man, the king to come to her.

The crowd shouts and cheers as the troops enter the gates. Ahinoam beams as Saul rides up to her, dismounts, hands the reins to his servant and kisses her gently on her forehead. Together they walk away from the laughter and the tears in the central square toward their home.

"You must have traveled high in the mountains," Ahinoam says. Saul is puzzled. "Why do you say that?" She grins and squeezes his hand, "your hair has streaks of white. Maybe snow?" He half chuckles, "Ah, your hair would be as white as wool if you'd seen all I've seen."

She wraps her arm around his waist, "Well, now you can feast your eyes upon your daughters and your new grandson."

He embraces her in the doorway to their courtyard. "And upon my beloved." As his arms enfold her she can feel the heavy mantle of his weariness. Ahinoam begins to prepare for the evening meal. Saul stands gazing at the comfortable, familiar things of home—the cooking pots and baskets set against the courtyard wall, the ladder leading to the rooftop. The memory of that night on the rooftop of Samuel's house –the last night of his former life—flits behind his eyes. He moves inside the darkening front room and lets his eyes drift over the rugs on the floor, the wide pallet in the corner where he and Ahinoam have shared so many of their nights. The bench against the wall burnished by decades of rough robes shines dully in the fading light. He is awash with warm memories of nights spent telling stories, roaring with laughter, and passing the wineskin around the circle of friends. He sighs. *How easily I took all that life for granted. Will I ever taste those simple joys again?*

The screams of children at play in the street slice brutally into his thoughts. His body stiffens, his brain quakes and instantly he is back on the streets of the Amalekite city. He is surrounded by wailing mothers and terrified shrieking children. He grips the wooden post holding up the roof, squeezes his eyelids shut so intensely that his

148

face aches. He shouts, shivers and moans as the vivid, horrifying scenes engulf his mind.

Ahinoam gasps in alarm, runs to him and presses her body against his back. "What is it? Are you sick? You want to lie down?"

Saul's mind flails desperately. He strains to escape from the visions of carnage that pummel him. Minutes pass and at last he manages to slam the gruesome scenes behind a door in his brain. His trembling gradually ceases, his breathing slows. At last he turns and holds his wife.

"No, not sick." How can he explain what just happened? He's not sure himself. He presses his face into her hair, "Glad to be home, just glad to be home. I'm going to wash and find a new robe."

Ahinoam watches him and guesses at the demons he is battling. She heard rumors of their last battle and does not even dare to imagine the bloody scenes. Her daughters join her as she prepares the meal. She anticipates the evening as a quiet family affair. A dinner of lentils, olives, figs and cucumbers, cheese and fresh bread, melons and for this special evening the best wine. She and the girls bring a hint of laughter and light to Saul's face. He savors the fresh food and they are just finishing the last of the melon when it begins.

Ahinoam hasn't fully realized that Saul's family no longer has first claim upon him. He is Israel's king. He belongs to the entire country. One by one the elders of the village arrive to pay their respects. The next hours are filled with endless greetings and well-wishes. Throughout the evening, Saul sits, graciously smiles and accepts the accolades heaped upon him. Their words along with the wine infuse his body with warmth. Glimmers of the old Saul, the laughing, carefree Saul appear through his weariness.

The evening stars already pierce the velvet night when Kish comes through the door. He moves slower than he once did, yet at sixty-five he is still clear-eyed and steady. He stands before Saul and leans into a small bow. "Welcome home son. You are our king. You've done well."

All evening Ahinoam has been standing discretely against the back wall, as tradition requires. She's seen her husband relax and mellow in the welcome bath of praise from the elders. Now she hears Kish's words and anticipates the glow in Saul's face. How deeply and often her husband has yearned to hear these very words from his father.

What she sees stuns and confuses her. As the oil lamp flickers on the table, the sparkle in Saul's eyes dims and his cheeks sag. A vital breath, a lively spirit flutters away into the night. Before her eyes, Saul ages ten years in an instant. He drops his head and is silent. She cannot imagine what thoughts are spinning through her husband's mind.

Ah father Kish, you've come at last. If you'd said those words five years ago my heart would've burst in gratitude. I suppose I should be grateful. Yes, yes, I am grateful for what you say, for what all the elders said tonight. For these few hours, I've let myself believe all the flattering words. I've savored them like tonight's fine wine. But when I saw you coming through the door, all those tributes fell to the floor and shattered like a pottery plate. I remember again the truth. I'm naked and weak.

Saul raises his haggard face. "Sit, father, sit here beside me." Kish slides onto the bench. They sit in a silence broken only by the cooing of the doves upon the house beams. Neither a king, nor a son can give voice to the bitter torrent raging through his mind.

Ai… father, you praise me. You applaud how well I've done. Maybe in your eyes, maybe in the eyes of the men of Israel, that is so. But no, father Kish, I've not done well. I'm an imposter. Thus says our God---at least according to Samuel. Evidently I deserve no praise or applause. Evidently I'm the failure you always believed me to be. Everyone, including you, still calls me king. But the prophet declares that God calls me a disappointment, a divine mistake. I've been rejected, I'm going to be replaced. I'm rejected from a position that I never asked for. I was chosen, then unchosen.

Saul slumps back against the wall. He draws a breath that fills his lungs and releases it as though he were a bellows puffing upon hot coals. "Thank you father for coming, and for your kind words. These last weeks have been exhausting. Please excuse me, I need to rest."

The two men rise and embrace. Ahinoam joins Saul and they walk with Kish to the courtyard doorway. "Shalom, Father Kish" she says as the old man slowly walks into the night. Saul closes the door and puts his arm around her shoulder as they walk to their bed pallet. He mutters more to himself than to her.

"I will be king as long as the people call me king. I will not surrender." Ahinoam feels the muscles in his arm around her tighten as he speaks these puzzling words. She wants to question him, but the hour is late, and one look at his face convinces her; asking will be fruitless. And then, after the lamp is extinguished and they finally lay down together, she does not ask, but only shivers when he whispers harshly into the darkness.

"My days are numbered but I will not give in."

***

Jakeh lowers himself creakily onto the hard-packed soil between the roots of the ancient oak tree in the center of Gibeah's plaza.

"Good morning and shalom Abner," he rasps without turning his head to the stocky soldier sitting against the same tree.

Abner looks quizzically at the aged servant. What would induce this elder to suffer the pain and indignity of sitting on the hard ground? But he is a soldier and closely guards both his curiosity and his words. "Good morning and shalom to you."

The morning breeze plays in the tree top and the sun filters through the leaves. Spots of light and shadow dance across both men.

"So, have you and your troops rested well in your months at home?" Jakeh asks.

"Some want even more days, but too much rest makes soldiers soft."

"Maybe your rest is coming to an end. I suppose you've heard the rumors?"

Abner spits into the dust. "Philistine dogs! Mustering their troops to the southwest, near the valley of Elah. Claiming territory that is ours. Sons of dogs!" He spits again.

"So, will the king lead you into battle?" Jakeh asks quietly.

Abner cautiously chews on his query before replying. "Yes, surely. Why do you ask?"

Jakeh shrugs. "Well, lately Saul seems to be…" He pauses and searches in the leaves overhead for the right words. "The king seems distracted by other matters."

"Ahh yes. The new rooms to his house, and the special bed; a raised platform made of cedar, I've been told." Abner turns his palms outward. "Being the king does have privileges I suppose."

Jakeh shakes his head. "No, no. Those things were Ahinoam's idea. She contacted the masons and the carpenters. She wants him to have a larger room to receive visitors and she hopes that he can rest better with his own bed. Saul hasn't put his hand into any of this."

Abner slowly turns to face the Jakeh. "Then I don't know what matters you're referring to."

Jakeh meets Abner's eyes then shifts his gaze out over the village. "Ah, well, I mean… you must notice that his eyes often look beyond you, appear to gaze into some invisible distant land. And when he walks alone his lips move as though he were in conversation with an unseen companion."

The cautious commander answers, "Maybe he is praying."

Jakeh sniffs loudly then falls silent. A perilous undercurrent swirls beneath this encounter. Abner yearns to escape, but sits out of respect for the elder. The voices of children at play and of the women sharing gossip at the well fill the warming air. After minutes of charged silence Jakeh stirs and gathers his robes.

152

"Abner, I mean no disrespect to Saul. He's my king too. I'm sorry if my questions trouble you. I only thought…I wondered if maybe he has shared some concerns with his commanders." He groans and struggles to his feet. Abner leaps up and grabs his elbow.

Jakeh sighs. "I'm just an old man crammed full of fears. It's just that I've seen too much…Best you forget my fretting." He shakes out his robes and shuffles off.

Abner stands with arms crossed over his broad chest. The disquiet whispering in his own mind for weeks grows louder. He and the soldiers are doubtless more confused and bewildered than Saul's household.

Last week the king appeared in the camp at first light. He stood like a proud lion and roared.

"Wake up my soldiers. The day is already glorious. Come and run with me." Saul grinned and slapped the backs of his waking troops and then began trotting across the plain. The young men fell in behind and for an hour they ran. Saul's enthusiastic whoops and laughter filled the morning air. They returned puffing and glistening with sweat. Though Saul too gasped for breath, he never stopped joking and laughing with the men.

Two days later it was midmorning when Saul arrived at the camp. Several soldiers paused in their exercises and greeted the king with hearty shouts.

Saul lifted his chin and snapped, "Silence. This is no festival. Focus on your training." He stalked around the edges of the field, mumbling to himself. The confused men shot sidelong glances at their king who was as morose and moody as the gray, scudding rain clouds hovering overhead.

Abner watches Jakeh enter the king's gate. Then there was yesterday…

Yesterday Saul stalked into camp in the heat of the day. The men had eaten and were resting in the shade of their tents. He rolled through the grounds like a summer thunderhead boiling up over the mountains.

"You lazy curs. I know you'd all rather be home sleeping with your women. What chance do we have against the Philistines with feeble men like you?" For an endless hour stalked between the tents pouring out his venomous, caustic comments. Then he stopped in the center of the camp, roared until his face was florid, spun on his heel and stalked home. His men sat stunned and bewildered. Who was this man they called king?

Abner steps out of the dappled shade into the bright mid-morning sun. He strides back to his troops, trying to focus on the day ahead but he cannot avoid musing. *Something or someone is gnawing at my cousin's heart and mind. Lord God, I'm only a soldier. These things are a mystery to me.*

Ahinoam observes all her husband's moods, racing like the shadows of windblown clouds across the landscape of his heart. She sees all of this and more. Her hip and ribs bear bruises from his flailing during the nightmares. Many nights Jakeh and the other household servants have come running across the courtyard to their pallet as Saul shouts and screams from his dreams.

***

For weeks Ahinoam watches helplessly as her husband fights his demons. She prays to her God and finds, if not answers, at least comfort in the ancient prayers.

"I call upon you, for you will answer me, O God; incline your ear to me, hear my words."

Tonight, she lies on her side, presses her body against Saul. He's lying on his back as she strokes his brow. The guttering oil lamp throws their shadows against the stone wall.

"Husband, I know you're troubled. Blood, death--you've seen too much. I can't imagine the agonies that torture you. Maybe, maybe if you pray to God for relief--."

154

Saul snorts, "Pray to God for relief? I've told you more than once. God gave me this burden, this agony in the first place. Besides, now God has decided to ignore my pleadings."

Ahinoam rises on one elbow. "But, but…we're promised that God hears all of our prayers."

He painfully turns and gazes into her face. She sees the bottomless pools of grief in his dark eyes. He says, "Maybe that's true. But between God hearing and God responding lies a very deep chasm." He groans and rolls onto his side away from her. "Enough of this talk. My mind is already full of gloom."

After months of tortured nights, she convinces him that they need separate sleeping arrangements. She hires the local bricklayer to add a room for Saul's sleeping and meeting quarters. She has a raised bed made for him, the first in the village. One morning the carpenter's two workmen bring in the bedframe. It is solid and heavy. The young men's foreheads glisten with sweat as they ease the frame through the gate. The sharp fresh tang of cedar fills the room. After they leave she lays mats and sheep skins upon the frame and steps backs up to examine the work just as Saul walks in.

"Look at your royal nest my dear", she teases, "A king deserves at least some privilege!" Her eyes flash with delight but Saul's eyes are dull black stones. He growls.

"Fine work, well made. I can't sleep no matter where I lay my head. But I suppose there's no sense keeping you awake too." He spins on his heel and without another word marches out, followed by his four guards. Ahinoam's eyes glisten with tears.

Saul has once more become convinced that he needs to be protected by guards, though enemy rumblings are still far away and the hometown populace hardly poses a threat. He stations his guards at the courtyard entrance. He orders them to restrict access to all but family. Now both the home and its owner have the air of a besieged fortress.

Chapter Twenty-three

Why wake up? Why bother rolling over? The day is black, Sheol black, and as bitter as my heart. My head is filled with nothing but viperous slippery thoughts; writhing, leech sucking thoughts. Even here in bed my heart twists like a furtive fox desperate to escape. Escape? Abandon that effort! I already know. This will be another of those days: No portal unlocking, no gate swinging open. I'm a prisoner in this lowering, glowering cloud. Bitter, myrrh bitter.

Still… O God I fling this into your gray sky…or have your ears gone deaf to my cry? Have you possibly forgotten that I didn't ask for this? None of it. I didn't seek it, nor covet it. I couldn't even have imagined it. No. The oil that drenched my hair and dripped off the end of my beard, that wasn't mine. Was it yours? The hand that poured it? Yours surely, for it absolutely wasn't mine.

So, now what, O silent God? The old man says I'm no longer king. But the soldiers still call me king, the people still hail me when I march through the villages. But Samuel says you've denounced me, turned your face away from me. So now here I lie on my sweat-stinking pallet, sinking into a fetid swamp dragged down by a millstone that you and you alone have chained around my neck. Why should I even open my eyes?

"Good morning, sir." Saul's morning lament is broken by a placid voice. He rolls onto his back, props himself up on his elbows and reluctantly opens his eyes. A young man in a simple shepherd's robe stands at the foot of his bed.

"What do you want? How'd you get past the guards?" The haggard king swings his feet to the floor and roars, "Guards, guards!"

A tall bearded soldier rushes into the room and stands at attention. "Are you men sleeping out there? How'd this sheepherder get in here?"

The young guard anxiously stammers, "Excuse me, sir but this is the person you requested."

"I requested?! I requested?! You worthless piece of dung. I requested! Ha! Either you're insane or I am. Why would I request to see a sheepherder? Look at him. His face is still smooth as a child's. Get him out of here or I'll kill you both."

The guard begins to fidget. He knows what the king in his rages is capable of. He edges back toward the doorway. "Not a shepherd sir, a musician. To play music for you sir, when the evil spirits come. Your servant Jakeh sent him. He said you'd asked for someone."

Saul's shoulders slump. Righteous rage surrenders to glum despair. He falls back onto his bed, with a groan. "Ah, yes, I remember. You're not the insane one after all. Go then." The guard ducks quickly out of the room.

If tortured Saul would possess even a sliver of Samuel's prophetic gift, he would now leap out of bed, lunge for his spear, fling it and skewer the boy against the wall. This is another of those crossroad moments in his life. But that gift has not been granted to this rejected king. Instead Saul lies groaning in bed, the boy sits down on a stool and begins plucking the strings of a small lyre that he's been holding at his side.

He plays no clear melody, but with his slow plucking, he allows each note to sing its song. Together the notes sing of wild birds welcoming the dawn, they whisper of the wind playing in the branches of the cedars, and they murmur of the spring waters tumbling over the stones. The boy does not look at the king. He gazes at a world beyond this melancholy room. This other reality floats into the king's chamber on the crystalline notes of the shepherd's music. Saul's groans cease, his breathing eases and he sleeps.

An hour later, he wakes, stretches and yawns like a hulking cat. He blinks at a fading shimmer in the morning air at the foot of his bed. The room is empty but it feels as though someone slipped out only an instant ago and the spirit has lingered an instant longer than the body.

Ahh, what a refreshing sleep. I believe I slept the whole night through. I remember fragments of a dark dream—serpents and shouting guards. But then, ahhh. I came to the meadow. Green pastures, still waters; gratefully there I lay down and rested.

He rises and stands in the doorway to his bedroom. The soft light sifting through the leaves of the grape arbor in the courtyard coaxes a smile to his lips. Ahinoam sits on her stool grinding grain and he playfully creeps up behind her, stoops and kisses her neck.

"Shalom, my good wife!" She turns in shock, stunned at what she sees: her husband's eyes dancing with glee, his lips smiling. She's lived so many weeks with his pursed lips, guarded eyes, stiff jaw. Even in the unguarded moments, back when they still shared a bed, he'd been distant and reserved.

"Good morning, dear husband," she smiles back. "It looks as though the music worked its magic!"

He grins and wags a finger. "You know wizards and magic are against the laws of Moses!" He lifts her up into an embrace. "But I did wake with silvery music in my dreams."

She leans away from his embrace. "Don't you remember the young man with his lyre?"

He pulls her back into his arms. "Oh, I thought he was part of my dream."

She leans her head against his chest. The sunshine warms her neck. She savors the strong arms that envelop her. The rough cloth of his cloak presses against her cheek. She tries to rein in her thoughts, keep them focused on this place, this moment. But fears and memories jerk the reins away from her. She speaks with quiet sadness.

"Husband, you've been in one of your moods for many days, weeks. You seemed so confused and sad. We didn't know how to help." She pulls back her head and looks up at him. "Finally, Jakeh and Jonathan and the others convinced you to let them look for a musician. They thought maybe music could soothe your mind, help you sleep. His name is David; he comes from a good family. He seems like a bright young man."

Saul is pensive. "Yes, I… The past days feel like a leaden dream. I remember things, but all broken, fractured. Only shards, pieces of days. I can't explain it." He releases her and throws his arms into the air. "But this morning, the colors, the light, the sky—it's as though creation has just dawned. Let's invite our sons and their families for the evening meal. I've not seen enough of them and the grandchildren."

The house of Saul overflows with laughter—riotous roars from men filled with wine, giggles from children tossed and tickled, and chuckles from women sharing their tales. Ahinoam bustles everywhere; her cheeks are flushed and her eyes dance with delight. A few times during the evening she catches Saul winking and grinning at her. She smiles at him and rolls her eyes. She knows, and the thought is like a plump grape, bursting with juice, teased by her tongue. She knows that she will finish this glorious day helping her husband assess the qualities of his new cedar bed.

The morning light seeps through Saul's eyelids. He hears the voices of the women in his courtyard and the sounds of men outside in the plaza. He keeps his eyes closed a moment longer and luxuriates in the memory of last night's party and pleasure. The taste of Ahinoam still lingers on his lips and his groin aches deliciously from their lovemaking. Today will be a good day.

Saul steps out of bed, grabs his robe and orders one of his guards to summon Abner. He is sitting on a cushion eating figs and bread when the commander appears. It has been many months since Saul has summoned him so early. He is suspicious, but hides it behind his stone face. He sits down across from Saul.

"Good morning King. You're awake early."

"Ah cousin. Have you eaten? Take some figs. I'm often awake at this hour but usually not in a mood to see anyone. Too many mornings the sun rises before my eyes have even closed." Saul throws out his arms and stretches. "But these past few nights, I've slept, genuinely slept, and this morning, I feel reborn."

"That is good news…. for all of us." Abner hesitates to say more.

Saul looks intently at his commander. "Abner, I know…. Thank you for coming so quickly this morning and…and for keeping order among the troops while I've been… well, I think you know. Thank you."

Saul rises and Abner follows. Saul puts his hand on Abner's shoulder. "Go now, send messengers and gather the commanders. We've…I've delayed long enough, too long maybe. We need to plan our campaign against the Philistines who've gathered at Elah."

So begins the sixth year of Saul's kingship. Over the next weeks, the commanders gather and discuss strategies. Calls go out to regather the tribal armies. The latter rains come and then give way to the month of flowers. The bold luscious red flowers of the pomegranate trees and the subtle white flowers of the olive trees bring splashes of color to the green countryside.

Saul enters each day bursting with energy and lies down every evening to the music of young David's lyre. He soon realizes that not only does the music soothe his troubled thoughts but the young man himself, his quiet, clear face and his direct firm voice, are like a healing balm. He also discovers that David is not as young as he appears. He is only two years younger than Jonathan. When he learns that Jonathan and David have become good friends, Saul is delighted. He is confident that David will bring joy to the entire house.

***

The king finishes his tea and steps out of the courtyard into Gibeah's plaza. The rasping buzz of cicadas fills the air. The day will be hot. Jonathan and David stand under the oak tree laughing and hooting at a story one of them has told. The urge to join them tugs at Saul. Both young men are so alive and hearty. Saul is hungry for camaraderie. He takes a step, then hesitates. Burned onto the retina of his mind is the vision of himself beside the fire after the battle of Michmash raising his sword above his own son's bowed head. His longing to join these two men does battle with his shame at what he might have done, what he almost did.

Jonathan has never said anything about that night, though he has been present at all the gatherings of commanders, and at the family events. Still, Saul fears that the bond between father and son has been deeply lacerated by his own disgraceful deed.

David sees him standing by the wall and waves. Saul waves back and dares to move toward them, keeping his eyes and attention on the young musician. He is shorter than Jonathan. Both his skin and hair are lighter. Like Jonathan his shoulders are broad and he moves with easy grace.

David greets him. "Good morning King. We're just talking about how nasty the Philistines are, weren't we, Jonathan?" By the laughter in his light brown eyes it's clear that their conversation went beyond analysis of the perpetual enemy.

Jonathan doesn't answer his friend. He gives Saul the hint of a smile and then murmurs, "Good morning King."

Saul keeps his eyes focused on David. "Ah yes, the Philistines. We'll be marching soon to run them out of our lands. That reminds me, I've been meaning to tell you, I've decided to name you my armor bearer so that you can accompany us to Elah. And of course, you will bring your harp."

David shoots a glance to Jonathan, then stammers, "An honor, o King. I am…yes, honored, surely. It's just that... Well, my father is old, all of my brothers have joined your army and I'd hoped…I thought maybe when you set out for Elah I could go home to visit my father and to look after the flocks."

Saul strokes his beard and wonders. *I imagine the two of them have already discussed his plan. Did they anticipate my offer? Have I already spoken of it to someone? I can't even be sure of my own memory anymore. Permission to visit an aged father—how can I deny such a request?*

He nods and lays his hand on the young man's shoulder. "David, I respect your wish. You may go. You can leave tomorrow if you like. Carry my regards to your father. But when you return you'll be named my armor bearer and officially part of my troop."

David bows deeply, "Thank you sir. You are kind and I am in your debt." He turns and leaves the two men in the shade of the oak. The buzzing of the cicadas fills the awkward silence.

Saul wonders if words can ever bridge the chasm between them. The silence deepens, grows so heavy that finally he is compelled to speak. He turns to face his son. "Jonathan, I want to say, 'I'm sorry,' but the words seem too trite. I hope we can…"

Jonathan holds up his hand and cuts him off. "If you're talking about what happened at Michmash, you don't need to apologize. You did what you had to do."

Saul is stunned. "What? How can you say that? I nearly killed you, my own flesh and blood." He wrings his hands as that horrific vision flickers again in his mind's eye.

"But you'd made a vow before God." Jonathan speaks quietly and shrugs. "What else could you do?"

Saul shakes his head. "No, no, it was a stupid vow. How can you be so calm about this? Even on that horrible night, you knelt so calmly before me."

Jonathan shrugs. "I trusted that God's will would be done. I left it in His hands."

Saul sputters, "But if I had… if the commanders had not intervened…"

Jonathan smiles, "They did what they had to do. Just as you did, just as I did. You are king, <u>my</u> king, but God is the commander of you and of me and of us all."

Tears film Saul's eyes. He lays his arm on his son's shoulder and Jonathan surprises him by stepping in and embracing him. Saul gulps back a sob. He looks over his son's shoulder at the dazzling white of the city walls. They seem to swirl before his eyes. His mind teeters on a precipice.

One of us must be living in delusion. How can my son trust so simply and I doubt so completely? What gift has he been given that's been withheld from me? How can I have faith in God when God's lost faith in me? He grips his son in a hard embrace.

"Ai, son, if only I had trust like yours. Doubts, questions—I have plenty of those. Lately, I don't know if I can even trust myself.

Jonathan steps back and looks up at his father. His eyes are clear and bright, like his mother's.

"But father, you're still our king. I follow you, we all follow you. I believe you are still God guided."

A sad ghost of a smile flits across Saul's face as the two of them walk together to the troop camp. Jonathan's words momentarily warm his heart but they do not melt the icy premonitions in his soul. One thing his son's words have accomplished. He reaffirms his own vow: *As long as he and the troops are loyal to me, I will lead them. I will be their king until I die.*

The evening sun dissolves into a gray film of clouds hovering over the western hills. The wind moans through the olive trees in the midnight darkness. Flickers of lightning illuminate the purple air. Grumbling thunder rolls down the hillside. The first drops of rain splash into the dust, thud against the mud baked roofs and splatter upon the thirsty leaves of the oak tree in the village plaza. Then an eye searing bolt ignites the sky, thunder cracks open the heavens and rain pours down on the grateful earth. When the first rumbles began, Ahinoam padded quietly to Saul's bed. Now they cling to each other and the passionate pounding of their hearts matches the rhythm of the rain.

Chapter Twenty-four

The sun rises into a scrubbed sky. The day has arrived: the day Abner the warrior has been lusting for, the day Saul knows cannot be put off, and the day Ahinoam and the other wives have dreaded. The troops muster and march out to confront the belligerent Philistines. The rally order went out the week before and the solders from the other tribes have gathered as Saul and the Benjaminite troops march toward their encounter with the enemy.

Saul swings his long leg over the back of his horse. He sucks his lungs full of the fresh rain-washed air. The early morning sun dances off the many metal plates of his armor. His long hair reaches his shoulders and ripples brightly in the breeze. He is warmed by the memory of last night's love with Ahinoam. He feels rested and strong. A faint, fluttering buzz has begun somewhere behind his eyes, but he forces himself to ignore it. His eyes linger on Ahinoam holding their youngest grandchild. At last he lifts his formidable sword into the blue sky and roars, "death to the infidels." The troops echo his shout and the children, elders and women lining the road cheer and wave.

The seasoned soldiers savor the warmth of the sun, the buzz and hum of voices, and the camaraderie of old warriors. They have battle in their bones and this stage of the conflict, this marching and soaring of spirits, warms their hearts. The young men joke and shout, full of piss and bravado, hiding any fear or anxiety behind blustering talk, teasing and bawdy stories.

Saul continues to ride alone at the front of the march. The clouds are high and cottony white. The birds wheel and dip above them seeming to share in the excitement. An hour into the march the raucous rumble of the troops fades in Saul's ears and that earlier dim buzzing grows to a dull throbbing hidden somewhere deep within his head. He massages his eyes with his thumb. Two spirits wage war within him. One spirit is an eagle, sharp and eager, delighted to be back in action and facing an enemy that is visible. This spirit swoops and snaps with fierce joy, like the deep blue battle pennant that flaps in the head wind. The other spirit lurking in his mind is a grim ghost clutching a heavy gray blanket. It keeps trying to throw the shroud over the lively spirit. *Do you know what you are doing?* it whispers. *Aren't you forgetting--God has abandoned you, renounced you, disowned you? Aren't you marching blindly into disaster?*

Saul rides statue still. Teeth clenched and jaw locked, he leads his troops westward. His horse trots steadily forward and the troops march onward unaware of their king's fierce interior battle. Their boisterous shouts and songs of the morning give way to the steady cadence of feet pounding the trail. The hours stretch into the hot afternoon. Repeatedly Saul shrugs off the heavy gray ghost spirit. Repeatedly he frees the eagle spirit. But the soul, like the body can grow weary. Saul's silent battle saps his strength. As he marches into the setting sun, he casts a long shadow back upon his troops. The last sunrays pierce his eyes, he bows his great head, the dark spirit triumphs and his heart brims with lead.

When they reach the Valley of Elah his guards set up his black tent beneath the largest terebinth tree on the slopes. The troops arrive, set up camp and soon small cooking fires freckle the dark hill sides. The time is too late and Saul is too weary to meet with his commanders. He flops onto his pallet with a groan. The night is endless. His dreams are turbid, full of endless running through bleak fog. He wakes up exhausted. In bleakness, the campaign against the Philistines begins.

The monster is bellowing. Forty days, every day the same. I awake in my black tent, crawl out and eat my bread and drink my tea. The sun sends its first arrows through the trees out onto the valley floor. And the monster comes to meet them. He stands and lets the sunrays dance and shimmer on his massive metal chest plate. He throws back his huge helmeted head and roars. "Dogs of Israel, wake up! Cowards cowering in your holes, arise. Have you all skulked away with your tails between your legs? Send out your best, send out your hero. If he defeats me, we'll all be your servants. If I defeat him, you will be our slaves." The shadow that stretches behind this giant is as dark and monstrous as the one in my soul. For weeks, I've sat with the commanders arguing about our next move. Our spies assure us that our troop numbers are equal to theirs. But the Philistines, all of them, have weapons of steel… and they have this giant from Gath, Goliath is what he calls himself. Day after day, his challenge for single combat goes unanswered.

Two nights ago, I was sweating and cursing in my tent, plagued by that familiar evil spirit God keeps sending to torture me. In the midnight of my torment, I glimpsed a light, like a candle flickering through a crack in the door: a way out, an escape from this torment, this godforsaken burden of a life that God has inflicted upon me. I myself would step out onto the valley floor and face this behemoth. The perfect solution! Wasn't I the tallest and broadest of all the Israelites? Wasn't I the leader of this army? Who better to meet their champion? I'd die, but I'd die as a valiant son of Israel. And who's to say, maybe even God would be pleased. Like a moth drawn to a flame, I was drawn to the silent nothingness of Sheol, a place free of all feeling, free at last of all remembrance of God. This dark hope calmed my spirit and finally I slept in peace.

In the morning, I came to our meeting carrying my armor. I dropped it at my feet and sat down. Since we arrived and set up camp, my tongue has been as vile as an asp's. The commanders all stared but sat in painful silence. I grimly enjoyed their discomfort and stared out over their heads. Finally Jonathan asked, "King, what word do you bring us today? Are we finally going to engage the Philistines?"

I stared at him, then swept my eyes around the circle of seated leaders. I clambered to my feet. "Today I myself will face this filthy pagan. I already hear him roaring in the valley. He drags our honor through the dirt. Enough." I began to strap on my sword. Abner leapt to his feet.

"Saul, you can't do this, you dare not do this. Even if every one of us faces this Goliath and is slaughtered, you must live." I stared dumbly at him. What did he mean?

"Cousin, can't you see the difference between the two of you?" I snorted and the other commanders laughed. More than twenty inches and hundreds of pounds—the difference was obvious. Abner growled. "No, not that. This giant is a soldier. He's one of a kind,

but he's still a soldier. If he's killed, his fellow soldiers will run when he falls and they will lose this battle. But their nation will still rule the coastland. They'll still be free. But you Saul, if you're killed, we lose more than our battle leader. We lose our king, the leader of our entire people. You dare not face him."

The commanders all rose to their feet and agreed with Abner. I closed my eyes and held back bitter tears. I hungered for escape, death, rest. Yet, even though God had rejected me, I felt responsible for my people. My scheme of escape was suffocated by the weight of my duty. I backed down.

And so, here I am again this morning. My mind is muddy and my vision is cloudy. Sadly, my ears are still sharp. I hear Goliath slandering our nation, our soldiers and our God. I grind my teeth. I dare not meet him. I lack the will to force any of my men to face him. Who else has the courage to die?

***

David carries a woven bag over his shoulder. He has been walking since before dawn. He watched the rising sun melt the mist in the valleys, heard the owls flapping to their nests after their night hunt, and saw a flock of sand grouse swooping to a pond for their morning drink. Now at last he descends the hills into the Israelite camp. Jonathan sees him first as he wanders among the tents.

"David? What are you doing here?" David drops his bag and hugs his friend.

"Father sent me to see how my brothers are doing and to bring them bread and cheese. I'd guess the troops don't always get their fill."

Jonathan grins and is readying a quip when the sound of the shofar blaring on the hilltop fills the morning air. He groans.

"Ahh. You're just in time for our morning ration of shame. Come." He claps David on the shoulder and they join the throng of soldiers moving slowly through the trees to the edge of the open field. David is baffled.

"Wasn't that the call to battle? Why are they lingering? Some haven't even drawn their swords."

Jonathan grunts. "We've been here almost six weeks. Every day begins the same way. You'll see."

They step out of the terebinth's dappled shade and gaze across the field at the line of Philistine soldiers. Even at this distance David can see their lackadaisical stance.

"Jonathan, what's going on? I don't –."

Jonathan interrupts. "Wait. Just watch." He points toward the Philistine ranks just as a roar floats up from the troops across the valley. The line of Philistine soldiers parts and out through the gap strides the tallest man David has ever seen. This mountainous hulk stomps across the plain toward them. The Israelite army answers the roar of the Philistine troops with a cursory and weary reply.

The giant stops at the edge of the dry stream bed that runs through the middle of the shallow valley. His head is the size of a boulder and is covered with a gleaming bronze helmet. His legs are as thick as oaken tree trunks and are overlaid in bronze. From their positions at the edge of the tree line, every Israelite soldier can hear the rattle of his chest plate and see the enormous spear that he carries.

The giant raises the massive headed spear, shakes his chest and they all can hear the rattle, like a distant avalanche. He opens his mouth and bellows like a wounded bear, "Cowards! Dogs of Israel. Give me a man to fight!" He rages and curses, the air throbs with his blasphemies.

David looks up and down the ranks of his countrymen. Some stand with heads bowed, others stare blankly into the empty sky.

Jonathan mutters, "Our daily dose of humiliation: Goliath of Gath challenges and no one steps forward."

David shakes his head. "Every day we are disgraced like this? What happens now?"

Jonathan shrugs, "He rants for an hour and then lumbers back to his camp. They hold onto our territory. They're camped on it and are content to let us rot here in the forest."

"Has no one dared to fight him?"

"None of us desires death. The king won't let me go and he won't command anyone else to face the beast. He's offered a bounty and even the hand of sister Michal in marriage for whoever kills him. So far, no takers. Besides, if one of us fights and dies, our men will no doubt run like terrified rabbits."

David sputters, "But..but why should he be allowed to defy the armies of the living God? This should stop." He shakes his head and marches off to look for his brothers.

***

Saul stands with his arms crossed behind his back staring out at Goliath. The sky is pale blue, the sun golden white but Saul sees only a gray pall.

'Do whatever you see fit to do, for God is with you.' The prophet's words on the day I was conscripted to be king. Hollow words, words proven false a hundred times over. How many times have I decided to act only to have Samuel appear and announce God's displeasure? Then yesterday when I decided to challenge Goliath myself, my commanders protested and again I relented. Has the Lord God abandoned me completely as the seer declares? Ha! I've no way of knowing whether Samuel speaks the truth or not, since from the Lord God I receive only thunderous silence. Truthfully, with or without the Lord, I can't see what is the fit thing to do here in this wretched valley of Elah.

"King, we've found a man." Saul slowly turns his head. Medad, his out-of-breath aide, reads the query on the king's face. "We've found a man willing to face the giant. Jonathan is bringing him to you now."

Saul turns away from the bright field and looks back into the cool shadows. *What man is this who has a death wish?* A crowd of animated men comes through the trees. At its head is Jonathan and beside him walks…David? Saul tries to shake the mist from his eyes as the crowd approaches.

"David, didn't I send you home to spend time with your father?"

David steps forward and bows, "Yes, my King, and I did that but he sent me here to bring food for my brothers."

Saul smiles and his spirit lifts as he gazes at David's grin. "Come, let me greet you properly." He waves David forward into his vast embrace. His heart warms as he recalls all those nights when David's music drove away the evil. He releases him and turns to the crowd.

"Now, where is this warrior willing to face Goliath?"

The crowd is silent but all eyes lock on the young man beside him. Saul turns. "You? You David? You want to fight this monster? Are you drunk, or insane?"

David steps back and speaks loud enough for the troops to hear, "I'm not afraid, we shouldn't be afraid. I'll face him."

Saul's disbelief turns to concern. "David, that giant is a hardened professional soldier. You're young, you're…you're a shepherd and a musician."

Once more David speaks, loud enough for the crowd to hear. "My king, I've rescued sheep from the jaws of bears and lions. I've killed those beasts and I'll kill this beast too. The living God was with me when I attacked those animals. The living God will go with me when I attack this pagan dog."

Saul's spirit plunges. *No! I don't want to give up this young man into the hands of that unwashed Philistine. I've been cornered by God again. Everyone hears David declare that he trusts in the Lord God. Now how can I, supposedly king of God's chosen people, dismiss him without revealing my own doubt? 'Do what you see fit to do.' Damn that prophet and his empty words.*

Saul reluctantly strangles out a blessing. "Go and may the Lord be with you."

A nervous buzz sweeps through the throng. After all these days, the impasse will be broken for good or ill. Men hurry off to the battle line to await David's entry onto the field. But Saul hasn't totally surrendered to the inevitable. Pious belief in God may have hemmed him in but he can still do something. As the soldiers scuttle out of the shade into the sunlight, he clutches David's arm and shouts for Medad to fetch the king's armor.

"Here, put on my helmet. And here, take my best suit of mail." Amid his concerned flurry, Saul has forgotten that last month he chose David to be his armor bearer. David staggers under the weight of the heavy armor, and winks at Jonathan. The two young men chuckle at the irony of the moment.

David takes a few faltering steps in the armor. He stops, shakes his head and pulls off the helmet. He hands it back to Medad. "Thank you my king for your concern, but I can't move with all of this weight. I'm not as big or as strong as you are. I've got to face this giant on my terms, not his."

Saul ruefully watches the young man stride through the trees. Years ago, before God had invaded his life, he'd been like David-- unburdened, light, free to face the world on his own terms.

Saul's stomach cramps in fear. If, or more likely, when the giant crushes David, most of the Israelite troops will turn and run. They all heard David claim that God would be by his side as he faced the Philistine beast. Should the young man fall, it will become obvious to his troops that on this day, the Philistine gods are more powerful than their own deity.

Saul watches David weave across the sunlit grassy field and thinks of the many battles he's led in the past five years.

How many times did I lift my sword and roar, "death to the infidels, God goes with us!" I shouted it even when I was unsure, even when I doubted. Did God go with us? Many of my men believed He did. But how did they know? How do any of us know? One thing I do know, the faith that God went with them, didn't guarantee their survival. I saw young men, fervent and fiery in faith, lie slaughtered on bloody ground. And veterans, solid faithful men—I saw them slashed to pieces by enemy swordsmen. And against the Amalekites, Abihail, one of my commanders, a chosen leader of God's chosen people was struck in the neck by an errant arrow and died in his son's arms. David may have God by his side but that doesn't mean he'll walk off this field alive.

Jonathan stands next to his father. He watches his friend move confidently toward the hulking enemy. *Look at how the sunlight gleams on his air. He glides across the field like a lion on a hunt. Such courage! I should've gone out there with him. He's more brother to me than my brothers ever were. Such a calm spirit, so alive. I've no doubt he walks with God. His faith is so…alive, so real. Stronger than any coat of mail. He isn't afraid. Why should I be? O God of our fathers, cover him, protect him. Strike down this beast.*

Farther down the line of soldiers stands Abner. He watches David with the eyes of a veteran warrior. *Ah, he's zig zagging across the field. Now he slows down, then dashes forward. He's noticed what I've suspected all along. The brute's eyesight is weak. You can tell by the way he tilts his head back and then sweeps his eyes back and forth as though searching for movement. This David is no naïve shepherd boy. He's got a warrior's instincts. He's trying to confuse his enemy. Now he stops completely. Ahh, he's choosing stones from the riverbed, just out of reach of the giant's spear. This young man has the cunning of a fox.*

Out in the valley of Elah the giant finally spies David moving through the grass. His bellow fills the valley. "Who do you Israelites think I am? A dog? Why do you send out this pretty little boy? Are you mocking me? Come closer and I'll turn you into buzzard food."

Soldiers on both sides of the valley hold their breath, straining to hear David's reply. The words, though softened by distance, pierce the stillness.

"You come at me with mighty weapons, but I'm coming with the Lord of all creation, the God of our army. Today you and your army will be food for jackals, your bodies will be picked apart by vultures. By the time the sun sets tonight the whole world will know that God is on our side."

The giant roars, raises his spear and lumbers forward in rage. David charges toward him, swinging his sling as he runs. The Israelite army can hear the whine of the leather thong as it whips through the air. Then with a blur, one strand of the sling is released and the rock flies to the giant's forehead, striking the one bit of forehead not covered by his helmet, right between his eyes. Goliath stops his striding, straightens up and stands frozen. The entire battlefield is transfixed. For some of them, especially for Saul and his family, this is another crossroads moment. The next seconds will decide which road they will travel into the future.

Goliath begins to lean forward. If he had been without armor he would have crumpled in a heap. But sheathed in metal he does not bend. He topples like a downed tree. The crash of his armor booms across the valley and breaks the spell of silence. The Philistine army screams in horror, the Israelite army charges out toward the Philistine lines, howling its war cries.

David scrambles to the downed giant and grunts as he unsheathes the huge sword. He is hacking at Goliath's neck as Abner leads the first troops across the field. Abner pauses before the red faced, exultant young man. "Well done. You're a true soldier of the Lord." He salutes and rushes away with his men.

Jonathan mounts his horse and reaches David just as the giant's head rolls to the ground. He sits for a second in the saddle, gazing first at the gory sight and then grinning down at his friend. Then he slides off his horse and the two men embrace, laugh, and shout. David grasps the head by its hair and swings onto the horse behind Jonathan and they gallop back toward the Israelite camp.

King Saul has not moved from the shade of the trees. He can breathe again. The two young men ride toward him in the bright sunlight. David is swinging his macabre trophy. Saul raises his arms and revels in their mad joy. But as they approach, shimmering in the sunlight behind David's triumphant smile, Saul catches a fleeting glimpse of the future, and a shadow races across his heart.

Chapter Twenty-five

Saul steps from his tent and draws into his lungs the sharp tang of the cypress trees. Their spires sway gracefully in the pale blue morning sky. *Tonight, if the Lord wills it, we'll reach Gibeah and I'll sleep in my own bed.*

He smiles to himself as he reviews their six-month campaign. Yes, the first weeks, the stalemate at Elah, those were frustrating. But on that day, the day the giant fell, his troops decimated the Philistine army and sent the remnants fleeing. When his troops returned, they plundered the enemy camp and recovered many fine steel spears and swords, even some chariots. His spirit and the morale of his army were bolstered by that victory. He led his army forward, they took the offensive and drove the Philistines back toward the coast.

"Ahh, thank you Medad." He takes the plate of olives and bread from his aide. "How are you this fine morning?"

The young man smiles and nods. "I'm well, O king. A little tired. Some of us began our homecoming celebration last night."

Saul laughs, "Oh, I heard you all laughing as I tried to sleep. I could hear David spinning his stories."

He savors the salty bite of the olives and chews on the decisions he's made regarding David. He had insisted that the young man stay with them on this drive. He felt he had no choice after David had killed the giant. Jonathan quickly saw to it that David was properly outfitted. He gave him his own best robe and out of his personal store had given David a sword and bow. Wherever the two young men went, high spirits and laughter followed.

Saul tears off a piece of the hard bread and nods to himself as he eats. *Without a doubt, the morale of the men has never been higher. After every battle, they admire David more. He's got an instinct for strategy, we all can see that, and an uncanny ability to detect enemy weakness. All the commanders, even Abner, listen hard when David speaks. Last week when I named David to command the armies for*

the next battle, not one commander raised a voice, or even any
eyebrow against my decision.

David has brought another significant change to the past months, one more obvious to the commanders than to Saul. Every evening, Jonathan and David sit with the King outside his tent and review the day. David does not have his harp or play music but his presence, his spirit seems enough to chase away Saul's night time demons. No mad plunging spirit followed by wild soaring moods. The commanders and troops have counted on a steady King. As for Saul himself, this morning he is physically weary from months of battle but his spirit is at peace.

What can surpass a victory parade? The men's spirits soar and swoop like the swallows in the breeze. No battles today, no pulsing adrenaline, no fearful sweat, no blood-soaked tunics. Today they drink up the cheers of the crowds. Every village has a welcoming party. Children run alongside the horses, young women flash shy, and sometimes bold smiles at the young soldiers. The elders, many of them once soldiers themselves salute and wave thin arms. Saul drinks it all in. Today he is the king of a great country, leader of a great army. He smiles and waves at the front of the parade. As they pass through the first village he notices that the cheering grows louder and louder after he passes. He turns to see what has delighted the host of onlookers. He detects a shout, a chant coming from the crowd but can't make out the words. When the same thing occurs in the next village and again he misses what is being sung, he changes tactics. He drops back in the troop line. Now from a point in the middle of the troops he waves and nods to the admiring crowd and then the catches the words of the chant that the people, especially the women have been shouting. "Saul has killed his thousands, but David has killed his ten-thousands". The crowds reach out to touch the horse David rides, they toss flowers to him, wave palms as he passes by. And David beams, laughs, pumps his fist in the air, waves his sword, the crowd roars with delight.

The din of the crowd fades for an instant and Saul hears the echo of his last confrontation with Samuel. "God has torn the kingdom from your hand and given it to another, to one with a heart like

God's." Could this David, this barely bearded shepherd be the one? The black snake of jealousy stealthily uncoils in Saul's heart. The rattling, hissing spirit of fear and anger drowns out the hosannas and alleluias of the crowd. The dark spirit pounces and Saul feels its coils constricting his heart. How quickly it strikes, how sharply it plunges him back into the dark swamp. He blinks and is submerged. In an instant, he feels as though he's always lived in this murk. The lightness of the morning is not only gone, he cannot even remember how it felt.

The arrival in Gibeah was what Saul expected. Ahinoam's eyes glistened and she embraced him with pleasure and relief. The elders bowed to him in proper respect. Saul smiled and waved to the crowds but inside dwelt only hollow darkness. Even here in his own hometown, he heard the children and the women shout when they saw the handsome young shepherd soldier: "Saul has killed his thousands, but David has killed his ten-thousands." Even here, in his own town, eyes and hearts were captivated by this David, the one Saul himself had brought into the family, into his own house.

Now the crowds have gone home and the evening chill settles like a soft cloak upon Gibeah. Saul is at home. He sits on the bench against the wall with his spear beside him. Ahinoam is preparing the evening meal. David sits on a low stool, and Jonathan sits on a pillow beside him. David plucks the strings of his lyre. The melody is pleasant, yet for Saul it begins to buzz and ring in his ears, a fearsome wasp set to sting. Saul stares at David out of hooded eyes. David stares back and his eyes burn into Saul's soul.

Saul's eyes widen. *This golden boy, he is the enemy, the usurper, the threat. He is the one, God's favorite sent to destroy me. I see it, right here, right in front of me. I see his black heart.*

Saul flushes, his fingers twitch, his eyes go red. He roars, snaps up his spear and in one motion flings it at David. David's fingers have been on the strings but his eyes have been on Saul. He ducks as the spear clatters to the floor behind him. Jonathan shouts, Ahinoam screams and Saul growls and bounds up after the spear. David crouches as Saul, bellowing in rage, grasps the spear and flings it again. This time David steps behind a pillar and the spear crashes against the wall. He dashes toward the door. Jonathan shouts, "David! Wait!" but his friend is gone into the temporary safety of the night.

Saul stands paralyzed and mute in the center of the room. His eyes flutter, he pants like an overheated dog. Jonathan and Ahinoam rush to him.

Ahinoam grasps his arm, "Saul, what...? Why…?" She shouts over her shoulder. "Jakeh, bring us wine." She and Jonathan each grab an arm and help the king shamble to the bench. Saul groans, drops his head and presses his hands against his eyes. Jakeh shuffles to them with a cup.

"Here husband, drink." Saul raises his head and stares at her with red-rimmed eyes. He silently takes the cup and drains it in one long draught. Ahinoam takes the cup from him, "Now, tell me, what's happened? Why try to kill David? I thought you and he…"

Saul turns from her and in a raspy whisper speaks to Jonathan. "Did you hear them today? The women in the villages? Did you hear them singing?"

Jonathan is dumbfounded. "Father, since when do we care what the women sing? David is young, he attracts their eyes like a flower attracts bees. Don't tell me you tried to kill him because you're jealous? You're the king, the king of Israel."

Saul drops his hands onto the knees of his wife and son. He squeezes and says through gritted teeth. "He's come to throw me down, to take what is mine. Can't you see it in his eyes?"

Jonathan and Ahinoam exchange a quizzical glance. *Has Saul gone mad?* Ahinoam pats her husband's arm. "Saul, you yourself invited him to Gibeah. Think of the many nights he helped you sleep with his music."

Jonathan adds, "Father, are you forgetting the giant? David fought for you and for us all. You called him to lead your army. Hasn't he always been obedient, always deferred to you?"

Saul brings his hands to his cheeks and shakes his head. "Can't you see? I've invited a wolf into the sheepfold. I've got to kill him before he kills us all."

Jonathan leaps up in exasperation and begins to pace. His instinct is to shout and denounce this insane babbling. But he's wise enough to realize that at least for tonight his father won't be argued out of his conviction. "Father, let's suppose what you say is true. If you kill him, won't that reveal to others that you're afraid of losing your crown? Might that not plant a seed of rebellion in other men?"

Saul stares at him then slowly nods, "I suppose so. Yes, I can see that. But what are we going to do?"

Jonathan has a quick answer. "Let him continue to command the army. The more times he faces the Philistines, the closer he is to death. You can stay here at home and let the Philistines remove him from your life."

Saul draws a bleak, scratchy breath. "I suppose that's a better way. But, not the whole army. That's too dangerous. I'll let him take only a thousand men. Tomorrow I'll send him off to the eastern line." He slowly rises and then growls, "We'll see how long he lasts."

As he walks to his bedroom, Ahinoam wipes away her tears and wonders when his shoulders got so stooped and his hair so gray. Jonathan watches his father shuffle away and wonders what he will tell David.

Saul lies spread eagled on his bed. *How can this be? Twelve hours ago I grinned in anticipation of this homecoming. My loins tightened at the thought of Ahinoam's breasts pressed against my chest? Now my bed is cold, my manhood shriveled and I am afraid. How can this be? This sudden, intense red hot rage erupts from my heart. I am shocked and afraid of myself.*

Saul groans as the miasma of memories swirl about him. Once his reminiscences were sweet: The passions and pleasures of his youth, delicious warm nights with Ahinoam, tossing his laughing children into the sunshine and hugging their sweet-smelling bodies against his neck. Now all these comforting remembrances have been savaged and ripped by that horrific beast birthed at his anointing: 'God's call, God's unescapable choice,' Samuel had called it. Saul groans and slaps his fists into the bed. All the good in his past has been shredded and replaced by that relentless demand: Be the king, lead the people. Battles, blood, and men's screams--these now invade and inhabit his brain. Then Samuel or God, he'll never know which, decides to rip the kingship from his hands. Victories, parades, honor and respect—now even these are going to be ripped from his life. And tonight, sitting on a stool in his own home he thought, for an instant, that he saw the future—a young warrior scheming to replace him.

Saul stares up into the blackness and is mystified by his own rage. He sees the spear flying, hears the bellowing roar, sees the flash of a robe disappearing into the night. He gazes at the ceiling and can see it all but the images are jumbled and garbled, alarmingly like the nightmares that invade his sleep and scream him awake.

Jonathan steps onto the hard-packed street in front of the house. He wonders where he'll find David. He hears his friend before he sees him. The sound of a lyre floats into the star sprinkled sky and Jonathan looks to a rooftop across the plaza. He crosses the plaza and climbs the stairs. David sits cross-legged on his sleeping mat, slowly plucking the strings, sending plaintive notes into the night. "You all right?" Jonathan asks as he lowers himself onto the flat hard clay roof.

David continues strumming, then looks up and shrugs. "I'm fine."

"David, you know how the dark spirits attack the king."

David gently lays his harp down. "Of course I know. But tonight, I'm not sure. Tonight he was… tonight it seemed personal."

Jonathan sighs into the darkness. "Ah, David, I should've known you'd see. You're right. He thinks you're after his crown, that you're a threat to his life."

Jonathan expects a sputtered protest but David simply asks, "What have I done to make him think that?"

Jonathan chuckles, "Maybe it's because you've stolen the heart of every woman in the land."

David laughs, "I can't be accused of stealing what is offered to me on a platter."

"So, you plead innocent. I've got to agree with you but that doesn't mean I'm not envious."

David leans forward. "Jonathan, I think there's more. When I walked out to face Goliath I felt the Lord God's strong spirit with me. When I've gone into battle, when I've led the men, I've sensed the mantle of God's spirit on my shoulders. Could the king be… Could he resent that spirit? Could the dark spirit be using the king to attack God's spirit?"

Jonathan is pensive. "I can't say. Father—the king—never talks about spirits. He never mentions the Lord God. All I know is that at least tonight he thinks you're his enemy. I've convinced him that personally eliminating you would cause unrest. So, tomorrow he's going to send you out with part of the army to attack the Philistines. He's hoping the Philistines will do to you what he thinks needs doing."

David turns up his palms and spreads his arms. "So, then I will go. He's my king and all I can do is obey. If the Lord goes with me, I'll return. If not…"

Jonathan stands and pulls David to his feet. He embraces his friend and speaks over his shoulder. "Go with God's spirit. Let's pray that the Lord changes the king's heart."

Chapter Twenty-six

The women of the clan keen and wail as Saul and his brothers carry the body into the cave carved into the reddish-brown dirt on the hillside outside of Zela. The Benjaminite clansmen have gathered to honor and say goodbye to Kish. The clan leader devoted his last month to this journey toward death. Last night he surrendered his *nephesh,* his breath of life. Long before dawn the clan began walking the five miles to this tiny town. Now this morning Kish joins his fathers in the bosom of the earth. Saul and his brothers step out of the cave and blink in the morning light. The elders now begin chanting and their voices float up, thin and wavering, like the wraiths of mist in the valley below.

"Those who love me, I will deliver, says the Lord.
I will protect those who know my name.
When they call to me, I will answer them;
I will be with them in trouble,
I will rescue them and honor them.
With long life I will satisfy them
And show them my salvation."

The crowd murmurs along with the elders. The words are familiar, sung at every burial. Saul doesn't sing. The beginning of the chant snares his thoughts. *Did I ever truly know the Lord's name? He's still a stranger to me. Is that why He's so silent? Samuel promised God was with me. He lied. Or was he himself deceived?*

The clansmen pile rocks in front of the cave entrance. Inside, Kish's body lies next to the bones of his father and his father's father. Without great ceremony, the group turns and winds its way back home, passing through olive groves and resting under scattered fig trees. Saul walks surrounded by kinsmen, yet he walks alone in his brooding.

The old man outlived most of his friends. Was this a sign of the Lord's favor? I doubt I'll have so many years. Still, favor or no favor, he's now gone into the darkness. Father Kish seemed satisfied with his life. He held his grandchildren and even his great grandchildren in his arms and counted it a blessing. He was a decent father. I could have been a better son. Too many stony words passed between us, jagged and hard words, meant to bruise and sting. Then when I was called 'king', we slipped into an unspoken truce. No more questioning or challenging. Did he respect me? Was he proud of me? Now I'll never know.

Ahinoam comes up alongside Saul. "Husband, have you noticed lately the look in Michal's eyes?"

"Her eyes? Is she sick?" Concern for his favorite daughter snaps Saul out of his thoughts.

Ahinoam chuckles, "You could say that, I suppose. Love can be a sickness, can't it?"

"Love? Who is she in love with?"

"Oh come on Saul. You're not that blind, are you? She's in love with David."

Saul stops his striding and glares at his wife. "David. Of course. The entire country's in love with David."

She grabs Saul's arm and they continue walking. "Maybe so, but not the way Michal is in love. The crowds love his victories over the Philistines. He wins battles, he's become their new hero."

Conscious of the clan walking around them, Saul drops his voice. "Hero, yes, and maybe on his way to be new king."

Ahinoam tugs on his arm. "Saul, has David ever disobeyed you? You send him out to battles, he goes. When he returns the first thing he does is bow down to you. Even after that night when you…." Her voice trails off. "Even now, he's still loyal to you. You admire him too, don't you?"

Saul slows his striding, allows the rest of the crowd to move ahead. "So, Michal loves our hero, does she?"

Ahinoam looks up at her husband. "I believe she loves David…hero or not. You gave Merab as a wife to Adriel so now she wants to follow her sister. She wants to be a wife, the wife of

David." She begins to walk through the grassy field and Saul trails after her.

The chirring, leaping locusts match the buzzing in Saul's mind. *Keep David at a distance or draw him closer? Which is more dangerous? A soldier who's captured the people's hearts or a son-in-law who's captured my daughter's heart. I'm the king. I need to do what is best for my people. How can I bend this situation to my advantage?*

Saul finally catches up and throws his arm over Ahinoam's shoulder and smiles. "So, Michal loves David? But does David love Michal?" Before she can answer, he laughs, "Leave it to me, wife. The king will see to it."

Two days later as the last rumblings of a thunderstorm fade into the evening's eastern sky, Jakeh approaches Saul who stands leaning against the doorframe at the entrance to his home. The aged servant bows, "O King, I have spoken to David of your offer."

"Thanks Jakeh. I can always rely on you. So, what did he say?"

Jakeh looks up with a trace of a smile on his lips. "He said he was honored but that he comes from a family without distinction and that he's too poor to pay any bride price. He seemed very humbled by the offer."

Saul sniffs. "Humbled or crafty…." He stares at the dark clouds hurrying into the night, still flickering with bursts of lightning. Then he grins. "Very good, very good. Tell the young man that the only bride price I demand is the foreskins of a hundred Philistines."

Jakeh steps back. "What?"

"Foreskins, foreskins, man. You're a son of Israel, your rod was unsheathed when you were eight days old. You don't have your foreskin, but every Philistine dog still has his."

Jakeh is long accustomed to Saul's often twisted sense of humor but he sees a darker gleam in the king's eyes. He dares to ask, "Why this, this….? Why not an ear, or a nose? Anything from a dead Philistine would do?"

Saul smirks. "Jakeh, old friend, lopping off the foreskin reminds the Philistine survivors that we are the chosen people. Can you think of a better way to defile a dead Philistine?"

"But why bother with defiling? It doesn't make our people any safer. It only infuriates the enemy more?"

Saul scowls. "You're clever Jakeh. Too much cleverness can be dangerous. Now go and tell David he can have my beautiful Michal when he brings me a hundred enemy foreskins. Tell him I'll give him seven days. No, make it five days...maybe if he hurries he'll get reckless."

Jakeh drops his head, mutters, "Yes O King,". Almost eight years ago he and Saul met the prophet Samuel. Ever since that day, the servant has been repeatedly bewildered by peculiar events. Today he feels a dismal chill in the air. He shudders and shuffles off to find David.

Next morning Saul stretches his limbs and rolls out of bed. He crosses his courtyard and opens the gate. The warblers and swifts are chorusing and carousing in the rain-washed sky. After the long months of heat and sirocco winds the early rains have come. The scrubbed leaves of the oak in the plaza glisten in the morning sunshine. Across the plaza, a horseman trots slowly toward the gate, followed by a company of soldiers. David is off on his grisly venture. He spies Saul and raises his arm in salute. Saul returns the gesture, then grins as he walks back into his courtyard. This might be David's last campaign. What a glorious day to be king.

Hours later he is the expansive host. "Welcome, brothers," Saul receives his fellow kinsmen with arms spread wide and his broadest grin. The men leave behind the glare of the afternoon sun and gather under the grape arbor in Saul's courtyard.

"Sit, have some figs." Ahinoam and Michal bring in baskets of fruit and set them on the mats before the bearded elders. Now that his father Kish is gone, Saul is the chief of the clan. The baskets are passed; the men relax and the meeting begins. As usual it begins with bantering and joking.

"Pagiel, have you still not married off your second daughter? You might need to get a thicker veil to hide her face!"

"Abed, your goats are getting so thin, I can see sunlight through them."

But amidst the glib comments, more serious issues soon appear.

"Brothers, once the spring rains are over, where should we move the herds?"

"Ahira and his cousin Ochran still have not settled their dispute over the boundary line between their orchards. What will we do to resolve this?"

"Shall we organize a salt buying expedition? Who will lead it?"

The conversations are lively, opinions are animated. Whenever the group reaches a stalemate, they turn to Saul. "O King, brother Saul, what do you say?" Saul pauses, then speaks quietly and forcefully. Local issues, clan concerns about life and health: if only these things were his chief responsibility, instead of blood and battles, how different his world would be. The gathering goes on into the lazy afternoon hours. Finally, when all the matters have been chewed, Ahinoam and Michal return, fill cups of wine and the meeting ends as it began with banter and laughter.

***

Four days have passed since David set out on his grim mission and Saul calls for a meeting of his commanders. The king sits on his bench and smiles to himself as he waits for them to gather in his courtyard. Ahinoam and Michal are setting out baskets of fruit and he catches a glimpse of Michal's downcast face. Her eyes are red, her cheeks flushed. He aches to enfold her in his arms, to comfort her. He begins to rise from his seat. Ahinoam puts her hand on his shoulder and murmurs, "Don't bother. She'll probably push you away. She talked with David before he left." He slumps back onto his seat. A grimace supplants his hidden smile. *What choice do I have? How else can I save my country from the threat of chaos that comes with David?*

Suddenly Michal squeals, drops her basket and runs outside. Saul jumps to his feet when he hears the cheers and laughter out in the street. He runs to the doorway and the sunlight stabs his eyes. What he sees stabs his heart. On their way to the meeting at his house, the commanders have encountered David. Now their boisterous laughter and shouts surround the young soldier as he leads his horse toward Saul's home.

Michal and her mother stand holding each other against the outside wall. Michal's eyes flood with tears of joy and relief. Saul stands palm tree straight just outside his door. He strains to unlock his jaw and force a smile onto his face. David hands the reins of his horse to one of the commanders and walks toward Saul carrying a bundle in each hand. He pauses for an instant and with a half grin on his face looks directly into Saul's eyes. Then he goes down onto one knee before the king.

"O King, I have obeyed your command. I led my men against the Philistines at Aijalon. We attacked just before sunrise. The hand of the Almighty Lord was with us. Here are the spoils that you demanded."

He throws down the bundle in his right hand and it spills open onto the hard-packed dirt. The shriveled, bloody pieces of flesh already smell of decay, flies buzz over them and the sniffing stray street dogs move in closer, risking kicks from the soldiers' boots. Saul and the rest of the commanders stare at the shriveled foreskins with gruesome fascination. Clearly they represent at least a hundred dead Philistines.

But David hasn't finished. Without rising from his knee, he announces loud enough for the whole company to hear, "We lost three men in that first attack. To avenge their death, we moved on south to Elon and the next morning assaulted their camp and killed another hundred." He throws open the bundle from his left hand and another clump of withered, reeking foreskins pour onto the ground.

The commanders and curious neighbors roar with delight. Not only have their hated enemies been killed, they've been defiled. Saul does not share their euphoria. The forced smile disappears from his face.

So, now I'll have to make him my son-in-law. He not only fulfills my demand, he proves his prowess in front of everyone. The crowds laud him, but I know he mocks me. He mocks me. His humility is false. It smells as rank as these damned filthy foreskins.

Saul raises his arms and stills the crowd. "Commanders, we will not meet today. I must meet with David. We have to prepare for a wedding." He turns stiffly and stalks back inside. David stands, Michal runs to him and they follow Ahinoam into their courtyard. The commanders and neighbors cheer then turn toward their homes. The dogs snarl and snap over the bloody, rotting flesh of the Philistines.

***

Every inhabitant of Gibeah is gathered around the oak tree in the center of the plaza. Saul and Michal stand with their backs to the rough trunk. Facing them is David. His oiled hair shimmers, his white wedding robe glistens. He sits on a low stool holding his lyre. Standing by his side is Jonathan, the ceremonial best man.

David sweeps his hand across the strings and sparkling notes rise and float suspended in the crystalline sky. The murmuring crowd hushes in surprise. This young bridegroom is not reading the traditional marriage contract. He is singing it. The elders listen solemnly, the women's eyes overflow with tears, even the children are quiet as David sings.

"Love is stronger than death, passion fiercer than the grave. Beloved, set me as a seal upon your heart. By the power of my arm I will protect you. In my house you shall always eat the choicest foods; you shall be dressed in the finest raiment. Beloved, I am yours, and now you are mine."

Saul feels Michal's hand tremble against his rough palm. He glances down at her. Her glowing smile radiates through her veil. He allows David's song to carry him back to those many evenings when the gentle waves of this music calmed his soul and rocked him to sleep. How tranquil and untroubled were those nights. He looks out at the entranced crowd and sees again the enraptured faces of the villagers when David returned from his many victories.

Ai, why deny it any longer? The Lord who is a stranger to me, is a friend to David. The Lord who never speaks to me, clearly speaks to him. He holds my daughter's love, he claims my son's loyalty, and he embraces the people's adoration. He's been sent to replace me. He's the one Samuel claimed was coming. And yet…

Saul looks down into the clear face of his son-in-law. The young man's eyes brim with tears. He looks down and sees the tears caressing his daughter's smile. Saul clamps his own eyes shut and his mind is a torrent of fragments

And yet…it was me Samuel ordered to kneel in the gravel, the scorching Spirit filled my limbs with fire and I slashed my own oxen to pieces. I hear the thunder of my soldiers at Gilgal hailing me as king. And I see the men, so many good men who followed me into battle and spilled their blood for me and for my people. My people still call me king. Surely they'd soon forget David if he were to disappear.

David sweeps the lyre one final time and sings, "Arise, my love, my fair one, and come away." The last words float in the air and the crowd breaks into cheers. Jonathan takes the lyre and leads David toward his sister. He then takes her hand from Saul's and puts it into David's. He takes Michal's other hand and leads the bride and groom to the newly built house that will be their home. The tambourines rattle, the women chant and the villagers sing as they follow the new couple down the street. Only one man in Gibeah does not share in the community joy.

Chapter Twenty-seven

Jakeh hears Saul's courtyard door slam. He opens the door of his tiny room and calls out to Jonathan as he strides by.

"May I have a word?"

"Jakeh, of course. But it's late. Why aren't you asleep?"

The servant snorts, "And why isn't the king's son out with his friends? Please, come in, only a few minutes."

Jonathan has known Jakeh all his life. Since the death of Kish, the elderly house servant is the closest person to a grandfather that he has. He politely follows the stooped shoulders of Jakeh into the tiny windowless room. The sleeping mat takes up one half of the space. A bench stands against the opposite wall and in the corner a small table. The flame of the oil lamp gutters until the door is closed then it burns clear and straight in the stuffy room. The two men sit side by side on the bench.

"So, what is so urgent Jakeh?"

"Jonathan, you were just with your father, weren't you?"

Jonathan stares straight ahead and nods.

"And is his mood still dark, feverish?"

Jonathan stops his nodding and turns to Jakeh.. "Ahhh! I can't make any sense of this. He mutters, he growls. When I try to tell him how rich the fields are, how the sheep are fat and the orchards heavy with fruit, he spits in disdain. When I tell him that the enemy has backed off from our borders, he thunders that the enemy is close and dangerous. Tonight, he called David the enemy and raved against him with such passion, that I finally got up and left."

"My son…Jonathan, I need to tell you that the king is saying such things to everyone in the household. All of us hear him day after day ranting about killing David, eliminating David, removing David. I'm afraid the whole village will soon know the king's intentions, if it doesn't already."

"I know, I know. You're right. I only wish I could understand. David's given him no reason for such hatred."

The two sit, brooding in the dim, silent room. Their leaden thoughts weigh down the darkness. Then Jakeh points.

"Look at that moth. See it circling the flame. If I move the lamp, the moth follows. It's drawn to the fire. It's been captured by the brightness so it flits and darts closer and closer. But if it flies too close it'll burn and die."

Jonathan watches the tiny gray insect flutter above the lamp. "So to save the moth do we douse the lamp? Is that the only way?"

"As long as the king is wrapped in darkness he'll be drawn to the light of David, tormented by the thought of him. Can you find a way to lift his mood? Change his vision? Tomorrow—maybe tomorrow you can visit the fields and the orchards, walk and talk in the sunlight. You might be the only one who has a chance."

Jonathan silently stands and moves toward the door. From his bench, Jakeh rasps as Jonathan slips out, "I think you should warn David."

The next morning, despite his grumbling resistance, Saul is walking the fields with Jonathan. The summer breeze ruffles their light robes. Jonathan says, "Look at the heads on this wheat. Nearly the length of your finger."

Saul idly sweeps his hand over the waist high stalks and walks in silence.

Jonathan tries again, "If this heat holds do you think we could harvest within two weeks?"

Saul looks blankly at his son. "What? Did you ask me something?"

"I asked if you thought the harvest could be soon?"

"Maybe, maybe not."

They enter the olive grove and climb the hill. "Father have you ever seen the trees so full? The Lord is showering his bounty on us this season, don't you think?"

They reach the summit. Golden fields of grain and gray green olive orchards stretch in all directions. But Saul's head is bent and his eyes are fixed to the ground. Jonathan is confounded.

What can I do to shake him up? How can I break through his darkness, his indifference? How can I help him see beyond the black night of his own soul? Maybe if I surprise him...

"Father, do you remember the story of the Levite's concubine?"

"What?" At least Saul raises his head and looks at him.

"The story of the Levite's concubine. Do you remember it?"

Saul picks up a dead branch and slaps it against the rocks.

"Huh. What Benjaminite boy doesn't have that gory tale drilled into him."

Jonathan laughs. "True. But why did the entire tribe have to pay for the sins of that rowdy crowd of men in Gibeah?"

"It was the blood. Innocent blood was taken; innocent life was destroyed. And our tribe was responsible." Perhaps Saul's interest has been piqued.

"So if someone in the tribe sins, the Lord punishes the whole tribe."

Saul stops and cracks his branch on a rock. "I don't know if it's the Lord who punishes, but I do know the tribes hold each other to account if innocent blood is taken."

Jonathan can't hold back. "So, why then do you want to kill David?"

Saul snaps up his head. At last he is fully present. His eyes flash and he opens his mouth but Jonathan plunges on.

"David took his own life into his hands against Goliath. He's led your armies to great successes. Has he ever been disloyal?"

"No, but he's…he's..." Saul is tempted to repeat the rants he's been delivering for the past weeks. But out here, in the vast open sky, surrounded by the bounty of field and orchard he suspects those words will sound cynical and ring hollow. He grunts, then sighs.

"No, I can't say that he's been disloyal. Haughty maybe, and proud. But not disloyal."

Jonathan keeps pushing. "So, to kill David is to kill innocent blood. And if in the times of the judges the tribes rose up to punish our tribe because of the death of a concubine, a woman none of them even knew, what'll happen to us, to mother, to your grandchildren, to all of us, if you kill David who is loved by all the tribes?"

Saul stares out over the green valley. He imagines the smiling face of Ahinoam and then of Gebar his little curly haired grandson. Between heartbeats a red knife slashes across his vision and he is gazing into the open mouth of that screaming Amalekite mother. Suddenly he's slipping on the blood in those streets. The animal shrieks of the children being slaughtered lacerate his eardrums. He clutches his head, a herd of stallions thunders in his chest, and sweat streams down his face. He stumbles to a boulder and sits gasping as though he's just run up the hill. His shoulders quiver as though the sunshine were icy rain.

Jonathan dashes to him and lays his hands upon Saul's shoulders. "Father, what's the matter? Are you sick? Do you need to lie down?"

Saul shakes his bowed head. His frantic gasping breaths gradually slacken. At last he looks up. His eyes are red rimmed and spittle hangs from the corners of his mouth. His voice is hoarse.

"It was…I…a vision, an evil memory—You'll not speak of this to the others."

"But what..?"

Saul struggles to his feet and stares at his son. His words are brittle. "You will not speak of this. And as for David…I know what I've been saying. Today I've heard your words and I say this, 'As the Lord lives, David shall not be put to death'."

The two men stride down the hill toward the walls of Gibeah. Jonathan is hopeful and prays that now things will be different. Saul is exhausted and fears that some things will never change.

***

Ahinoam sings as she hikes toward the wheat field. Perfect weather—cloudless sky, dry air, and the sun a warm blanket upon her shoulders. Her children and grandchildren move along the trail with her. The harvest is finally here.

For days now the elders have been walking through the grain fields, plucking a few heads from the stalks, grinding the heads in their palms to remove the husks, then slowly biting the kernels. If the wheat is cut too soon, the kernels will be too soft, and will shrivel as they dry. No good for grinding into flour. Cutting too soon would be regrettable. But cutting too late would be catastrophic. Once the kernels are hard and golden red, the stalks must be cut quickly, lest a windstorm blast over the fields and break the brittle stalks, or worse yet, a hailstorm pound and slash the field until the ground become a muddy red carpet of wheat—food fit only for the birds.

So yesterday when the elders announced, "Tomorrow we harvest," the entire village hummed with anticipation. The men sharpened their scythes, the woman baked extra bread to take to the fields, and the children, infected by their parents' excitement, chattered into the night. Harvest was a community event, men and women working together in the fields and the children, when they weren't bringing water to their parents, frolicking with their friends.

Ahinoam's spirit dances this morning. Last night for the first time in many nights Saul slept long and without the torturous dreams that always leave him drained and dour. He walks up ahead chatting with the other men. His hair is now gray streaked and his broad shoulders sag. She remembers before---not so many years ago--- when his hair gleamed like hidden fire in the sunlight, when he walked lightly and laughed easily. She is proud of his success as the warrior king but she, more than anyone else, sees the price he has paid for that success.

The next days, from sunrise to sunset, are crammed with feverish activity. Across the land, on every wheat field, the scene is the same: First comes a line of men and women, each one with a short, curved scythe in one hand. Each person grabs a handful of stalks and cuts it. Behind them comes another line of people who tie this bundle of wheat together with a cord. Another group of people carry these sheaves of grain to an oxcart. When the cart is full, it is driven to the threshing floor. The sheaves are poured out onto the hard-packed surface, then the cart is driven back and forth across the sheaves until the grains are freed from their husks. Later, when the breeze is blowing a group of men with forks begin to toss the stalks into the air. The breeze carries away the chaff and the stalks. The precious golden red grains fall to the ground, and will be carefully gathered up and stored in the underground granaries.

"Where is the king today?" Reuel, one of Ahinoam's neighbors, asks on the fourth day of the harvest as they carry their sheaves to the cart.

Whether present or not, Ahinoam hears in Reuel's voice a greedy desire to glean a bit of gossip. Saul's night was a horrific cycle of nightmares, stumbling treks around their patio, followed by tossing and cursing on his bed.

Ahinoam tosses her bundles onto the cart with a grunt. "The king has matters to attend to with some of his commanders." She'd asked Abner to stop by their house so this isn't a complete lie. She shares Jakeh's and Jonathan's concern. If too many more people know about Saul's black moods, his kingship might be in danger. She stretches out her aching back and walks back to the field softly praying that the Lord take away the dark spirit that troubles her husband, and that he might not be crushed, threshed and blown away by this burdensome office the Lord has chosen to lay upon him.

***

"This has been a glorious God blessed day!" David says as he and Michal stand on the edge of the the threshing floor of Gibeah, looking out over the valleys below.

"Why so silent? Don't you agree?" He looks down at his wife who leans against his side. Instead of answering she turns to face the hard-packed floor. It glimmers dully in the moonlight. Earlier the floor was full of dancing and music. Now only David and Michal and a few other young couples remain, chatting in the warm evening air.

The wheat harvest began seven weeks ago. Now the fields are clean and the precious grain is safely stored in the village's underground silos. This evening marked the end of the festival of weeks. The lambs, rams and the bull were slaughtered. Parts of each were given as a burnt offering to the Lord. The prayers and blessings were pronounced. Then the feasting and dancing began. All the frenzied labor, the tension of racing against the weather, the aching muscles and blistered feet—all released and forgotten in the exuberant celebration.

David looks down at this wife nestled against him. A tear slips down her cheek. "Michal, what's wrong? Did I say some—"

"No, it's me. It's been over a year since our wedding and I've not…I should be with child. I want to give you a son." The tears on her cheeks sheen in the moonlight.

"Do you think I love you less because of that? Michal, you're more dear to me every day." He presses her against his chest and kisses her hair. He holds her and they sway slowly back and forth, then with her arm around his waist and his arm over her shoulder they walk to their home. They do not notice Saul standing in his doorway nor feel his heavy eyes following them down the street.

Three hours later the exhausted village sleeps. Only a lonely cricket's melancholy chirping breaks the silence. Saul's eyes snap open. Fear paralyzes him. Every muscle tenses and he is terrified of his own breathing. He is convinced the pounding of his heart will betray his location. His mind tells him it's only dream, but his soul will not be convinced. Isn't that the spectral figure of David slinking across the courtyard with a gleaming knife in his hand and murder in his eyes?

A minute passes. His heartbeat slows and his taut muscles slacken but the roaring tumult in his mind continues. He sits and swings his feet to the floor and mutters to himself, "Enough!" He moves quietly across his courtyard and opens the door. Two of his guards have just come on duty for the second watch. They snap to shocked attention.

Saul steps out, closes the door and stands between them. "Shhh. No sound. Just listen and obey. Go, get the other two guards and cover the front of David's house. In the morning, when he tries to leave, grab him, bind him, and bring him to me. Understand?"

Saul lowers his head and looks deep into their dark eyes. He sees their confusion and their fear. Like a horned viper, he hisses at them.

"If you don't obey, you'll feel the bite of my sword between your ribs. Now, nod if you understand."

Their heads bob and Saul dismisses them with a wave of his hand. He returns to his bed and a wave of unexpected peace rocks him to sleep.

***

"Oh King, excuse me." Jakeh gently prods Saul's shoulder with his gnarly hand. Saul grunts, rolls over, blinks in the morning light and then jerks upright in bed. "What? Oh. Where are my guards?"

"I'm sorry to wake you, O King, but one of them is at the door and says he must speak to you."

Saul throws on his robe and hurries to the door, steps out and closes it. His whisper is harsh.

"What is this? Didn't I order you to bring David to me this morning?" The guard tries to disguise his fear but his voice quivers.

"Yes sir, but he hasn't left the house. Your dau--, his wife says he's sick. She took us in and showed him lying beneath the blankets in his bed."

Saul growled. "Enough. Bring him to me, bed and all if you must. Go now." The soldier trots off down the street and Saul goes back inside. He begins to pull on his breastplate and scabbard. Ahinoam rushes in from the orchard.

"Saul, what are you doing?"

"What I should have done long ago. You and the servants, go back out to the orchard."

Ahinoam knows who torments her husband and can imagine what he is planning. She throws back her shoulders. "This is my house as much as yours. I don't know what madness you intend to do but I will not leave."

"Stay if you wish but the servants—." The courtyard door bangs open, Michal bursts in and runs into Ahinoam's arms. One guard steps in and the rest shuffle nervously in the doorway.

"Where is he? Why don't you bring him in?" Saul fumes as he marches toward them.

The guard retreats and bumps into his fellows. "O King, we didn't... Sir, he's gone."

"Gone? But you said he was in bed."

The trembling guard glances to his fellows for support. "When we pulled away the blankets we found a tarnished idol statue and the curly hair of a goat skin."

Saul bellows like a wounded ox, then pivots to his daughter who sobs in her mother's arms. Rage, grief, regret and love distort his face.

"Why? Why? I'm your father, I'm your king. Why did you deceive me? He's my enemy and you let him escape."

Michal pulls away from her mother's shoulder and murmurs. "He said if I didn't let him go, he'd kill me."

Even though his thoughts tumble like rocks in a flood and his mind seethes with frustration, Saul can hear the lie in her words. He turns back to the soldiers. "So how then did he escape?"

"Their back wall, O King, is the city wall. It has a window high above the ground. Someone must have lowered him down from that window."

Saul spins back and looks at his daughter. She stares back at him and rivulets of tears run off her cheeks. He unbuckles his breastplate and lets it fall. He drops his sword and it clatters on the courtyard stones. The king shuffles back to his room.

The soldiers are gone. Michal has gone back to her empty house. Saul lies spread eagled on his bed. Ahinoam stands outside his room and prays.

O Lord my God, I'm your humble servant. You're my maker and all things come from your hand. O God what are you doing to my family? My husband hates the very one my children love. Since our first joining, I've loved and served my husband. Since their first breath I've loved my children with a mother's heart, tender and fierce like a mother eagle. But now my love has been ripped in two. What should I do?

O Lord, why have you laid this burden upon our family? Why must Saul be king? He lies in bed, fevered and cursing David. Michal sits in her empty home grieving for her fugitive husband and loathing her father. Jonathan is furious and bereft. My God in heaven what do you expect of me? What's happening to us? Have you abandoned us? Help us. Save our family O God.

Ever since he slid down the rope and his feet touched the ground, ever since he waved to the pale, sad shadow of Michal in the window above, David has been running. For hours, under the shroud of darkness he has run northward on the road that leads to Ramah. Now the sky on his right pales and the sun begins to melt away the night. He leaves the trail and moves into a grove of ficus trees. Here, beneath the branches, it is still dark and chilly. He leans against the rough bark, tries to quiet his breath and listen for the sounds of Saul's pursuing soldiers.

O God, hear my cry. I'm alone, hunted like a wild beast. Why have I become the enemy? Where are you Lord? When your servant Samuel came to my father's house and called me from the field, when he bade me kneel and anointed me with oil, then I felt the power of your Spirit. When I stood in the valley of Elah and faced the giant, I felt the power of your Spirit. When I led Saul's army, your Spirit was with me. But now I'm alone and I can't find you O Lord. I run like a frightened deer through the bushes. I've become the King's enemy. Where are you? Help me, save me O God.

Saul stares up at the ceiling of his bedroom. He doesn't see the rough wooden beams nor the hard-baked clay. He sees only a vast darkness and in the center a bright figure, David, glaring straight into his soul.

I don't see you God; I see only my enemy. I don't hear you God; I hear only David's laughter as he prepares to destroy me. He's stolen the hearts of my children. He's turned me into a fiend. What have I done to deserve this? O God, for me you are as dark and as silent as Sheol. My words and thoughts never reach you, they never leave this dark room. Why do I even try to pray?

Chapter Twenty-seven

"Again? Are all of you as feeble as newborn lambs?"

The six soldiers stand with heads bowed, awash in Saul's caustic wrath. They had fared no better than the two preceding groups sent out to capture David. A week after David's escape a traveler came to Gibeah and reported that David was living with the prophet Samuel in Ramah.

"I should have known he'd go there," Saul mused when he heard the news. Obviously his two nemeses would sooner or later join forces against him. But, as far as he knew David had no soldiers with him and Samuel's powers were not of the military nature. He'd sent only four men to capture David and return him to Gibeah. But they returned and claimed that as they'd approached Samuel and his school of prophets they'd been struck by a whirling spirit and had fallen into the dust in a frenzy. Saul had sent out another band of soldiers but they'd suffered the same fate. Now, before him stands the third group reporting they'd been victims of the same ecstatic frenzy.

"Get out. What use to me are soldiers who can't withstand the spirit of an old man?" Saul paces back and forth across his courtyard. His encounter with the prophets at Gibeath-Elohim was nearly ten years ago. He retains only broken, chipped fragments of that event.

Maybe that all happened to someone else in another lifetime. It most certainly happened to a naïve, tender hearted young man, to someone who still trusted in God. David is my enemy. He's after my throne. I'll go get him myself.

Saul takes his aide Medad and three other men and they ride the eleven miles to Ramah. As they trot past the fields of ripening melons and the fig trees, Saul considers his strategy.

"I'll approach Samuel's house first and call out for David. He's no coward and I think he'll step forth. I'll dismount and call him to me. Then I'll begin to walk toward him and as I do I want you to ride to either side of him and keep him from retreating."

The soldiers listen in silence. They've heard their comrades' stories and wonder how they'll escape the same fate. But the King is leading so they have no choice but to follow.

It's nearly noon when they begin climbing the hill to Ramah. Shimmers of heat waver and dance above the earth. The clouds are clumps of dirty wool and the air is leaden with the threat of storm. They ride forward another fifty feet and Saul feels his scalp begin to tingle. He turns to his men.

"Stay here. I'll call David out." He rides ahead a few more yards, dismounts and hands the reins to Medad. As he walks toward the gate his hands begin to tremble. He opens his mouth and prepares to shout. But by now his jaw and entire torso are shivering so intensely that he only manages to bellow out a strangled, "David come…" before he falls to the ground. Medad and the other three men are transfixed and dare come no closer. Saul now begins to roll and flop in the dirt. Then he flies into the air as though tossed by a mad bull. He grabs his now filthy tunic with both hands, screams and rips it entirely in two and tramples it in the dust. He spins frantically as though stung by a million wasps, then yanks at his loincloth and snaps it away. Now everyone can see his shameful nakedness. For ten, fifteen, then twenty minutes he spins and jerks hysterically. Spittle spews from his foaming mouth and dust clings to his sweat streaked body. When it seems impossible for anyone to endure such prolonged frenzy, the tall, naked king collapses unconscious in the dust. Medad begins to approach, then hears a ragged shout.

"Don't touch him." Samuel steps out from the gate and walks toward them. "He's been struck down by the Spirit of the Lord and you'll suffer the same fate if you try to wake him now. Wait until the Spirit goes. When Saul wakes, you may give him water and take him home. But only after he wakes." He turns and walks back to the gate. Before he enters, he turns and shouts. "Tell Saul he is not welcome in Ramah. And tell him that David is no longer here."

Medad and the men are petrified. They do not doubt the prophet's words, so they wait. All afternoon they wait. When the sun sets and Saul still lies unmoving they build a fire near him, and try to keep him warm despite his nakedness. The night is endless. The threat of rain passes and the wind blows the scudding clouds across the face of the moon. The dancing flames throw grotesque shadows on their naked king. Their fitful sleep is tormented by visions of Saul being flung into the air by the Spirit's power.

The swallows are already singing their welcome to the morning when Saul begins to stir. He groans and the soldiers leap to their feet. Medad, still unnerved by the tumultuous chaos of the day before, creeps hesitantly closer to his naked, groaning king. He holds a robe and a jug of water. Saul finally opens his eyes and grabs the jug and takes great gulps until it is empty. Then he lowers the vessel and sees his own nakedness. He bellows in shame and grabs the robe from Medad's hand.

It takes all four of them to get the still groggy Saul up and on his horse. They turn their backs on Ramah and begin the journey back to Gibeah. Saul groans and mumbles to himself. He sways in the saddle. The sun's warmth and the plodding of the horses slowly settles Saul's mind. In a subdued, exhausted voice he speaks to himself and his companions.

"This is how God's Spirit comes upon me. David says when the Spirit comes upon him, it fills him with power and he kills the giant. Samuel claims when the Spirit comes upon him it gives him a message for the people. But me? When the Spirit falls upon me it doesn't fill me. It doesn't give, it takes. It empties me, shatters my strength. God's fire consumes my will until I'm a scorched husk. I'm reduced to a naked, hollow man. What sort of God is this?"

The soldiers glance tight-lipped at each other. They're baffled and disconcerted by what they have witnessed. If they could they'd spur their horses and gallop home.

**

Saul sits quietly with Jonathan. They tear off pieces of bread and dip them into the bowl of lentils on the floor between them. Three weeks ago, Saul had his calamitous encounter with the Spirit in Ramah. Since then he moves and speaks as though recovering from a near mortal wound. He is subdued with his grandchildren. He is quietly attentive to Ahinoam and gentle with the servants. The entire household walks on tiptoe and wonders how long this will endure.

"So, have you seen David?" Saul's words are robed in menace. He takes a bite of bread and stares at Jonathan. Jonathan has known this question would someday arrive. Nonetheless it catches him off guard.

"What? What did you ask?"

"You heard me. I know David has left Ramah. And I know that you're close to him, closer to him than your own sister is. So? Have you seen him?"

Jonathan looks up from his bowl and stares back at his father.

"I.... David still doesn't understand your hatred of him."

Saul's subdued voice rises. "He's a liar. He's taken you in, seduced you. He wants to be the king."

"But when has he ever said that?"

"Ha! He says it with his eyes every time he looks at me."

Jonathan sets down his bowl and glowers at his father. "You're imagining this. You've created this idea and now it's poisoning your mind. Your hatred is blinding you."

Saul turns his face away. His neck reddens and he springs to his feet. Jonathan scrambles up to face him. Saul stares down on his son.

"You're blind because you love this beautiful shepherd. Your love is shameful to us all. And what's more you're utterly ungrateful."

"Ungrateful? I've no idea what you're talking about."

"Jonathan, don't you see? While he lives you'll never be king after me."

Jonathan snorts and walks away from his father.

"What makes you think I'd ever want to be king?"

Saul retorts. "I didn't want to be king either. But that didn't stop the Lord from taking me by force and shoving the job upon me. So now I'm going to hold onto it until I die and see to it that you follow me as king of Israel."

He walks over to where his weapons lie upon the bench. He turns and thunders at Jonathan. "I want you to go out now to wherever your friend David is hiding and bring him to me."

Jonathan turns back to his father with hands outstretched. "He's innocent. He's done nothing to deserve death. I won't let you slaughter him."

Saul's face flushes. He screams and with eagle swiftness swoops up his spear and flings it at Jonathan. The spear whistles past Jonathan's ear and clatters against the wall. Jonathan stands with his fists on his hips. Flickering anger flares in his eyes, tears of pity tremble on his cheeks. He sighs and marches out of the house.

***

In the feeble gray of predawn Jonathan slips out of Gibeah and hikes three miles east into the hills. He sits on a boulder and mimics a mourning dove's lament. David steps out from behind a clump of thorn trees. The two meet in a long embrace, then Jonathan steps back.

"David, I'm afraid you're right. The king is convinced that you're after his crown. He won't rest until you're dead. I told him he was crazy. All that got me was a spear flung at my head."

"Are you alright? I'm sorry for dragging you into danger."

Jonathan grabs both of David's arms. "Danger? You're the one in danger. You've got to leave. Get as far away as you can from his fuming rage."

Again the men embrace and David's voice is full of tears. "That means going far away from you. I…" He sobs as he kisses Jonathan.

Jonathan's tears wet David's cheek. "I know. But what choice do we have? I pledge my loyalty to you before the Lord, and I swear there'll be peace between us and our descendants forever."

The sun climbs above the horizon, the mourning doves fly to the shade of thorn trees, and the two men kiss once more. Then Jonathan son of the king trudges back to Gibeah and David the fugitive runs to the south. The two men will never meet again.

Chapter Twenty-eight

Even before the assembly begins, the mood is ominous. The gray green leaves of the tamarisk hang limp in the midday heat. The breeze that usually stirs here on the heights of Gibeah has died. Beads of sweat glisten on the necks of the military commanders and village leaders who've been summoned to this meeting. Each man tries to edge in and claim a bit of the tree's shade and moves uncomfortably close to his neighbor. King Saul sits on a stool with his back against the furrowed, dark trunk. His spear lies across his lap and bobs up and down as his knee bounces nervously. He has not slept through the night for weeks. He has grimly reconciled himself to the nightmares that routinely rip his sleep asunder. But he did not order this assembly to complain about his personal exhaustion.

Doeg the Edomite, the man appointed as overseer of the clan's shepherds, returned yesterday from a religious pilgrimage with news that reignited Saul's smoldering rage. He stands now at the King's right hand. The Edomite is as lean as a willow branch. A white scar slants across one cheek and his mouth is fixed in a painful grin.

Saul clears his throat. "Men, I want you to hear what I heard last night from my servant Doeg." He looks up and nods at the Edomite. Doeg takes a step forward, tips his chin forward and speaks in a voice that reminds his listeners of the bleating of a goat.

"I was in Nob for a ceremony. As I traveled home I heard from a traveler that David was in the caves of Adullam south of Bethlehem. People of his clan of Judah, malcontents, and debtors have joined him. Over four hundred they say. He claims to be their captain." He steps back with a self-satisfied look on his hawkish face

A buzz moves through the crowd and matches the droning that plagues Saul's head. Now the king stands and his head nearly touches the lowest branches. He jabs his spear into the packed earth beside him.

"Most of us here are of Benjamin's tribe and territory. Many of you have brothers and sisters near Nob or even Adullam. You know this rebel; you know what this pretty son of Jesse is doing, but you haven't told me, not one word. You've seen my own son slink off into the hills to conspire against me yet you haven't alerted me."

He jerks the spear from the ground and points it at the men. The entire crowd steps back. Saul is roaring now.

"What are you fools thinking? Do you imagine that when this shepherd boy of Judah overthrows me he's going to reward you with fields and flocks? Do you suppose he'll trust you to lead his armies? Maybe you think my time is over. Maybe you think it's time for you to change sides. But I'm telling you, it's too late for that. It's too late!" Saul pauses and the great bellows of his lungs, are the only sound breaking the oppressive silence.

Abner and a few other commanders glare at him, others stare down at the ground. Doeg the Edomite relishes their discomfort and steps forward and dares to speak again.

"When I was in Nob completing my vows at the house of the priest Ahimelech I saw David." All eyes, including Saul's swivel to him. Evidently this is even news to the king.

"Yes, I saw David come to the priest, and the priest spoke to the Lord on David's behalf. And then…" Doeg pauses and leans forward, "And then I saw him give David the holy bread and--" He pauses again and then bleats out, "and the sword of Goliath!"

The crowd gasps, not only at what happened at Nob but at what this knowledge will surely do to their ravaged king. Saul's knees buckle and he topples back onto his seat. He stares up into the dim canopy of leaves as though in prayer. At last he turns to Abner.

"Go to Nob and bring me Ahimelech and his family. Bring me all of the priests of the sanctuary." Abner salutes and without a word turns to gather his troops. Saul turns and wearily says to the crowd, "Go home, all of you. Go home and think about what you've heard here today. And remember, I am still your king."

Doeg lingers near Saul as the men disperse. He bends and leans close to Saul's ear.

"Oh King, with your permission I could join Abner on his mission to Nob. I can gather some of my countrymen to come with us. You know… in case of trouble." He pauses as Saul sits in silence, then hastily adds, "If of course you think it wise."

After a deep sigh, Saul simply nods and waves him off. He watches as Doeg scurries off after Abner. The king dislikes the Edomite. He is a distasteful blend of bootlicking and arrogance. But Saul admits the man has his uses. He was hired because of a local matter. All the sheep in the village go out together in one flock. The shepherds guard them and lead them to water and grass. But last year the five village shepherds were always bickering and debating. Saul grew weary of settling their many disputes, so he brought in someone from outside the clan, even outside the tribe, to be in charge. Doeg has no blood ties to any son of Israel. His only allegiance is to Saul. At least this is what Saul hopes.

***

Ahimelech and his retinue of white robed priests advance slowly up the sun-drenched hill. They flow silently past the young women who've intentionally lingered at the well to witness this unusual parade. As always Abner has been efficient. Only a day and a half has passed since Saul's order and here he is with all eighty-five of the priests of Nob. Abner and his twenty soldiers march in front of and behind the group. Doeg has managed to muster fifteen ragged warriors who march on either side of the holy men. Curious villagers stand on the crest of the hill and watch the parade approach the tamarisk tree where Saul is already seated.

Ahimelech the high priest marches at the head of the sinuous line of men. He is an impressive figure. His white turban is matched by his white beard and both stand in contrast to his obsidian eyes. His tunic is fine white linen and is covered with a deep blue robe. His breastplate is covered with twelve stones, one for each of the tribes. Around his waist is the ephod with pouches containing the Urim and Thummin.

As Ahimelech draws near, Saul gazes glumly at the pouches. He remembers his last bitter encounter with those stones. Saul rises, the high priest stops and the other priests gather alongside and behind their leader.

Ahimelech bows from the waist before the king and his rich baritone voice rings out over the hilltop, "Greetings O King. You have summoned us and we have come to do your bidding."

Saul quickly bows his head, then steps back and sits. The high priest fixes his eyes on the king. The king gazes blankly at the hard-packed dirt upon which the priest stands. The silence becomes painful. Whispers begin to slither among the bystanders. Without looking up Saul speaks.

"Listen to me, Ahimelech son of Ahitub." Saul is a sinister hissiing snake.

Ahimelech bows again.

"That is why I am here, O King."

Saul lifts his eyes and they are cold stones.

"Why have you conspired against me? You and this shepherd son of Jesse?"

Ahimelech extends his arms and stands with palms open. "Conspire? I would never conspire against God's chosen king."

Saul leans forward and puts his hand on his knees. Now he is growling. "Did you give bread to this shepherd? Did you give him Goliath's sword?

"Yes, I gave these things to David, but—."

Now Saul roars, "And did you ask God to give him direction, so he can rebel against me?"

The priest throws his hands into the air, "Yes, no, I... O King, yes David asked for God's direction. He is a religious man. He came just as he's done before. But never to rebel against you. Never. Isn't he your most loyal soldier? Isn't he your son-in-law? Isn't he honored in your house?"

"Honored? Honored?" Saul leaps to his feet and advances step toward Ahimelech. "He's a fugitive, an outlaw out to steal my kingship."

Now a ripple of fear washes over the priests. Saul's fury forces the high priest to step back. He gasps in frustration. "But I…we didn't know. We knew nothing of this. You can't blame us for something we did in good faith. We're innocent."

"Innocent? Hah." Saul spits on the earth between them. "None of us is innocent." He suddenly turns to the crowd of villagers. "Go home. Go inside the walls." The people stand confused. "I am telling you, take your wives and your children and go inside the walls. Now."

As the last stragglers enter the gates, Saul strides over to Abner, leans down to his ear and murmurs, "Take your men and execute these priests. They're all traitors, all on David's side."

Abner steps back and stares up at Saul. He's been a soldier most of his life and is quietly proud of his prompt and complete obedience to the king. He has done things that challenged his instincts as a soldier. But this… Today he has reached a line he cannot cross. Abner sees the sickly fire in Saul's eyes and quickly turns his head. He is willing to live with the consequences of his decision. "Saul, these are priests of the Lord, sons of Israel. I will not kill them and I will not command my soldiers to kill them." He spins on his heel and walks away from Saul. He would not be surprised to feel a spear in his back. He signals to his troops and they follow him back to their camp.

The unarmed priests teeter on the edge of panic. The clearing of the crowd was an ominous sign. And though they couldn't hear the exchange between Saul and his commander, the holy men sense it was about them. Some of the younger ones start to run up into the hills. The Doeg's soldiers herd them back.

The Edomite sidles alongside Saul. His voice is low and oily. "These men are no kin to me. What do you want me to do with them?"

Saul looks at the priests' faces sickly white with fright. He closes his eyes and hears again the rabble cheering for David, smells the rotting foreskins that a gloating David threw in front of him. He imagines these priests crowding around David, laughing and cheering for him. Without opening his eyes, he whispers to his mercenary, "Take them away from here and then kill them, kill them all. And get rid of the bodies."

He utters these words and senses a fracture, a fissure in his soul. A fragile vessel breaks and cannot be repaired. What has he done? A chill slithers down his spine.

Are innocent people going to die by my command? Yes, but are they more innocent than the Amalekite children killed by God's command? Who says kinsmen and holy men are exempt from retaliation? Didn't God himself teach me to be strong and eliminate enemies?

Saul twists his shoulders trying to free himself from these swirling thoughts. He shouts to the departing Edomite, "Doeg! Doeg, before you take them away, hear this. When you've finished with them, take your men to Nob. Destroy the city and everyone and everything in it. Understand?"

Doeg smiles and nods. He understands completely.

***

Saul crosses his legs and sits on the rooftop of his house. Thin clouds shine silvery in the moonlight. Earlier in the day the Edomite returned and reported that the city of Nob was no more. The king lets his thoughts drift into what in his life now passes for prayer.

Why am I still alive? If God doesn't want me as his king, why haven't I been killed long ago? Swords, spears and arrows--no lack of those. And enemies? Ha. They surround me, hide behind every tree. They lurk in my own household.

Now I've destroyed the priests' town. And still God is silent. Not even a roar of rage. What if God doesn't care that I've put all his priests to the sword? Does God even call them his priests? Did God make them priests the way Samuel made me king? Samuel, I curse the day you were born….

Ai, who can I trust? Abner refused to obey my order. How deep does his allegiance go? If he falters, then…then the troops will all…. No, I asked too much of him. He's still with us. Yes, I'm sure. I hope.

The Edomite? Ha I trust him as far as I can throw him. I trust him as much as I trust a snake. He is faithful to me while I am on top. But only that long. When the wind of power shifts, he will shift too. He'll be gone in the breeze.

My family? Only Ahinoam. I trust only her. At least I'm sure she won't stab me as I sleep. Jonathan, Michal…. both seduced by David. David, David, David--he's become the reason I live. His power, his name, fame, charm…they all whisper threats to me every minute of every waking hour. And since I barely sleep, those whispers fill too many hours. Does God care? Or is He only watching us with morbid curiosity. Maybe God is controlling every step I take. If that's so, then God is a cruel being, who enjoys watching his creatures suffer. David, David…if I could destroy him, maybe I could sleep, maybe God would begin to speak to me. Maybe if I showed God how wrong he is to trust this shepherd from the little house of Jesse, then who knows, God might change His mind. It wouldn't be the first time.

Chapter Twenty-nine

Three men stand before Saul as he sits beneath the tamarisk tree flanked by his guards. Their robes and faces are layered with dust.

"King Saul, we have good news for you." The short, broad shouldered young man is clearly the spokesman for the group. Bright eyes dance out of his round, dusty, and smiling face.

Saul looks at him and his two companions with brooding eyes. "Good news? I could use some of that. Speak."

The leader takes a small step forward. "We come from Ziph, south of Hebron. We know you're trying to catch the outlaw David."

Now Saul's eyes snap open and he leans forward. "You know where he is?"

All three men nod as their leader speaks. "He and his men are hiding out in the hills and caves in Ziph."

"You're sure of this?" Saul feels the blood throbbing in his temples.

"King, why don't you come down to Ziph and we'll hand him over to you." The leader turns back to his companions and they all smile broadly.

Saul lifts his shoulders and sits back. How long has it been since he's encountered men who so gladly and openly respect his authority and offer help? He smiles as he opens his arms as if to embrace the three. "You've brought me great news. Thank you for your kindness. May the Lord bless you."

They bow and their young leader responds. "Thank you King. Join us in Ziph and we'll capture him for you."

Saul grins at their braggadocio but he knows David better than they. "Look, you're not going to simply walk in and grab him as if he were a stray sheep. David is a fox. He's cunning and quick. Go back down and keep track of him, find out where he goes, where he hides. Once you've got that information I'll come down and we'll nab him."

Saul rises and embraces the dusty travelers. "Tonight, you'll dine with me and my family. Tomorrow you can return and begin searching for our enemy. Medad will take you to my house. You can wash and rest there until our evening meal."

He slaps the travelers' dust off his robes as he watches the three young men entering the city gate. *Can it be true? Here is proof. I'm not the only one. Others in Israel want David gone. Maybe the silent God is reconsidering his decision.*

***

The wilderness of Ziph is a bleak blanket spread out before Saul and his soldiers. Gray and ocher hills wrapped in gravel and rocks march to the horizon, fold after endless fold of slope and valley. The harrowing shriek of a hawk on the hunt pierces the arid air. The wilderness of Ziph, the wilderness of "flowing". The only thing flowing is sweat on the faces of the men as they follow a faint dusty trail across the hillside.

Saul looks out across the landscape. *How easy it is to convince yourself that every ridge and ravine is the same, to let yourself be lulled by the monotony of this land into thinking there can be no surprises here. That's why outlaws like David and his pack of men come to such places. Tucked away in this bland desert are caves, nooks, and secluded valleys. Hiding...David is a master at that. He hides from my soldiers; he hides his craven desire to be king from everyone. He pretends piety and hides behind God. David—the master at hiding. And me? My lot is pursuing, searching, hunting. Hunting for this outlaw who's just as adept at disappearing as is his God. Hasn't God spent a lifetime hiding from me? He hides behind the words of Samuel. He hides behind the dervish spirit that sends me reeling into the dirt. Hunting for a cunning outlaw, hunting for a hidden God...was I destined for this?*

Two days ago, the men of Ziph sent information claiming to have located David. Saul gathered his men and marched the thirty miles south into this barren land. The sun scorches the western horizon when two of these men meet them on the trail.

"Welcome King Saul. You bring honor to our land." The ever-smiling leader bows.

Saul thinks to himself, *this savage land needs more than honor.* But he graciously replies, "Thank you for your work. I hope we can soon capture this outlaw and leave you in peace."

The smile leaves the young man's face. "We've just heard that he's moved with his men farther south to Maon. He must have heard of your mission."

Saul scowls. "Who told him?" *Evidently not every man in Ziph sees David as an enemy.*

The young man shrugs and grimaces. "Who can tell with that one. He seems to have eyes and ears everywhere."

Saul and his men decide to make camp on the floor of a nearby wadi. A few gaunt trees desperately vie for the moisture that lies hidden somewhere below the hard sand. Saul sits outside his tent in the velvet night with his young aide Medad.

"Is this your first time in the far south?"

The young man answers, "Yes, my first visit."

"And what do you think of it?"

Medad shrugs, "Hot, different from home. What do you think of it O King?"

Saul gazes up at the slice of sky between the wadi walls and says, "This wilderness unnerves me. I think of our ancestors in the wilderness. Free from slavery but desperate for food. In that wilderness, God came close to them, gave them quails and manna. I keep wondering…thinking maybe God will draw near to us out here. But the only thing I ever feel in this wilderness is a sweeping loneliness."

Medad sits silently and abashed. The king has never spoken so intimately to him.

Saul muses. "David is out here in this barren land. No doubt he claims that God is with him. I suppose that's why God is gone from us."

Medad asks, "But King, can't God be with David and with us too?"

Saul sighs. "Ah Medad. Don't confuse what God can do with what God chooses to do. Remember the story of God hidden in the cloud at Mt. Sinai? The people heard only thunder but Moses went up and came down with the law. God is a mystery wrapped in a cloud. Some claim to talk to God and to know God's will, but who can say? As for us, here in our wilderness, we have nothing--no mountain, no thunder, no cloud."

***

The morning sunlight paints a fringe of fire on the wadi's upper rim. A few birds awaken in the scrubby trees. A horseman charges into the camp and shatters the calm. He flings himself off his panting horse and salutes Saul.

"O King, the Philistines have mounted an attack in the west. Abner asks that you come at once to lead the forces."

Saul hears the news in stoic silence. *Enemies on all sides: A rebellious outlaw covets my crown, a belligerent well-armed nation determined to destroy my people. I must choose....* Within the hour they are back on the trail retracing yesterday's journey.

The campaign against the Philistines is grim and costly. Saul's armies fight efficiently, as they have for many years. But like the king the troops grow weary of this insidious arrogant beast that keeps chewing at the borders of their land. The Philistines retreat but not before inflicting serious injuries and death upon Saul's forces. Saul and the army return to Gibeah to recover and recuperate. But when a messenger arrives announcing that David and his followers are now hiding at En Gedi, Saul hastily musters his soldiers and once again they charge south.

***

En-Gedi. Saul's mount trots ahead of the dust raised by his troops and for a moment the king forgets his mission and journeys back to when he was nine and visited that magical place. Near the end of their hot, long journey to buy salt he and Kish's men found relief at this beautiful oasis tucked in the mountains just west of the great sea. He can still see the date palms soaring upward and piercing the sun-bleached sky. He hears again the laughing and squealing when he first bit into the red jujube fruits. He licks his dry lips now and recalls the icy waterfall slicing into the deep, blue-green pool at its base. Walking from the floor of the desert plain into the canyon where the water fell was like walking into another world. The air was chill, thick with moisture. The swallows swooped and crisscrossed over the water with delight. He closes his eyes and remembers how all was green and cool.

After a hard, twelve-hour march, they reach En-Gedi and Saul exclaims to Abner, "It's a miracle. I can't believe it. The water, the air, the birds. It's all just as I remember it. Everything out in the world changes but not here at En-Gedi." He slides off his horse and runs to the edge of the pool, stoops and throws water in his face. He stands and with arms upraised fills his lungs with the moist cool air. There is no debate: tonight's camp will be right here, near the water and everyone will be lulled to sleep by the sound of the falls.

Hours later Saul slips noiselessly from his tent. By the moonlight, he sees the night watchmen at their posts around the camp full of sleeping soldiers. His own skin quivers as if preparing for a rush of cold water, his muscles coil as though preparing for a race. Sleep is a distant and estranged friend. He strides to the edge of the pool and stares at the moon's reflection, a mother of pearl plate on the black rippling water. He crosses his arms and slaps his shoulders nervously.

Ai, God you haunt me here. The living water, the joyful green, the exalting birds. God, God, God... you must be here making and

*keeping all of this. Why can't I feel you, hear you, sense you?
Forget, deny, ignore…I've tried it all. But always there's a hum, a
trembling inside, as though a taut string within me has been plucked.
God, you haunt me. Do you haunt David too? Or is he your friend?
Does his heart truly keep rhythm with yours or was that Samuel's
malicious notion? If only…. Ai, let the night race like a wolf in the
wind and let morning come so I can exchange this fruitless
pondering for the hunt.*

The morning air is soft and cool. The guard on patrol approaches
Saul who already sits in front of his tent. "O King, we saw men at
dawn, moving up on those heights, the ones they call the Rocks of
the Wild Goats." Saul looks up. The blinding white, sun-bleached
boulders slash across the pale blue sky. His eyes flicker and he pants
in excitement.

"Roust the men, now! We'll find the trail and climb. Hurry man.
We can't let this weasel escape."

Saul leads the charge up the rocky switchbacks like a man
possessed. Even the young soldiers strain to keep up with the pace of
their forty-eight-year-old king. The coolness of the En-Gedi oasis is
replaced by the fierce sunlight and blazing heat of the heights. Yet
Saul charges on without stopping for rest or breath. He scrambles
around boulders, all his senses aquiver, alert for any clue that his
enemy is near.

Abruptly he stops. His heart thumps and the skin on his neck
tingles. His entire body senses his nemesis. Saul licks his dry lips
and is a statue trying to locate David's presence. The king's troops
catch up to him and then hush before his silent intensity.

Saul breaks the silence with a groan. He stoops and clutches his
gut.

"Hold here men. David is close, I can feel him." He grunts as he
moves off the trail. "We'll get him. But first, I've got to relieve
myself."

He spies what looks like a shallow shelter under an overhanging
rock ledge. But when he steps into its shadow he realizes that he's

entered a cave. He moves back far enough to be out of sight and then groans again as his intestines cramp. He'd like to dash back out into the sunlight but it's too late for that. He pulls up his robe and squats on the gravelly floor. Even as his bowels relieve themselves he feels the pressure of the immense blackness behind him and hears a whispering moan from deep within the bowels of the mountain. A shiver trickles down his spine. Caves are the home of dark, baleful spirits.

His ears thunder in the silence. It takes all his willpower to force himself to finish before rushing out of the cave. He stands and dashes back to his troops. "Now, men, let's be quick. Our quarry is close." Saul begins trotting on the trail which now begins to descend. They go down one switchback, then another.

A shout cascades upon them from above, "Soldiers of Israel, stop." Saul and his men skid on the dusty trail, shield their eyes and look up. On a ledge, just out of arrow shot stands David. He glows in the sunlight. He holds both arms aloft. In his right, he holds his sword; in his left he waves a piece of cloth. He shouts again. "O Saul, my lord and king. Does this look familiar? Look behind you. Look at your robe."

Saul sucks in his breath and stands frozen. Slowly he turns to see threads and the jagged edge on his robe. Reluctantly he turns his face back up the slope.

"See, O King, see? I'm not your enemy. I was so close to you I could've killed you. The men that were with me in that cave whispered, 'Look, God has put the enemy into your hand. Strike now.'"

Abner, standing beside Saul, mutters, "Ha, if he'd have killed you there, we'd have cornered them like rats in their hole." Saul holds up his hand and shushes his commander as David continues.

"My men wanted me to kill you, but I don't listen to my men. I listen to the Lord God and the Lord has declared that you are the king. Saul, I still honor you. I'm still loyal to you. I'm sure that God will see that justice is done between us. But I won't be the instrument of that justice. You've nothing to fear from me."

David falls silent and the soldiers all turn to look at Saul. The flaming energy that drove him up the mountain vanishes. He stands like a candle whose flame has been extinguished. His panting, hungry desire for David's capture has been displaced by woeful tears that trickle down his dusty cheeks and disappear into his graying beard. He throws out his arms and shouts, "David, today I see that you're a better man than I am. You repaid my evil with good. God will reward you for that." Saul pauses, then gulps back a sob, "I'm more sure than ever that you're going to be the king. All I ask, all I beg of you, is that you don't destroy my entire family. Please let my ancestors live. Please swear you won't let my name be forgotten." Saul's soldiers lower their heads, embarrassed by their king's tears and his begging.

David shouts from his ledge, "O King, I will never raise my hand against your family. I swear this before God and before you."

Saul nods, turns and mutely starts down the trail. Every jolting step drains away more of the frenetic energy that powered him these past few days. Into that void now seeps a gray mist of guilt. *How much damage I've caused. My wife, my daughter, my son—how my fear has harmed them. How much hardship I've laid upon my soldiers to hunt down this one who claims he's my most loyal subject. Is he telling the truth? Today he could've killed me but didn't. And if he'd cut more than my robe? I'd be in the empty, dark silence of Sheol. At least there I could rest.*

The pace of the return to Gibeah is sluggish. Wispy gray veils of cloud promise rain but deliver only paltry drops. The troops are exhausted and disheartened. With each passing mile Saul grows quieter and more lethargic. By the time they reach Gibeah he is somnolent and without a word enters his home and lies down. The sleep that has so often slipped away from him now drops upon him like a leaden shroud.

Chapter Thirty

In Ramah, a dozen miles to the north, Samuel exhales on his pallet. He has outlived his wife, one of his sons and most of his friends. His youngest son came earlier in the morning to see how he'd passed the night. Now he is alone. The house servant is outside in the courtyard, making bread and visiting with the neighbor. Out in the village a mother scolds her child. Inside the small house, the sunlight falling on the wall opposite his pallet tells the aged seer it is nearly noon.

The Voice has been silent for many months. Now, as it has done for decades it breaks through Samuel's drifting consciousness without warning.

Your journey is nearly over. Your work is done.

Samuel's eyelids are heavy but he whispers into the quiet of the morning, "At last. Too long…. I've lingered too long."

Your time, all time is in my hands.

"All time. And all deeds….I know, I know…In your hands. But I've had to carry them all, suffer them all. I'm the one with heart scars and soul wounds."

You have been obedient, that is enough.

"For you, yes. But I'd hoped…I'd hoped that my work would matter more in this land, to my people."

You need not seek their approval.

"Ha! No chance of that. The messages you gave me to deliver seldom brought approval. But still…I thought my life would make more of a difference here."

No one ever promised you that.

"I'm not saying you did. But still…I spoke hard words. I delivered crushing messages that pained others and took their toll on me. Saul's bewilderment when I anointed him…. His shock when I chastised him at Michmash…. His horror filled eyes at Gilgal when I told him You had changed your mind and he was no longer king. All those words…they burned him but they scorched me too. And for what? For what? Saul is still king; David hides like a rabbit in the hills. And the Philistines? They hover like vultures on our border. My eyes tell me we are worse now than when I began my journey."

Samuel, you know not to put your trust in feeble eyes.

"Yes, yes, I'm old enough to know that. And I'm old enough to know never to argue with you. So, what comes now? What happens after the end?"

Samuel waits. And waits. The Voice does not answer. The only sounds in the room are the last rattling breaths of a worn out man. Then at last, silence.

"Samuel the prophet is dead!" From village to village, the news is carried by travelers and messengers across Israel. In Gibeah, Jakeh brings the news to Saul. He steps into the king's bedroom. Though the sun charged into the sky hours ago, Saul lies dozing and listless. Since he returned three weeks ago from his failed mission in En-Gedi, he has grown more and more lethargic. Some days he does not open the gates of his courtyard. He can sit for hours staring at the shadows as they move across the floor.

"O King, the news came this morning. Samuel is dead."

Saul slowly swings his feet to the floor and sits up. His eyes are encircled by pools of purple. His hair is tousled and stiff. His voice is hoarse and rusty.

"So…. even God's prophet doesn't live forever. When did he die?"

"Two days ago. Everyone is going to Ramah to mourn his death."

Saul snorts. "Not everyone. I had enough of that man when he was alive. Let others weep for his passing. Do you want to go, Jakeh?"

The aged servant slowly shakes his head and smiles ruefully. "No. I carry too many years for such a journey. I'm older than that dead prophet. The last long journey I made was with you when we went out looking for the donkeys. I'm staying home."

Saul puts his arms behind him on the bed and leans back. "Ah the donkeys. How our life would be different if they'd not run away."

The winds of memory blow and break up the thick clouds in Saul's mind: Kneeling inside the gate of Ramah, staring into Samuel's fathomless eyes and feeling the oil dripping down his cheeks; Wincing as the furious prophet grinds his staff onto his foot at Michmash; on his knees grasping in desperation for the seer's cloak at Gilgal. His last memory of Samuel is the old man's vicious slaughter of the Amalekite king. He cringes as the nausea from that day threatens to return. Saul stands up.

"Samuel claimed to speak for God. Whenever he spoke to me, I suffered. I don't know if I should blame him or God for my misery. But Jakeh, what I do know is that I'm not going to travel anywhere close to Samuel dead or alive. I'm going to stay here with you. I believe I'll be safer."

Chapter Thirty-one

The three men climb the slope toward Gibeah's walls. They see the tamarisk tree, site of their first contact with the king. Today the tree is a solitary sentinel. At the city gates, one of the two guards, a tall young man with a fierce black beard challenges them.

"Who are you and what's your business here?"

"We're from Ziph," grins the leader of the group, "And we have news for King Saul."

The bearded guard consults his partner. The man from Ziph interrupts, "It's about the outlaw David."

"Ahh. Very well. The house on the opposite side of the plaza belongs to the king."

The three travelers scurry across the plaza and knock on the courtyard door. A stooped, wizened Jakeh opens the door and squints at them. "Good afternoon, how may I serve you?"

"We've come to speak to the king. We were here months ago. We have news about David."

The manservant winces. "David, you say? Aii. No. Well...Please wait here." He hastily closes the door and the men hear him grumbling as he walks away. A minute later the door swings open and the men stand face to face not with the king but with a grizzled soldier.

"I'm Abner, the King's first commander. What's this about news regarding David?"

All three men bow as the leader begins, "We're from the wilderness of Ziph to the south, just past the city of—."

"I know where Ziph is," Abner growls. "What's your news?"

"We've come to tell the king that David and his men are again hiding near our territory, on the hill of Hachilah, opposite the plain of Jeshimon."

Abner stares at them with one eye shut then snaps, "And why do you come all this way to tell the king this news?"

The three look at each other in consternation. Last time they'd been welcomed by the king himself. Now they need to defend themselves? Finally, the leader lifts his chin and manages to smile at the scowling commander.

"Sir, we are loyal to our king and want to serve him. This David and his men are using our own lands for their dens. We do not support him. We belong to King Saul. We know he hunts this outlaw so we want to help."

Abner forces a smile. "Your loyalty is appreciated. I'll bring your news to the king." He steps back into the doorway. As he closes the door he notes the slump of disappointment on the men's faces. He anticipates their request.

"No, you can't see the king today. He's not... He's not feeling well. Maybe we'll see you on the hill of Hachillah." He closes the door. The disappointed travelers turn and start their journey home.

Inside, Abner strides across the courtyard to where Saul sits on a bench. Saul's face is like wax melting in the sun. His eyes are focused on an unseen far country.

Abner stands directly before Saul and tries to seize his attention, "O King, the men from Ziph report that the outlaw David again hides in their land."

Saul shoots a flickering glance at Abner but quickly returns to staring at his far-off country. When he returned from his confrontation with David at En-gedi, Saul slipped ever deeper into a doleful pool. Now, since Samuel's death, he spends hours staring into the sky or at some invisible spot on the courtyard wall. He devotes more and more of his hours to sleep.

Fog hems me in. Fog as thick as wool. Murky, heavy. Voices from faraway; dream voices. Dark shadows move, far away, out there. In here I'm not afraid, not sad. I can rest. Let the fog fill my head, it stops the pounding. If I stay in here long enough, the pain may never find me.

Abner backs away and stands beside Jakeh. "What's happening to our King?"

Jakeh whispers. "The dark spirits, the ones David's music could drive away--they've returned and invaded. Now they possess him."

Abner shakes his head. "David, David. Somehow it always comes around to David. If only we could rid ourselves of him."

Jakeh protests, "But he helped the King once. Maybe he could still soothe him."

Abner shakes his head. "No, that possibility is long dead. I think David himself is the dark spirit. Saul believes David covets his kingship. I don't know if that's true. But now we face something even more serious than a battle over power. We're dealing with a matter of life and death. David must die if Saul is to live. I don't think the king sees that way but I believe it's true."

"So, what will we do?" Jakeh asks as he stares at the catatonic king.

Abner paces in the courtyard. "We know where David is hiding. We've got to capture him. Can we rouse Saul enough to travel? He still needs to lead or at least appear to lead. Can't you do something?"

Jakeh shrugs. "Me? I'm an old servant. Besides if God has sent these dark spirits, who are we to question His authority....?"

Abner's face twists and his eyes flare. He points to Saul frozen upon his bench. "Are you saying we abandon our King to this?"

Jakeh cringes and stammers, "No, I don't.... Listen, the king... Saul has always been most alive when he's moving—walking, running, riding. Maybe...maybe if you could get him out of this house, out into the field, get him to breathe, stretch, shout..."

Abner snorts. "We can get him out of this house. I've got enough men to do that. But getting him out of this black pit…" He shakes his head and then tosses up his arms. "Very well, we've got to do something. I'll get Medad and some of the others. We'll try to get him moving."

As Abner turns to leave, Jakeh says, "I will pray that Saul be healed."

Abner keeps walking toward the door. "Do what you can old man, do what you can. If we don't act soon that fox will escape again."

***

Saul rides alongside Abner at the head of a column of marching soldiers. Two days have passed since Jakeh made his suggestion. The king's face no longer droops and he sits tall in his saddle. His hair hangs limp and lifeless but at least it is clean. The flash of fire has not returned to his eyes, but at least his eyes are open and he is scanning the landscape in front of them. Nearly a year has passed since he and his men entered this same sterile territory only to be called back to face the Philistine threat.

The afternoon wearily slumps into evening and the troop enters a region of soft chalky barren hills. When they reach a small plain surrounded by low bluffs, Saul raises his hand and announces, "We will camp here for tonight."

Abner is gratified and hopeful. The king did not shout, but at least he did not mumble. He commanded and he sounded like Saul—a fatigued Saul—but at least like the man Abner still calls king. Abner organizes the camp with his customary efficiency. He pitches his tent alongside Saul's in the very center of the plain surrounded by the rest of the troops. The king and his commander gaze at the western horizon. A handful of purple clouds lie low on the horizon and melt the sun into a flaming lump of molten iron. As the light dies Saul quietly speaks, "Cousin, this assault is more your venture than mine."

"Yes, Saul, I know."

"I keep asking myself, why do I keep hunting David? How often I've tried and failed to kill him, or even capture him…. Abner, if he's God's anointed one, aren't we doomed to fail?"

Abner protests, "But YOU are God's anointed one. Samuel announced it at Mizpah and confirmed it at Gilgal. Saul, as long as David lives you're ensnared by a curse. If we can get rid of him, you'll be liberated from that curse."

"If only it were that easy." Saul sighs. "I'm entangled in more cords than those tossed out by David."

Abner does not respond. He's already said more than he meant to say. And what's more, he secretly agrees with Saul. Killing David will not resolve the king's plight. Still, the commander believes, or hopes, it will be a helpful first step.

Saul shuffles to his tent. "I am utterly drained. Place extra guards tonight. We've many more men than David and his band of outlaws, but we can never predict what he'll try."

"Of course. We'll be vigilant." Abner goes out to set the guard. Saul jams his long spear into the ground, collapses on his mat and within minutes is softly snoring.

Abner walks the perimeter of their camp and satisfies himself that the guards for the first watch are in place. As he picks his way through the sleeping soldiers toward his own tent, he fails to notice the silken, pale tendrils curling down the hillsides. Because he is nearly as weary as his king he does not see these slender white wisps coming together to form a low cloud. He crawls into his tent as the white blanket silently begins to roll over the camp. The guards see the cloud and think it is the evening mist. Before they realize otherwise, it's too late. They slump to the ground. Breathing slows in every tent, on every pallet. Every man in camp slides ever deeper into sleep. They dream they are gliding like eagles and have no fear. The soaring is everlastingly peaceful, and they are content.

Now, it is time to change the watch. The guards of the first watch lie snoring on the ground. Their replacements, the second shift guards, dream deeply on their pallets. The white fog has disappeared but it has accomplished its purpose silently and efficiently. The camp is a sheep lying on its back with its belly exposed. Two figures slither down the soft-sided hills. David and his aide Abishai weave their way around the slumbering troops and reach the center of the camp. In the pallid moonlight, David picks out the black goatskin tent of the King. The night air is sultry and the tent flaps are wide open. Stretched out on a pallet outside Saul's tent, David recognizes his former commander, Abner. David and Abishai step across his snoring form, stand at the entrance to the black tent and stare down at Saul. His hair fans around his head, his arms and legs stretch out beyond the sleeping pallet. Each exhaling breath ends in a fluttering whimper. Saul's spear stands vigil at his feet.

Abishai strains to keep his voice down to a whisper. "Here he is, our enemy! God has put him into our hand like a lamb ready for slaughter." He hefts his sword and steps into the tent. "Let me have the honors. One blow is all I need."

David extends his arm. "No. You won't kill him. Neither will I. Why should we risk it? He's still God's anointed. We don't need that guilt on our heads. Besides, when the time is right the Lord will strike him down, with God's own hand or He'll use the hand of an enemy in battle. No, let's do something more devious. I'll grab his spear. You take his water jug. Let's leave before this sleep from the Lord fades away."

The two men hurry past the dreaming soldiers and scramble back up into the hills. David makes his way to the highest peak overlooking Saul's camp. The moon has set. From his perch, he can see the first intimation of dawn. In the dark camp below the soporific effects of the white fog fades and the troops stretch and stir. David peers down into the darkness and shouts.

"Ho! Army of Saul! Ho! Army of Saul." He hears a faint muttering but no answer. He roars louder, "Abner, son Ner! Abner, son of Ner!"

Abner jolts up from his pallet as if bitten by a scorpion. He spins around in confusion and tries to disperse the fog from his head. Did he hear his name being called?

"Ho, Abner, son of Ner, are you afraid to answer?" The voice reverberates from high above. The still groggy soldiers gasp and even Abner feels a chill shiver. Could this be the Lord's heavenly angel?

Abner clears his throat and bellows into the darkness, "Who are you? Who calls me in the middle of the night?"

Once more the voice rings out from the sky. "Ha, Abner, you're truly muddled. The night is long past. Dawn will soon surprise you. Abner, aren't you the commander of Saul's army? Aren't you the great man of Israel? Aren't you in charge of the king's safety? Abner you're a failure."

Abner chokes at the heart in his throat. He spins, stumbles and peers into the king's tent. He grabs the tent pole in relief when he sees Saul stiffly rising from his pallet. He turns around as the voice pierces the silence.

"Abner, the king is still alive, no thanks to you. Where were your guards when I walked down the hills into your camp? Where were you when I walked up to the king's tent? If I was king, I'd have you executed. Look around you. Where's the king's water bottle? Where's his spear?"

Abner does not turn around to look. He dreads what he will see, or not see.

Saul comes out of his tent and stands alongside Abner. The two stare up into the darkness. The pre-dawn breeze begins to stir. Saul tugs his robe tight around his shoulders, then shouts into the sky with hollow sadness, "Is that you, my son David?"

Every soldier now stands staring toward the peak to the west. The voice echoes eerily across their camp.

"Yes, my lord and king. It is I. Why do we keep meeting like this? You hunt me down and I run like a rabbit. Have I committed a crime? Is there guilt on my hands?"

Abner hears the hint of arrogance in David's words, but Saul hears only the plaintive plea of his son-in-law.

"David, no. I'm in the wrong…again." Saul gulps as David continues.

"Saul, think about this. If the Lord God is the one who keeps goading you to capture me, I can make Him an offering to appease Him. Maybe then God will stop bothering you. But if some of your soldiers are stirring you up against me, let them be damned before God. They've driven me out of Israel and turned me into an outlaw against my will. They deserve to die."

Saul looks across his shoulder at his commander. Abner feels the cold steel of the king's gaze but continues to stare fixedly into the now graying sky. The battle-hardened soldier is not afraid of Saul. Their destinies are like two grape vines grown up side by side: Intertwined and interlaced by battles fought, orders given and received, quarrels and compromises, promises and pledges. He does not fear Saul. He and Saul will live and most likely die together. Nonetheless, this morning Abner is afraid. He fears that what Saul said last night is true. Pursuing David is futile. God has switched allegiances. Last night's heavy sleep… It felled them all—clearly God's doing. God has surely turned against Saul and must also have turned against his commander.

High above them all the sky lightens. The entire company can now see the dim outline of David. He shouts down to them.

"I'm a single flea, one lonely partridge in the mountains. Just forget about me."

Saul shakes his head. "Forget? That's impossible. David, I've been a fool. I give up. You can come back home and I promise you'll be safe."

Abner hears these words, spins and stalks back into his tent. How many times in the past decade have Saul's sincere promises gone up in flames, torched by Saul's fiery rages? Too many dark spirits pummel the King. He is no longer the ruler of himself.

Now everyone in camp sees the crisp silhouette of David against the dawn. His arm is raised.

"O King, send one of your young men up here to fetch your spear. I didn't take your life and I won't keep your weapon. Your life was precious in my sight and I pray that my life will be precious in God's sight. Hurry now and send up your man."

Saul's young soldier scrambles up the steep slope to salvage the spear. Saul watches him climb toward David. Now the sun strikes the peak and glints off David's breastplate. The line of light flows down the slope until Saul too feels its warmth. The young man reaches the summit, he bows and takes the spear from David and begins his descent. One last time Saul shouts into the clear morning.

"David, my son, God has blessed you. You will succeed." David waves once then slips over the summit and Saul never sees him again.

Chapter Thirty-two

A dozen barking curs and a covey of little boys welcome Saul and his army back from Hachilah. Gone are the cheering crowds and smiles that once graced their homecomings. The men march glumly up the hill in the heat of the afternoon. Word of the failed mission reached Gibeah earlier in the day. Inside their homes, soldiers embrace wives and children. Everyone is quietly grateful; no battles were fought and no lives lost. But no one dares celebrate this publicly. The entire village knows how David's past escapes tormented the king and no one wants to the target of his searing fury.

Surrounded by his four guards Saul trudges home. Ahinoam greets him at the courtyard entrance. Silently she pulls him inside and closes the wooden door. She grips both of his arms and probes his eyes searching for a vestige of the man she once knew. After a few seconds, beneath a layer of sadness and fatigue, she detects a glimmer. She leans back and sees a wry smile on Saul's face. She throws her arms around him with a sob.

"I don't know how long I can do this. This endless hunt…It torments you and when you ride off I'm left in agony." She shudders against his chest and he wraps his long arms around her.

"I know, I know." He strokes her hair with a sigh. "I'm sorry, so sorry."

She's not heard those words from his mouth for many months. She is grateful but puzzled. "Saul, I miss you," she murmurs as they walk together to the bench against the wall. He drops with an exhausted thud.

Days earlier, when Abner and his men carried Saul out of his bed and set him onto his horse, she feared she'd never see her husband alive again. Secretly she believed that some part of his spirit had already departed. Yet now here he sits beside her, more vital than when he left. His voice and eyes tell her he is fully at home, totally present in this moment, in this place. He's physically drained, she can clearly see that. But she senses something else. During the days and weeks when he was unreachable his muscles were knotted and stretched like old leather thongs. Now his entire frame seems to have unclenched.

She holds onto his hand and compelled as much by curiosity as love she asks, "What's changed? You're different. Wasn't this just another failed hunt?"

Saul closes his eyes and shakes his head as Jakeh approaches with a cup and a jug.

"Welcome home, O King. Here is cool water, just drawn from the well." He hands the cup to Saul and pours it full. Saul drains it in one long draught and lowers it with a satisfied 'ahhh'. He hands the cup back to Jakeh, and says, "It's over."

"Sir?" Jakeh is puzzled.

"Ah sorry, Jakeh. I'm answering Ahinoam's question. No, this wasn't just another failed hunt. It was the last hunt. It's over. Whatever happens to David is now in God's hands." He recounts the events of his strange nighttime encounter with David.

"Everyone—every soldier, all the watchmen, even Abner—they all slept as though drunk while David marched boldly into our camp. I've no doubt. This overpowering sleep came from God's hand. Who can fight God?"

Jakeh dares to ask, "And what of David?"

Again, Saul shakes his head and opens his hands. "Who knows? I told him he could return here to Gibeah, but he doesn't trust me. Can't blame him."

Ahinoam can hear the new tone in Saul's voice, a tone unscorched by rage. She dares think of her daughter Michal who grieves for her husband and her son Jonathan who laments his lost friend. "So, do you trust David? Do you believe him when he pledges loyalty to you?"

Saul replies, "What difference does my trusting or not trusting make? He's gone. He's out there somewhere. God alone knows what he'll do. All I know is that my hunt for him is finished.

Ahinoam wants to shout, 'Thanks be to God!' But she bites her tongue. "Enough talk for now. Jakeh, go prepare the bath. I'll see to dinner." Her step is lighter. She does not yet realize that Saul's rage has not vanished like smoke. It may have burned out but its molten core has congealed into a misshapen stone pressing upon his heart. Jakeh shuffles off thinking about the candle and the moth and wonders if the candle can ever move far enough away to save the desperate moth.

***

Only six times up and down the field and already my shoulders ache. Already I have a blister on my hand. Once I could plow all day. Once, before I became king….

Saul grips the oaken handles of the plow as the oxen plod across the south facing hillside. He is glad to be doing what he once did so well. In the weeks since his return from Hacilah he has been haunted by hollowness. Like a child on the day after a great festival, he surveys his world and is disturbed by its drab ordinariness. This morning, in one of those gossamer moments between dreaming and waking, it came to him. What was missing was his compulsion to destroy David. On those days when he'd been bursting with zeal, that compulsion throbbed with white heat at the center of his thoughts. And when his energy ebbed, even then the hunt for David dwelt at the center of his brooding. Without that compulsion, each day meanders meaninglessly from sunrise to sunset. This morning he resolved to direct his restless energy to the fields.

The sky is cloudless but a pale white sheen stretches across the firmament. The late rains will soon be here. Best to have the soil laid open, ready to drink up each precious drop of moisture. Saul stops the oxen at the west end of the field and picks up the clay water jug he'd set in the shadow of the thorn tree. The cool water sluices down his parched throat.

Ahhh! No drink sweeter than fresh water, even for a king. King...what has being the king of Israel given me? Soft hands and a hard heart; my own children despise me by day, the children of the enemy haunt me at night---these are my rewards as leader. In the beginning the clan laughed that I could be king. Now somewhere above this firmament God laughs too. I'm sure he's numbered my days. No escape from that. But I'll be king until that day comes. I'll do what I must do. Today...Today, at least I can finish plowing this field.

The King of Israel steps back out into the sun, grabs the plow handles, signals the oxen and begins scratching another furrow across the field.

That evening Saul stands outside the doorway and jokes with the guards and pounds the dust off his tunic. "Look at these nasty blisters! Your king can at least still command the oxen and direct the plow." He steps inside the courtyard and the chuckle dies in his throat.

"Ahinoam, what's wrong?" His wife sits on cushions near his bedroom and tears trickle down her cheeks. He kneels and wraps his arm around her. She leans into him and for a moment is silent. Then she sighs and murmurs, "I knew it would happen. It's Michal. She left. She went to be with David."

Saul tightens his grip and rocks with her. "When did she go?"

"This morning, as soon as you left the house, she came and said goodbye. Jonathan sent three soldiers with her. She told me…She said to tell you she was sorry."

Saul releases his hold and sits cross-legged beside Ahinoam.

"Sorry? I'm the one who should be sorry. I made the offer of marriage, I named the bride price. It was all my scheming."

Ahinoam wipes her tears with the back of her hand, "Are you forgetting that it was Michal who loved David before all of your scheming? You tried to take advantage of that love but you didn't produce it. This isn't totally your fault."

"Ah wife, I don't deserve your kindness. Michal is lost to us and I'm to blame for that. She's left to be with her husband, that much is as it should be. How she'll find him…I don't know."

Ahinoam pats his hand. "I wouldn't worry about that. They will find each other soon enough. She's as stubborn as her father."

Saul smiles. "And as beautiful as her mother." He rises with a grunt and moves toward the bath. He stops halfway across the room. "If I thought it'd do any good, I'd pray that her life with David be calmer than ours has been."

Ahinoam does pray but she too shares her husband's doubts.

***

Abner's news is as gloomy as the sky. He sits beside Saul on a bench under the awning of the king's house. It is the eleventh month, the month of rains, and the sky is a furrowed field of mud brown clouds from horizon to horizon. The rain began again during the night and has continued into the afternoon.

"Could this be true?" Saul is wrapped in a gray robe and stares out into the rain.

"Well, it comes from a Moabite traveler." Abner shifts on the bench. "Moab is no friend of Israel, but why would this man lie?"

Saul snaps back, "Because we're the enemies? Because they hate us? I don't know. But I can't imagine the Philistines moving troops in this weather." A swirl of wind tosses a spray of raindrops into their shelter. He's in no mood to muster his forces in this dark, dour month. The rain comes down now in sheets and his chest tightens against the cold.

"The traveler thought he heard the Philistines were heading far to the north. Maybe the rain isn't falling there." Abner sounds unconvinced of his own words.

"Well, it's raining here and I won't drag my men out and march them north until I've heard from someone besides a treacherous Moabite."

Abner stands. "Of course. I'll send out two men today." He lowers his head and steps into the pelting rain.

Saul shouts to his retreating back. "Wait until the morning. Maybe the rain will slacken." He stands and moves inside. Even the inner walls of the house are damp from the persistent rain. He knows he should be thankful for the moisture. The trees, plants and fields all rejoice. The farmers and the shepherds live in harmony with the pulse of the seasons—ploughing, planting, raining, growing and harvesting. They have a comforting rhythm to their lives and they accept each day as it comes. But kings mark their time by a different calendar—marching, warring, disputing, and sometimes, rarely, reconciling. Their time lurches, jerks, stalls, then races.

Another windy squall races across the hillside and rain drums against the roof. The cold seeps deeper into Saul's bones than it once did. He tugs his cloak tighter around his aching shoulders. *Philistines, cursed Philistines…they've infected every day of my rule. Could they truly be on the move again?*

***

Ahinoam walks in the glorious light of the new day. Every blade of grass, every leaf on every tree shimmers, washed clean by last week's rain. Clouds like white washed clumps of wool dot the brilliant morning sky. Amidst this paradise stand the almond trees. Delicate pink and white five-petaled blossoms cluster star-like on every branch. As she walks through the trees she hears the busy hum of the bees searching for nectar. These past months she has tried to reclaim a bit of Saul for herself. From the beginning their marriage had been marked by sharing unlike most couples in the village. He gave her respect and listened to her thoughts, unlike many of the iron fisted men around them. But once he'd been seized by God to be king, his time for her was scant and his sharing was meager. Then, when his hatred for David consumed him, he was inaccessible to everyone.

But these past few weeks, since he's given up his pursuit of David, Saul has spent time with her: talking, laughing and simply walking. Last night they'd agreed on a morning walk through the orchard. She is beginning to wonder if he's forgotten when she sees him striding down the hillside.

"Good morning, master Saul," she teases. "Did you oversleep again?"

His grin is small and stiff. "No, queen of the land. I was meeting with Abner."

"Ah, and by your look, the meeting wasn't pleasant."

Saul takes her hand and they walk under the canopy of pink. "No, I'm afraid not. The spies Abner sent out returned last night. Their news isn't good."

"The Philistines?"

"Who else! These pagans will never rest until they rule our entire land."

Ahinoam can already feel the coiling tension in Saul's hand. "Are they already marching?"

"Some have already arrived. In the north this time. More of them are pouring in. They threaten to swallow the lands belonging to the tribes of Manasseh and Issachar, near Mt. Gilboa. Will this never end?"

Ahinoam pulls down a branch and smells the gleaming flowers. "I suppose as long as there are Philistines there will be war."

Saul shakes his head. "I think as long as there is Israel there will be wars against us. Today it's the Philistines. Tomorrow…Who can say? It seems as though I'm doomed to spend the rest of my life in battle."

They reach the bottom of the orchard and they walk along its bottom edge.

"So, how soon will you leave?"

"Abner is organizing the troops already and sending out messages to all the villages. We'll march out tomorrow. Who can say when, or if, we'll return."

Ahinoam protests, "Don't talk like that. We're God's chosen people and you're their king. The Philistines can't win."

Saul starts climbing back up the hill and Ahinoam follows. He speaks over his shoulder to her. "Even the great warriors of our ancestors sometimes lost battles. Who can say what will happen? And what if the Lord God himself has planned our destruction?"

Ahinoam tries to drown such thinking, her own as well as his, with more immediate plans. "Since you leave tomorrow, we'll have a feast tonight. We'll gather the children and grandchildren. I'll go now and start the preparations." She charges up the hill oblivious to the serene, beautiful almond blossoms.

***

Saul sits on the carpet at the head of the low table. All night he's been served the finest meats and cakes. Twelve years ago, in Ramah on the evening he first met Samuel there'd been a feast like this. On that night too, he'd been served the best. Everyone deferred to him. Back then he'd been bemused but hadn't let that spoil his enjoyment of the evening. Tonight, he is conflicted.

How blessed to be loved by a family. To eat and drink and laugh together. Yet--this feels like a farewell meal. My eyes delight in the food but my stomach rebels. And I can't help noticing the absent ones, the ones I've driven away.

Saul's jaw drops in shock. The room hushes as Jonathan walks through the door. Saul stands and Jonathan comes directly to him, embraces him and kisses him on each cheek. He puts his mouth next to Saul's ear and whispers, "David has joined the Philistines."

Saul steps back in shock. He blurts out, "What? How…how do you know this?"

Now Jonathan addresses the entire household. "David has sided with the enemy." Gasps and cries fill the room. Jonathan continues. "One of our spies came this afternoon from Judah. King Achish of Gath has given David and his people the town of Ziglag as their own."

Saul repeats in disbelief, "The son of Jesse now fights alongside the Philistines? Jonathan, do you believe this?"

Jonathan taps his head with a fist, "I have to believe it with my mind." He thumps his chest, "But I can't accept it with my heart. I can't imagine David as a traitor." He stares at his father and declares, "Whether true or not, tomorrow I march north with you to fight the Philistines."

Jonathan sits with Saul as they finish the meal. Conversations have lost their thread and laughter has disappeared. The children are taken off to bed. The dread of what might lie ahead drives everyone home early.

***

Saul stands in front of the towering door. He senses it behind his back, a looming beast preparing to crush him. Before him stand his troops. Their huge eyes glow red with blood lust. The ranks stretch out to the horizon, a horde of crazed men. Behind him, on the other side of the door a horrific cacophony erupts. The shrieks of Amalekite women and the pitiful wails of their children fill the air. The ear-piercing cries grow ever louder and shriller. He clamps his hands over his ears but the sounds invade his head and claw viciously at his brain.

Abruptly the door swings open and the soldiers swarm in, voracious ants attacking a piece of rotten fruit. Now Saul is staring into the city and sees the terror-stricken faces of the mothers and the desperate wailing children. He sweeps his eyes across this bloody panorama. No! O God no! What a hideous mistake. Ahinoam stands in front of the first house clutching their youngest grandson. Her eyes are white with panic. Her mouth moves but he cannot hear her over the roar of the troops. She extends an arm toward him. She beseeches him to stop the swords and spears. Saul opens his mouth, tries to order his troops to halt but his tongue is a lump of lead. He cannot lift it. He manages only feeble grunts. He strains to run toward her but his legs are knee deep in mire. He cries now in frustration, and watches helplessly as a burly soldier reaches his wife. One of his own men, one of his soldiers, roars like a crazed beast, raises his sword, slashes down on her skull and her beautiful face splits in two.

The blow fractures the spell, frees his tongue and Saul shrieks, "No, no, no!" and twists up out of bed. He thuds to the floor like a downed tree. He lies there gasping as Ahinoam rushes in and kneels beside him. His eyes are frantic. He is an animal caught in the snare of his past.

"Saul, what's wrong? Are you sick?"

His panicked eyes finally focus and he pulls her onto his chest and whimpers.

"I couldn't save you. I couldn't save you. I'm sorry, so sorry."

Ahinoam sits up and pulls at him. "Shh. Enough of that. I'm right here. I don't need saving. It was just a dream. You were only dreaming."

Saul sits up and moans. "Dreaming, dreaming. Another damned tormenting dream. Will they never end?" She has no answers so she ignores his question and tugs him up.

"Let's get you back into bed. You'll need all your strength for tomorrow." Like an obedient child, he allows his wife to tuck him in. She covers him with a blanket and strokes his broad forehead. Once it had been smooth but the years and the battles have carved deep creases across it. Once his sleep was deep and refreshing. Now it is crowded with fragments of fear, shards of piercing memories, and only scattered bits of rest. At last she returns to her bed and Saul desperately hunts for a few fleeting moments of sleep.

Chapter Thirty-three

Saul leads the soldiers down the long slope out of Gibeah. Droplets of mist cling to his beard. Above, the sky is a filmy blue but a thin fog drifts like smoke nearer to the ground. The king sets a steady pace but does not push the troops. They must travel over sixty miles to reach Mt. Gilboa and face the enemy. If they are to have any chance for victory they will need strength to fight.

Saul looks down at Jakeh riding a donkey beside him. Saul had pleaded with him and promised him a mount and finally he agreed to join. Unbeknownst to Saul, it was Ahinoam's pleas that finally convinced Jakeh to travel with her troubled husband.

Saul asks, "Remember this trail, old friend?"

"I'm old but my memory still clutches a few things: Looking for runaway donkeys, Samuel the rusty-voiced prophet…I remember you coming out of the gates of Ramah looking like you'd just met a specter from Sheol."

"Now that troublesome man's spirit rests in Sheol and I'm still stuck with the yoke he laid upon me." They ride in silence as the last wreaths of mist dissolve in the warming sun. When they reach a fork, Saul takes the road to the right.

"We'll leave Ramah for the ghosts. This trail leads north to Michmash."

Michmash. How my head throbbed that morning when I met that despicable priest. Then the earthquake and the battle. I remember only bits and pieces of the chaos. But that night on the hilltop—the hissing fire, the shadows flitting in the trees, my sword poised and trembling above my head, and Jonathan, my son kneeling in the dirt, staring into my eyes—that cursed night is engraved, every detail, into my mind. I would have killed him. Yet here he is, still riding with me. Ai, a blessing I don't deserve.

Throughout the morning they march northward. At every village men join the ranks and Saul's army grows. They reach the rocky plateau of Michmash by mid-afternoon. They drop down into the wadi and march through the pass. They continue north but as they travel past road running east to the Jordan River and Gilgal, Saul allows his thoughts to follow that trail.

Gilgal, the circle of stones, Israel's beginning. A beautiful site. But Samuel— his words, his face—they blight my memory of that holy place. There I was praised, then cursed. Raised up only to be torn down. Acclaimed then damned. Is it any wonder that all my dreams turn to nightmares?

At the end of the second day's march, they stop five miles south of Mt. Gilboa. Saul's guards set up his tent in the center of the camp. Saul lowers himself onto the rug in front of his tent and invites his armor bearer to sit. The king points eastward.

"Medad, do you know what lies a half day's march in that direction?"

The young man shrugs.

"Jabesh-Gilead. Remember? Our first battle?"

Medad grins. "Ahh, the day I became a man."

Saul returns his grin and asks, "So, you think it's war that makes us men?"

Medad shakes his head. "No, not war. Well, maybe some men think so. But I'm not talking about the battle. Jabesh-Gilead was where you gave me a mission, an important assignment. Remember, you sent me with a message to the city?

"I remember you were eager to go, but your eyes were full of fear."

"I was a boy when I left your camp, but the next day when the battle ended, when you praised me in front of the troops, I felt like a man."

Saul claps Medad on the shoulder. "You've done well. I'm grateful for your work. And if its led you to discovering who you are, then I'm glad."

The camp settles down for the night and Saul lies in his tent, listening to Jakeh snoring. He ponders the conversation with Medad. *I wonder, when I was a young man, how many times did I get recognition and praise for doing important work? Did it matter then? Does it matter now?*

The next morning, once the troops are on the march, Saul takes Abner and Jonathan and rides ahead. He wants to climb Mt. Gilboa and investigate the strength of the enemy forces.

They pick their way up the slopes. Purple irises bloom on every side and soon they are riding through a carpet of flowers. Abner, whose spirit lightens as the day of battle draws near, speaks in mock seriousness to his cousin, "The sea people, the Phoenicians, say that purple is the royal color. So here you are. A purple carpet for the King of Israel."

Jonathan laughs and teases, "What do you know of the sea people? I'll bet you've never even smelled the sea air much less seen the great sea."

Abner chuckles. "No need to see or smell the sea to know something about it. A traveler from Sidon passed through my village and offered to sell me some purple cloth. He's the one who told me."

Jonathan can't resist. "I'd guess that if his cloth had been red, then red would've been the royal color." Both men laugh. Saul rides on ahead in doleful silence. If he hears the lighthearted teasing, he shows no sign of it. He spent his night stumbling in and out of sleep. He so deathly feared the nightmares that whenever he felt himself sliding into deep slumber he scrambled back up and forced himself awake. This morning his head pounds and his heart lies like a stone in his chest. They tie their horses to one of the scattered shrubs and scramble up the last scree slope. They reach the summit of the mountain gaze north and westward into the Jezreel valley. Abner and Jonathan stand dumbfounded. Saul groans, staggers to a boulder and slumps down.

Their eyes are struck first by a band of white fire stretching across the valley. Rank after rank, hundreds and hundreds of Philistine chariots glint in the morning sun. To the north of this fiery band, on the other side of the valley, below the city of Shunem lies the Philistine camp. Even from this distance the three men gasp at its vastness. Thousands of tents stand in orderly rows, shields wink, reflecting the sun's rays, and the tiny men swarm like ants across the plain and hillside.

Saul doubles over and grunts as though he's been punched in the stomach. Jonathan and Abner run to him.

"Father, what is it?"

Saul pants, "my chest, my breath…" He gasps unable to say more. His face is ghostly pale. They take off his breastplate and lay him down on a level spot. Gradually his panting slows and color returns to his face. When he tries to sit up the two men each grab a shoulder and set him upon a boulder.

Saul murmurs, "Such a weight. It as though that entire army was camping on my chest." Jonathan holds out his water jar. Saul sips and stares out over the valley. "Has the Lord led us here only to be slaughtered?"

Jonathan refills the cup and tries to reassure his father. "The Lord has done great things in this valley. The stories of our people, don't you remember? Right here, in this very place, Gideon defeated the entire Midianite army with three hundred men. Only three hundred! And Deborah and Barak. Remember them? They defeated Sisera and the Canaanite army in this valley. You are the king of Israel and the Lord God gives victory to his people in the Valley of Jezreel."

Saul does not respond. He knows the stories but they do not comfort him.

Abner lays his hand on Saul's shoulder. "Can you walk? We need to return to the troops, set up our camp."

Saul nods, stands and they slowly descend to their horses. As they pick their way down the slope, Jonathan quietly asks Abner, "How do you see our chances?"

Abner's jaw is clenched and he growls, "I don't calculate chances. We fight with what we have, simple as that."

By late afternoon the rest of the troops have arrived and are setting up camp on the northern slopes of Mt. Gilboa, overlooking the Jezreel valley. Color has returned to Saul's face and he feels no pain, but he sits slumped over and his shoulders sag. He and Jakeh sit in front of the royal tent. Below and around them men are raising tents and sharpening weapons. Saul stares beyond them across the green valley toward the Philistine camp. He sighs and turns to Jakeh.

"I shouldn't have asked you to come with me."

"Why is that, O King?"

"I've brought you into great danger. I'm afraid this might be my last battle. This morning when I saw the Philistine army, my heart almost stopped beating."

"Jonathan told me. Maybe it was the climb. You went too fast, you'd not eaten…"

"No, Jakeh. It was fear, I know it was."

"But Saul, this is the valley of Jezreel where the Lord does great things for our people. Remember Deborah and Gideon and…"

Saul raises his palm in irritation. "Enough. I've heard all those stories since I was a child. Besides, Jonathan already refreshed my memory this morning. But he left out some details. The Lord God himself gave a message to Deborah about the battle. And Gideon? A prophet and then the Lord's angel came and spoke to Gideon. Whenever Gideon had doubts God reassured him with sign after sign after sign." Saul throws out his hands. "What do I have? Nothing. The Lord God has been so silent for so long. If only I had a whisper, one word, one sign…"

The two men sit silently amidst the bustle of the troops. At last Jakeh clears his throat. "O King, maybe it is time to ask?"

A smirk covers Saul's face. "Ask? For what?"

"For a word, a sign. Maybe the Lord is waiting for you to ask."

Saul snorts. "Do you know how often I've asked? Over and over, for twelve years. I've given up asking. The door is always shut."

Jakeh nodded. "Maybe the door is shut now. But God is still God and can open that door if He chooses."

"What are you proposing?"

"Beth-Haggan is just south of here. I've been told a prophet lives there. His name is Shuham. You could ask him for a word from the Lord."

Saul sadly grins and shakes his head. "Ai, old man. Haven't we done this before? You and I hunting down a prophet in a strange town?"

Jakeh shrugs and smiles. Saul turns to enter his tent. "Make sure your donkey is ready tomorrow at sunrise. We'll hunt down this prophet."

***

Saul and Jakeh arrive by midmorning in the quiet village of Beth-Haggan. Shuham the prophet sits on a stool in the shade of a mustard tree near the city wall. His robe is tattered and smudged and his left eye is glassy white. He is to Samuel the prophet as Jakeh's donkey is to Saul's proud stallion.

Saul tries to suppress the disdain in his voice as he and Jakeh approach the disheveled seer. "Sir, we've come to inquire of the Lord."

The prophet turns his head to look at Saul with his good eye. "Welcome King Saul to our humble town. What is it that you seek?" His voice wavers as though he lacks air in his lungs.

Saul is still the tallest man in the land so the king is not impressed that this weak-voiced man recognizes him. He takes a deep breath, bows, and continues. "Thank you prophet for your welcome. Soon

I'll lead Israel's army against the Philistines. Will you ask the Lord… ask Him if He will give us victory?"

Shuham's ghostly eye stares straight ahead while his right eye shifts back and forth between Saul and Jakeh. Eventually he closes both eyes and begins to mumble. After five minutes, still with his eyes closed, he moves a few steps away, drops to his knees and raises his arms and head to the sky. The two men can hear his wavering voice but cannot discern the words. Another five minutes pass. Shuham abruptly stops speaking and then fumbles his way back to his stool. He sits and tries in vain to brush the fresh smudges from his robe.

He turns his head from Saul to Jakeh, then back to Saul. Fear adds another tremor to his voice. "O King, I am sorry, but I hear no word of the Lord for you today. Maybe if you return tomorrow…"

Saul barked, "Tomorrow? I don't have time to ride back here tomorrow. This is not…"

Jakeh quietly touches the king's arm and interrupts Saul's rant. "Excuse me. Is there a priest who carries the ephod in this town?"

Shuham is relieved that he can give out some information that takes attention away from himself. He speaks in his watery voice.

"Yes, yes indeed. He lives down this street. Come, I'll take you there." He leads them to a small house near the center of the village. A young woman greets them at the door and invites them to enter.

Saul stoops to enter the doorway and he and Jakeh stand inside the dusky house of the priest. A young man enters from a back room, wearing the linen ephod with its jewels and pouches. Saul feels his gut tighten as he recalls his calamitous encounter with the priest at Michmash. *Why am I wasting my time here? Look at him. So young, probably Jonathan's age.*

He is tempted to do an about face and march back out into the sunlit plaza. But before he can move, Jakeh intervenes.

"The King of Israel has come to seek an answer from the Lord."

The young priest bows ceremoniously. "I am honored to be of service. Please sit with me." All three of them lower themselves and sit cross-legged on the carpet.

"What is the question you wish to place before the Lord?"

Saul repeats his query. "Soon I will lead Israel's army against the Philistines. Will the Lord give us victory?"

The priest drops his chin to his chest, then slowly draws the two stones, the urim and thummim, from the pocket on his ephod. He clasps them in both hands and prays quietly. Then he quickly stands, drops the stones into the pouch and raises both arms as though pleading to the heavens. Suddenly he drops his arms, shakes his head, draws both stones out of the pouch and holds them up once again. After a minute of praying he drops the stones back into the pouch, raises his arms to plead to the heavens. Slowly his arms droop. He looks down at the men seated before him. His voice is somber.

"The Lord has no answer for you."

Without volition, a pleading whine seeps into Saul's voice. "But, but the stones…one is yes, and one is no. Isn't it a simple…."

"Simple? No." The young priest's voice hardens. "I am a servant of the high God. If the Lord has no desire to answer, the stones must not be used. I cannot force the Lord to speak." He turns and leaves the room. Saul scrambles to his feet and helps Jakeh to rise. They blink as they walk back out into the sunlight.

"What do you say now, old man?"

Jakeh shrugs, "No one can force the Lord to speak. That's true."

Saul responds with sour sarcasm. "So, what's left to me? How else does the Lord reach out to his people? Oh, of course—dreams. I've had more than my share of those. Dark, vile nightmares. If those are God's messages…" He disgustedly spits into the dust. "Silence. That is what I get…except of course when Samuel lived. He always claimed to have the Lord's words for me…" Saul trails off into silence.

They lead their mounts toward the city gate. When they reach it, Saul stops abruptly and turns toward the servant. "Jakeh, how did you know there was a prophet here?"

Jakeh drops his head and murmurs, "We elders, we have our ways of staying connected."

"Jakeh, look at me." The servant looks up into Saul's dark eyes. He sees forlorn desperation. Saul quietly asks, "Do you know where I can find a medium?"

Jakeh's eyes take on a panicked animal look. He vigorously shakes his head. Saul persists.

"A medium, Jakeh, one who can communicate with the dead."

"No, no, no." The servant is near panic. Saul puts his hands on Jakeh's shoulders.

"Calm down. I know what the law says and I haven't forgotten my own decree. But I know they're still out there. I'm not asking you as your king. I'm asking as your friend. Can you tell me where to find a medium? Please, I don't intend to harm anyone."

Jakeh cannot escape Saul's grip, nor his plea. He takes a deep breath and wheezes, "They say there's a medium in Endor." He quickly adds, "But I don't know her name. I don't know where she lives. You can't simply walk in and look for her. She'll be in hiding."

Saul nods. "Of course. But Endor is nearby, only five miles away. Someone in this village…maybe that shabby prophet can lead us to her."

Saul and Jakeh return to the house of the prophet and call for him. Shuham steps into the doorway and trembles in terror when he sees them. Saul lets the old servant go ahead to speak to the frightened man. After several minutes of intense conversation, Jakeh waves for Saul to approach.

"Shuham has heard of this medium in Endor." As Jakeh speaks, the prophet shuffles his sandals nervously in the dust. "He can lead us to her but he fears she'll recognize you and run away."

"Ahh. Prophet, you are right. Might you have any used robes that I could use for a disguise?" Shuham grins at Saul's words and scurries off to his house. He returns within minutes with a bundle of ragged linen garments. Saul holds them up. Some are so thin from washing the sun shines through them.

"Yes, these will do. Thank you. Let's be on our way. Jakeh, you will ride your donkey. Prophet, I will leave my horse with your family. The two of us will walk to Endor."

The sun slides toward the horizon and their shadows grow long and thin against the eastern hills. By the time they reach the outskirts of Endor, the curtain of night has dropped. They step off the trail and into the shadows of the trees. Shuham and Jakeh arrange the threadbare robes over Saul's head and shoulders. They search the ground around the trees and find a stout stick to serve as a cane. Saul lowers his head and curves his long back. Though he is still as tall as Jakeh, they all hope the darkness will keep him unnoticed. He and Jakeh shamble down the road, following Shuham along the mostly empty serpentine streets. The prophet moves confidently and does not hesitate at any of the crossroads.

At last they come to a small shack, huddling like a whipped dog against the outer walls of Endor. Silently Shuham points to the building and steps back along with Jakeh opposite the shack's doorway. Saul creeps forward alone. The sagging, thin door stands open and the lintel is so low he must nearly double over to enter. The room is bare, save for a low stool next to a tiny table and a sleeping pallet in the corner.

A woman sits on the floor in the corner with a flickering oil lamp on the floor beside her. Saul was expecting a crone but this woman is middle aged, with long dark hair cascading down her back. Her face shines as though it has been rubbed with oil. She looks up at the hunched giant standing against the dark doorway. She gives no sign that she is surprised or frightened. Her voice flows, low and calm, from deep in her bosom.

"Who are you and what can I do for you?"

Saul keeps his head low and speaks softly, barely above a whisper. "I want you to reach out to a certain spirit in Sheol and bring him up for me."

The medium speaks quickly with a response she's clearly given before. "I'm sure you know that King Saul has banished all mediums and wizards from the land. Why are you asking me to do something that endangers my own life?"

Saul takes a step closer to her and raises his volume as he speaks, "As the Lord lives, I swear you will not be punished for doing this." He opens his hand to reveal a gold coin. "And you will be well rewarded."

The woman stares intently at the hooded figure. Saul feels a trickle of sweat rolling down his neck. After a long moment, she gives a small nod. She moves slowly and methodically, every movement a ceremony. She grasps the oil lamp and places it directly in front of her. From beneath her sleeping mat she draws out two candles, lights them and sets them on either side of the lamp.

Saul is transfixed and edges the hood over his head back just far enough to watch her actions. The medium reaches behind her and pulls out a bundle of herbs. She holds the bundle over the left candle and then the right candle while slowly chanting under her breath. Wispy gray smoke begins to waft upward. She closes her eyes and breathes deeply once, twice, three times. With her eyes still closed she asks in a voice that has gotten even lower, "Whom shall I bring up for you?"

Saul's throat is tight. "Bring up for me Samuel the prophet."

At the desperation in his voice and the mention of Samuel, the woman's eyes fly open. Shocked, Saul jerks back and his hood slips off, revealing his flashing eyes and anxious face.

The medium screams and scuttles across the floor until her back is against the wall. "You're Saul, you're the king. Why have you tricked me? Don't kill me!"

The screams summon Jakeh and Shuham and draw them into the room. When they appear, the medium redoubles her screaming.

Saul commands, "Get out, both of you. I'll handle this." With his eyes fixed on the hysterical woman, he slowly kneels in the middle of the room. He lowers his tone and speaks as calmly as own pounding heart will allow.

"Shhhh. Don't be afraid, please. It's all right. I tell you it's all right. No harm will come upon you. I'm the king. I will not hurt you. You have my word. Please continue. I beg you to go on."

The medium's unblinking eyes lock on Saul's face. She stops gasping and her breathing slows. Her terror subsides and she weakly moves away from the wall and returns to her place before the lamp and candles. She grasps the smoking herbs with trembling hands, closes her eyes and begins her chanting and deep respiration. Suddenly she gasps and stiffens.

"What? What do you see?" Saul whispers harshly.

She begins to shiver and her eyes flutter beneath her eyelids. "I see a..I see a divine being coming out of the ground."

"What does he look like? What's his appearance?" Saul himself begins to shake.

The smoke from the herbs thickens and swirls above the medium. "He's very old, ancient. And he's wrapped in a gray robe."

"Ai, it must be Samuel, it has to be Samuel." Saul closes his eyes and drops his head onto the room's dirt floor. His chest is full of thudding hammers.

He hears a voice, muffled as though spoken through a thick curtain, but with an unmistakable raspy growl. "Why have you disturbed me and dragged me up out of Sheol?"

"O Samuel, I'm in dreadful torment. The Philistines have mounted a horde, a monstrous army against me and God has turned away from me." Saul keeps his face in the dirt but pounds his fists on the floor in front of him. He tries unsuccessfully to keep the tears out of his voice.

"I've tried everything to get some word from Him. But nothing has worked. So I thought maybe…. maybe God has talked to you, like before. Maybe you could tell me what to do."

There is a long silence and Saul wonders if Samuel's spirit has left. Then a low murmur begins and grows into an unnerving rumble that rattles the little room. Saul hears Samuel thunder in his ears.

"The Lord has rejected you. Why come crawling to me? Don't you know I'm on the Lord's side? You don't need any new words. I already told you everything when I was alive." Saul presses his palms against his ears but Samuel's rumbling words drum into his head.

"You showed mercy on the king of the Amalekites when God ordered you to kill him. You mishandled your assignment as leader of the army. God is ripping the kingdom from your hands and giving it to David. And as for tomorrow's battle, it will be the last one for you, for your sons and the whole army. Tomorrow I will welcome all of you to Sheol."

Saul shrieks once, tries to rise and then faints. He pitches heavily forward onto the floor, knocking over the candles. The robes and garments of his disguise litter the room. The horrified medium stares at him. *What will happen to me if the king of Israel dies here in my house?* Desperation gives birth to courage. She reaches out, grabs his arm and shakes him.

"O King, please wake up. I listened to you. I did what you asked. I risked my life for you. Please listen to me, please." She tugs him into a sitting position. "Here's some bread that I baked. Please eat it and get enough strength to be on your way. Please. You can't stay here."

Saul sits slumped forward, head and eyelids drooping. "No, I won't eat. Why should I bother eating?" His body sways weakly, threatening to topple over.

The medium shouts, "Men of the king, help me." The two men bolt in and kneel beside Saul.

The medium repeats her plea to the men. "Please, the king needs to eat so he has strength to go home. May God have mercy on me if he dies here."

Jakeh lays an arm across the King's shoulder and murmurs, "Saul, this woman is innocent. Treat her with kindness. She's right. You're famished. You've not eaten since yesterday. Perhaps tomorrow we'll be in a battle. You'll have to lead. You've got to be strong for your troops."

Saul blinks and his eyes stop swimming. He turns his head and stares at Jakeh. A puzzled look sweeps across his face and then he speaks as though Jakeh has given him a new revelation.

"For the troops…. the troops, of course. I live for them and no one else. I serve them, and them alone. Yes, I'll eat. I must eat so I can be strong for my men."

The two men help Saul get up from the floor and sit on the low stool. The medium goes out behind her tiny shack and returns with a very fresh looking piece of meat. Within minutes she has a fire crackling on the ground in front of the house and the meat cooking in a black pot. While the water comes to a boil she finishes making cakes of unleavened bread. Jakeh and Shuham are impressed with the woman's alacrity despite the tumultuous events of the evening. Saul sits in the quiet room as the tumult in his mind fades away. Like the rain-washed air after a thunder storm his thoughts are clear and clean.

Why haven't I seen this before? I drag old Jakeh and that half blind prophet out into the night, I terrify a simple woman and force her to break my own law. All because I'm afraid. So selfish. My fate was set long ago. Why do I keep beleaguering God?

Jakeh is wise. I have to eat for the sake of the troops. I don't need it. No need for food in Sheol. But my men…They look to me because I'm still their king and need to be strong for them. They need to see my courage. Tomorrow? Tomorrow we might all fall by the swords of the Philistines. Yet we have no choice but to resist the enemy at our border. And, win or lose, aren't we still the children of Israel? Aren't we still the Chosen People? That is for God to decide. But since God has chosen to give me only silence, I'll insist that we are the chosen ones. And as long as I'm alive, I'm still the King. I'm king of Israel and king for Israel. Tomorrow I'll lead my brothers into battle and we'll defend our land.

The fat, juicy smell of cooking meat wafts into the room. Saul's mouth waters, his stomach growls and he is ravenous. He thanks the woman when she sets the food before them. The three men eat this unexpected late night meal in silence. After they have eaten their fill, Saul wipes his greasy fingers on one of the tattered robes that served as his disguise, then stands and bows.

"Kind woman, you've given us more hospitality than we deserve. I am grateful." The woman returns his bow and takes the coin he extends to her.

Saul turns to the two men. "Now I've got to prepare for tomorrow. Jakeh, I'm going to reclaim the donkey and ride back to our troops. I want you and Shuham to stay in Endor until tomorrow. Then I want you both to return to Beth-Haggan. When you get there, take my horse and go back to Gibeah."

"But King, I want…"

"Jakeh, I know what you want. But I don't want you anywhere near me tomorrow. After tomorrow Ahinoam and the rest of my family will need you more than I will."

Saul grasps Jakeh's thin shoulders and looks at his rugged face, then wraps him in an embrace. "You've been a loyal servant, a wise and faithful friend. Farewell." The king's throat tightens as he thinks of the many farewells he will not be making. He swings his long leg over the donkey's back and rides down the silent dark streets of Endor. He turns southward toward Mt. Gilboa where the great Philistine army waits for him.

Chapter Thirty-four

The cool sweetness of the night air fills Saul's lungs as he rides toward his camp. The crisp crescent moon pours out enough chilly light for him and his donkey to negotiate the trail. The silent, tranquil ride gradually eases the frenetic fire racing through his body. Midnight has passed when he reaches the guard post. Two figures loom in the darkness and a voice calls out, "Hold! Who enters?"

"Attention, men, your king is here." Spears raise and swords rattle nervously as he approaches the sentinels. Saul dismounts and his tall frame is silhouetted in the moonlight. They lower their weapons. Even after all these years no other man in the land stands so tall.

"Welcome O King. How is it you ride alone?"

"Alone, yes. Thanks for your concern. Sooner or later every man must…Well, it's late. Stay alert. The enemy is near." Saul tethers the donkey and quietly weaves his way between the tents to the mat in front of his empty tent. He decides not even to attempt sleep. He sighs and lowers himself and sits cross-legged looking out over the deeper darkness of the Jezreel Valley.

Dead or alive, Samuel always spoke the truth. Finally, I can admit it. No wasp sting of anxiety, no angry torch in my belly. These past years…ai…my mind has been a riverbank chewed and clawed by the raging current of feelings. Last night I heard the old man's final word, the truth I'd heard before but couldn't accept. On this last morning, the furious churning ceases, the current is smooth and gentle.

Did the Lord ever speak to me? Did the Lord speak and I didn't hear? In the end, does it matter? Some claim to have heard his word and some of us have gone deaf listening to the silence thrumming in our ears. Is there any difference between us? We all want to love our families, staunch our bleeding, and console our friends. All of us must face our enemies. And in the end, dust is the destiny of us all.

Out there in the darkness, the Philistines sleep. Does their king have questions like I do? Maybe he sleeps like a baby. Maybe he dreams of the brilliant battle plans given to him by his gods. Maybe he smiles. Who's more courageous? The leader who charges onto the field convinced he's doing a righteous, god blessed thing, or the king who plods out onto the battleground simply because he sees no other way to be faithful to his people?

Another sleepless night. Another dawn sitting cross-legged before my tent. This is the closest I've ever gotten to a throne.

The night's dark curtain dissolves into gray mist. Saul's soul darkness thins. The rising sun paints a bloody border on the horizon. He knows how this day will end.

CONCLUSION

The Jezreel valley glows emerald green in the morning sunlight. The watchmen on the flanks of Gilboa, high above the Israelite camp gaze northward toward Shunem and shout down to their comrades.

"The enemy is moving! The ranks are forming!"

Saul met with his commanders an hour earlier so the Israelite troops are already armed and prepared to move. At the watchmen's cry he turns to his commanders. He carries a mantle of weariness but his face bears a grin. One by one he looks deep into the eyes of the warriors who have stood with him, embraces them, slaps their backs and says, "God go with you."

Medad brings up the king's new mount, a stout ebony stallion. Saul rides up to the front of the army. Under his breast plate he wears a clean blue tunic. His beard and hair, both now heavily streaked with gray are freshly washed. The morning sun manages to find a hint of flame in the hair flowing down his back. His face is pale but his obsidian eyes flash. He tips back his chin and stares out across the plain for a long moment. Now he turns to his soldiers, raises his sword and shouts.

"We are Israel, the Chosen People. We fight to defend our land and our families." He lowers his sword halfway, pauses, then jabs it sharply back into the blue heavens and roars, "May God give us the victory!" He wheels his horse and leads the charge against the Philistines. Like a crazed bull the shofar blasts over and over, echoing across the plain.

The Israelite troops repeat Saul's roar, rattle their weapons and follow their king. The army of the Chosen People emerges out onto the plain from the trees on the lower slopes. At the sight of the enemy horde across the plain the roaring fades and is replaced by the resolute pounding of a multitude of boots and the grunts of a myriad of trotting men.

Heady exhilaration surges through Saul. He is a lion set free after years of captivity. He yearns to charge headlong into the enemy ranks and personally deliver death to them all. Instead as he races forward he calculates the distance to the first line of the Philistines. He is almost ready to set his line of shield men and archers when enemy arrows fill the air like a cloud of angry locusts. Apparently, the Philistine bows and bow men are stronger than his own. He roars "shields up," but it is too late. So many of the shield bearers fall in the first wave of arrows that now his archers stand exposed to the deathly darts that buzz through the air.

Saul's soldiers forge stubbornly ahead but the leading Philistine troop line opens and the shining chariots charge through, followed by rank after rank of armored men screaming and waving swords and spears. The spectacle is horrifying and the Israelite charge falters. Saul spins around bellowing words of encouragement but his voice is drowned out by the howl of the approaching horde.

The first chariots stampede into the Israelite ranks. The horses trample men, the archers on board shoot at deadly close range. The foot soldiers are close behind swinging their razor-sharp swords. For minutes that seem like hours Israel's soldiers stand their ground. Swords flash, spears and arrows fly, the screams of men and horses lacerate the air. Saul's men fight with a holy frenzy but for every enemy that drops two more step forward.

Saul has vowed he will not call for the shofar to blow retreat. But even amidst of his frenzied fighting, he realizes that the enemy is driving his men back, closer and closer to the slopes of the mountain. The Philistine advance is relentless. Medad, Saul's armor bearer, riding alongside the king, is unhorsed by a soldier swinging his spear like a club. Saul slows to pick him up but an arrow sinks deep into the chest of his own stallion and he is thrown to the ground. As he clambers to his feet he hears an animal shriek off to his left. He turns just as Jonathan falls backward with a spear in his chest.

Saul screams, "My son, o God, my son." But before he can even take a step toward him a tall, fierce Philistine hacks the young man's neck and swiftly moves on. Saul wails and starts running to his fallen son. His racing attracts the attention of the Philistine archers and in midstride the king gasps and tumbles headlong to the ground. He struggles to his feet and stares, momentarily confused by the arrow that protrudes from his side. He grasps it and yanks but it is too deeply sunk into his exhausted flesh. He tightens his fist around the shaft and with a sharp grunt snaps it off. The tumult swirls around him and he's lost sight of Jonathan. He and Medad now stand back to back fending off arrows. He risks a glance and sees, far off to his right, Abner and his men fighting and backing up one of the smoother slopes of the mountain. At least they have a chance of escape. Saul grimly notes that behind him and Medad stands a much steeper ridge. He and his men cannot fight and climb at the same time. The Philistine archers will pin them to the cliffs like skins stretched out to dry.

The king's tunic now blooms with bloody crimson blossoms. The enemy archers encircle him and Medad. The mad exultation that fueled Saul's morning attack flickers out. Jonathan is dead, no doubt his brothers are too, along with thousands upon thousands of his men. Saul's legs are leaden and his arms droop like willow branches. He clutches at the last strands of his energy and commands, "Medad, bring your sword and run me through."

The young armor bearer looks at him in horror. "Never. I'll never kill my king."

Saul moans now with each painful breath. "I order you. Come here and end my life. If you don't, these uncircumcised dogs will grab me, torture me, mock me and tear me apart."

Medad's face is frozen in panic. He backs up and shakes his head.

Saul groans, "Remember how Samuel chopped King Agag to pieces?" Not even this last horrific image is enough to move Medad. Saul snorts in disgust, turns his back on the young man. He drops to his knees, plants the handle of his sword on the ground and centers the point on his chest.

Not even my armor bearer obeys me. A fitting end. I command no one, I lead nothing. I'm king of only one last thing: my life. Before the enemy takes it, before the Lord God takes it, I will end it. Lord God, you rejected me once. Do you want me now? Here I am.

Saul thrusts himself forward. His fine Philistine-crafted steel sword slices skin, pierces viscera and penetrates his pulsing heart.

He grunts low and long, as though punched in the belly, his legs jerk out stiffly, and he topples onto his side. The rocky ground of Mt. Gilboa soaks up the blood of Israel's first king.

EPILOGUE

Saul's death does not go unnoticed. The next morning the victorious Philistine soldiers scavenge for weapons from the bodies on the low foothills of Mt. Gilboa. They reach the corpse of a tall man skewered by a Philistine sword. Since no soldier leaves his sword behind, it is obvious that this muscular soldier killed himself. They have no doubt: this is their nemesis. They yank out the sword from Saul's chest, strip off his armor, then hack off his head. They carry his armor back to their temple and display it as a token of their military prowess and a proof of the might of their gods. They drag his stiff, headless corpse to the top of their city wall, tie a rope around the arms and hang the body on the outside of the wall—food for carrion and a warning to any man or nation who would challenge the power of their army or of their gods.

Saul's death does not go unnoticed. When David hears of Saul and Jonathan's death he rips his robe in two. He picks up his lyre and composes a lament:

> Your glory, O Israel lies slain upon your high places! How the mighty have fallen.

> You mountains of Gilboa, let there be no dew or rain upon you, nor bounteous fields!

> For there the shield of the mighty was defiled, the shield of Saul, anointed with oil no more.

> How the mighty have fallen in the midst of the battle!

> I am distressed for you, my brother Jonathan; greatly beloved were you to me; Your love to me was wonderful, passing the love of women.

David summons his court and plays for them his song. He commands that they all fast for the entire day.

Saul's death does not go unnoticed. The citizens of Jabesh-Gilead learn of Saul's death and what has been done to his body. They remember that day more than a decade ago when Saul and his army rescued them from Nahash the Ammonite. Twenty men volunteer to restore the dignity of Saul and his house. They stage a raid and take Saul's body back to Israel. They burn the body with a solemn ceremony and bury his bones in Jabesh. Then they mourn and fast for seven complete days.

Saul's death does not go unnoticed. His spirit joins Samuel and the fathers of Israel in the everlasting shade of Sheol. Does the Lord God remember the one chosen to be the first king of Israel? We do not know. On this matter, God continues to maintain His silence.

Made in the USA
Thornton, CO
06/24/22 07:44:18

ce84bee2-c00d-4ffb-9a6e-aa21f076f167R01